MINISTER
OF MONEY

MINISTER OF MONEY

HENRY DUNCAN, FOUNDER OF
THE SAVINGS BANK MOVEMENT

Charles W. Munn

Foreword by Dr Paul Pester,
Chief Executive Officer of TSB

JOHN DONALD

First published in Great Britain
in 2017 by John Donald,
an imprint of Birlinn Ltd

West Newington House
10 Newington Road
Edinburgh
EH9 1QS

www.birlinn.co.uk

ISBN: 978 1 910900 14 7

The publishers gratefully
acknowledge the support of the TSB
in the publication of this book

British Library Cataloguing-in-Publication Data
A catalogue record for this book is available on
request from the British Library

Designed and typeset by Mark Blackadder

Printed and bound in Britain by TJ International, Padstow, Cornwall

*This book is dedicated
with much love to my wife
Rev. Fran Ruthven*

*and to my children
David and Kirsten.*

Little does one expect to find the Father of Savings Banks such an exceptional character – a man sought by the foremost literary and scientific men of his time as one of themselves – the humble manse a centre of all that elevates and beautifies human life.

The appearance of this village minister in London called there to instruct the Prime Minister and leaders of parties in Parliament upon the national value, moral and economical, of thrift and the merits of his plan, which provided for the first time the necessary feeling of security for savings, deserves a place in history as among the remarkable achievements of men.

Andrew Carnegie (1910) in a letter to Lady Sophy Hall,
the great granddaughter of Henry Duncan

The book is fitted to stagger our confidence in the old saw about the evil of having too many irons in the fire; for here we have one who had as many irons in as he could get hold of, and was always the better fitted for work the more he undertook.

Review of George Duncan's biography of his father Henry,
United Presbyterian Church Magazine, 1848

[Y]ou can never treat the emergence of a leader as an entirely isolated event. It is easy to see him as a solitary rebel protesting against the current trend. He is as often responding to fears and hopes and urges felt by many others. He acts on his own but soon he finds that there are others, often in surprising places, who are thinking the same thoughts and even doing the same kind of things. The success of any kind of experiment often depends a great deal upon this striking of the hour.

T. Ralph Morton, *The Iona Community: Personal
Impressions of the Early Years*, Edinburgh, 1977

Contents

Foreword

If you look back to the early nineteenth century, banks were elitist – they were there to make the rich, richer. It was impossible for normal, hardworking people to raise enough money to even open an account. In those days, it took the average annual earnings of a farm labourer just to be eligible for a bank account.

The poor were getting poorer. The rich were getting richer. A banking revolution was needed and one pioneer led the way.

That pioneer was the Reverend Henry Duncan. Henry created the first savings bank where people could deposit as little as a sixpence. So, hardworking local people at last were able to save and watch their money grow.

This revolution created a virtuous circle, which fuelled the local economy and improved the lives of people in the community, and in turn deposits grew to £3 million within just 10 years.

At its peak there were 645 different savings banks in 92 countries across the globe. Henry's one small bank in Ruthwell triggered an international movement that revolutionised banking for ordinary people.

Fast forward to 2007, and the banking crisis that rocked the western world. Banks had lost their connection with the communities they were created to serve. The results were catastrophic.

Trust was gone and there was significant rebuilding to do.

A few years later and a golden opportunity presented itself: create a new bank to increase competition and it was obvious where the inspiration would come from – Reverend Henry Duncan.

When TSB was re-launched in 2013 we started with a list of just over 600 branches and nearly five million customers. We took inspiration from Henry Duncan to recreate the virtuous circle between the Bank and the local communities we serve. We wanted to keep Henry's values alive and make sure we lived by them in everything we do – from how we communicate, to the products we offer and the way we provide local banking for Britain. And as we set out on our mission to bring more competition to UK banking and make banking better for all consumers, we challenged the banking industry to change.

As a result, we developed our Local Banking model which, simply put, means we provide great banking to more people, help more people to borrow well, and provide the kind of banking people want and deserve. And our approach is working for customers, our Partners, and for TSB. But without Henry Duncan, it wouldn't have been possible.

He was an ordinary person, who did something extraordinary for the benefits of others, and I'm proud to say his vision is still alive today within TSB.

Dr Paul Pester, CEO, TSB Bank

Acknowledgements

The idea for writing this book first arose when the BBC's Willie John-ston came to interview me about Henry Duncan in advance of the 2010 bicentenary celebrations of the savings bank movement. In anticipation of his visit a hasty search of the Internet and of my bookcases revealed enough to fill the subsequent interview. But it also revealed how little we knew about the man who gave birth to the savings bank movement and whose work impacted greatly not just on Scottish culture and society but on communities throughout the world, and still does. Moreover subsequent searches in libraries and bookshops revealed that Duncan's work has been all but ignored by successive generations of historians.

In writing this book I have incurred many debts, thankfully not of a monetary nature. The research and publication has been supported by TSB and I am grateful to them for their assistance.

The main source of research material was found in the Savings Bank Museum in Ruthwell in the room where Henry Duncan founded his savings bank in 1810, from where he ran the bank and the friendly society, and from where he dispensed food to the needy during the Napoleonic Wars.

The curator of the museum, Mhairi Hastings, provided open access to the museum and its archives and I am especially grateful to her for this and for many discussions, helpful suggestions and her comments on an earlier draft. I am also obliged to her colleague Rob Vallence for suggesting some books from the museum library that I might not otherwise have read.

Mhairi's predecessor as curator of the museum, Rene Anderson, also read and commented on an earlier draft. In a number of conversations she suggested sources that could be consulted, and I have drawn on her extensive knowledge of the Duncan family. She also transcribed a large collection of Duncan's letters, saving me the necessity of reading too much of his very poor handwriting. Her book *Crichton University: A Widow's Might* on Duncan's efforts to have a university established in Dumfries was the main source for Chapter 10.

Staff in Lloyds TSB Archives, especially Seonaid Mcdonald, provided me with an electronic copy of the letters that Rene transcribed; I am grateful to them for this and for giving me access to a number of other records.

In addition to Mhairi and Rene a number of academic colleagues have read drafts, in whole or in part, and I am obliged to them for their comments: Professor Christopher Whatley, University of Dundee; Professor Sam McKinstry, University of the West of Scotland; Professor Geoff Jones, Harvard University; and Dr Duncan Ross, University of Glasgow. I am also grateful to David Torrance for his editorial input and suggestions.

Librarians and archivists in the UK and USA have been extremely helpful including Ewart Library, Dumfries; Dumfries and Galloway Archive: Dumfries and Galloway Museum; Mitchell Library, Glasgow; National Library of Scotland; National Archives of Scotland; Baker Library, Harvard University; Amherst College Library; WEB Du Bois Library, University of Massachusetts; and the Jones Library, Amherst.

Most of this book was written in Amherst, Massachusetts, in a year spent living in the parsonage of South Congregational Church. I am grateful to the congregation there for their fellowship and for the lively interest that some took in this project.

I have given talks about Duncan to various groups and I am obliged to them for coming to hear about him and for their engaging discussions. These include the Crichton Foundation, Dumfries; the Library of Mistakes, Edinburgh; the Monetary History Group, London; the Department of Economic and Social History, University of Glasgow. In Ruthwell Parish I am especially indebted to Rev. Gerald Moule, Susan Broatch and the Kirk Session.

I am also grateful to Margery Wilkins of Annan who prepared the maps, Fiona Brown of the Church of Scotland who provided access to the Kirk's copy of the *Fasti* and to David Dewar for lengthy conversations and for his excellent play about Henry Duncan.

Bethan Thompson photographed some of the illustrations in the plate section.

I am also happy to record my thanks and appreciation to Mairi Sutherland, academic managing editor at Birlinn, and to Nicola Wood, freelance editor.

Finally I thank Mrs Catherine Davis-Osborne of Beverly, Massachusetts, who suggested the title for this book, and my wife Rev. Fran Ruthven who encouraged me to undertake the project.

Charles W. Munn

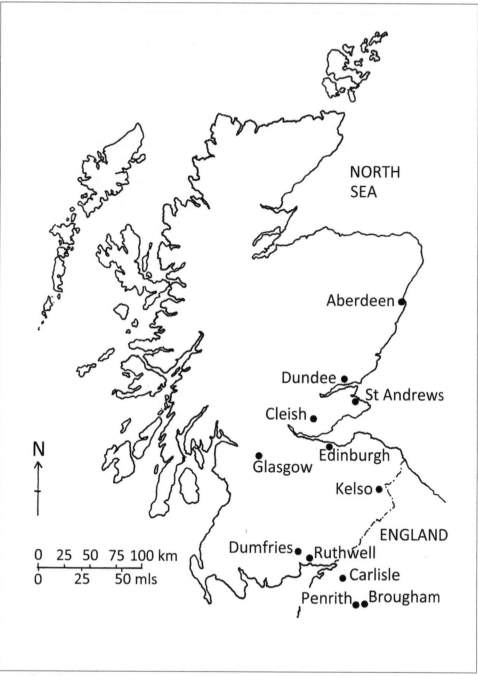

NORTH
SEA

Aberdeen ●

Dundee ●
● St Andrews
Cleish ●

Edinburgh ●
Glasgow ●

Kelso ●

ENGLAND

Dumfries ● ● Ruthwell

● Carlisle

Penrith ● ● Brougham

N
↑

0   25 50 75 100 km
0   25   50 mls

Map of Scotland

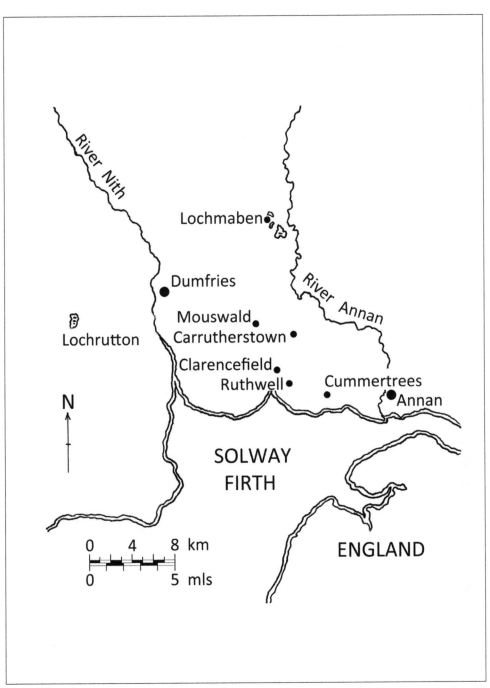

Map of Dumfriesshire

Chapter 1
Introduction

Rev. Henry Duncan transformed people's lives. And, in the process, he lived a life as varied, and as interesting, as it was possible to make it. He did not shirk his problems. Nor did he revel in his successes. He simply tried to make people's lives better than they would otherwise be. He was a true Enlightenment man.

He is best remembered as the founder of the savings bank movement, and while he may not have invented the idea he certainly gave momentum and energy to its great expansion and success, after he founded his banking 'experiment' in Ruthwell village, Dumfriesshire, in 1810.

The kernel of his idea was simple. It was that working people should be encouraged to save so that, if hard times came, they would have resources to fall back on and would not have to seek hand-outs from the parish poor relief system. He wanted people to be independent and his experience in running a local friendly society persuaded him that his ideas were sound. He believed that people could save some of their money provided that they had somewhere safe to keep it and that it would earn interest.

The bank was a great success. His friends and his brother soon followed his example and set up savings banks in their own parishes. Duncan spent an enormous amount of time writing about them in the newspaper that he founded and edited. He wrote a huge volume of letters to people in all parts of the country telling them about his bank. People came to see for themselves what he had established. And before the decade was out there were hundreds of savings banks all over the British Isles and his idea was spreading to the United States and to other parts of the world. It had become a matter of pride for towns and villages to have their own savings bank. A new 'culture' of saving had been created.

Henry Duncan was indeed 'a man of many parts'. His pen was never still and, in addition to the newspaper and the letters about the bank, he found time to write an anti-slavery book, poetry, short stories, a novel and a four-volume religious work in which he sought to reconcile Enlightenment ideas about creation with his religious faith.

He was also a devoted family man who surrounded himself with a wide circle of friends including many of the most influential men of the day: Thomas Carlyle, Thomas Chalmers, Henry Brougham, Andrew Thomson, David Brewster, William Buckland and Dugald Stewart.

Nor was Duncan the kind of man who sat behind a desk for most of his life. He formed and led a company of volunteers to resist a threatened invasion by Napoleon. He took an active interest in geology, he was a gardener and a landscaper, he farmed his fifty-acre glebe, he painted and built models. He established a Mechanics' Institute. In his later years he also practised dentistry – on himself. And he did all this in addition to his duties as a parish minister in the Church of Scotland.

This is the story of his life.

The world into which Henry Duncan was born in 1774 was undergoing great change. No part of the United Kingdom was exempt and Scotland, in particular, experienced a transformation. T. M. Devine maintained that 'The whole of Scottish society was being re-cast between the mid-eighteenth and early nineteenth centuries.'[1]

During the seventeenth century, Scotland had endured religious strife, repression and bloodshed. The matters in dispute – religious freedom and the monarchy – were not finally settled until the Battle of Culloden in 1746. By that time Scotland had merged its parliament with England's and, with certain important exceptions like education, religion and legal matters, Scotland was governed from London.

Political and military peace had arrived, at least within the British Isles. Culloden was the last pitched battle on the British mainland, although disturbances of another kind were coming. The union of the parliaments in 1707 had brought about commercial opportunities for Scottish merchants, of which they took full advantage. The Union gave Scots access to English and imperial markets and they soon came to dominate the tobacco trade across the Atlantic.

Trade brought profits which had to be re-invested in new business opportunities. The application of new technologies to the manufacturing of textiles was under way and the Scots were not slow to see the possibilities. Traditional industries such as wool and linen were transformed and new imported fibres, mainly cotton and later jute, came to prominence.

Nor did they come alone. Industrialisation brought urbanisation as people moved from the country into new factory towns, which, in turn, created increased demand for foodstuffs. Farming changed dramatically as the market economy came to dictate what was grown and what price it could command. These changes also altered the nature of relationships on the land. Modern historians Aitchison and Cassell addressed this issue when they wrote

> What seems clear is that certainly by the latter part of the eighteenth century the relationship between the Lowland tenant and his laird was an economic one: there was an expectation that a lease, even at the end of nineteen years, might not be extended or renewed. In other words there was no belief that the land they farmed was theirs by right or that the landowner held it in trust for the people.[2]

Bigger markets required better transport that, in its initial stages, meant canals and improved roads before railways began to be built in the 1820s.

The years between 1760 and 1830 are often referred to as the industrial revolution but it was much more than that – every aspect of life was affected.

This, then, was the world into which Henry Duncan was born and with which he would have to deal as he grew to maturity and assumed the role of a parish minister in the Church of Scotland.

If the worlds of business and farming were in ferment, so too were the worlds of religion and intellect. What became known as the Enlightenment was well under way in the second half of the eighteenth century and Scottish philosophers played a disproportionately large part in this movement. David Hume, Adam Smith, Thomas Reid, Adam Ferguson and Dugald Stewart were just some of the great names at the universities of Glasgow and Edinburgh. Henry Duncan read their books and was taught by some of them.

The Enlightenment and religion were not easy bedfellows, and as Henry Duncan's Christian faith developed he struggled with the challenges posed by scepticism and by the Enlightenment trend for putting man, rather than God, at the centre of things. American historian James Macgregor Burns put it succinctly when he wrote, 'Breaking from a universe in which God was the answer to any question, Enlightenment philosophers moved attention to human beings as the measure of all things.'[3] But, as a minister, Duncan also struggled with the difficulties faced by his parishioners in dealing with industrial, urban and agricultural changes.

He rose to these challenges and much of what he wrote sought to reconcile his faith with the transformations that were taking place in society. But his greatest contribution – one that impacts on millions of people to this day – was in creating and giving momentum to the savings bank movement. This was his way of helping those most affected by these disruptions to deal with what was happening to them in their daily lives. He provided a strategy for poor people to help them cope with a world that many would find hard to comprehend. This was a world that would go on changing, although no one at that time could anticipate the extent to which family and familiar routines would be disrupted and traditional ways of living and working would disappear.

Ultimately these changes impacted on the church, as people sought to have greater control over their own affairs and rejected the patriarchal manner in which matters, such as the appointment of ministers, had traditionally been arranged. Aitchison and Cassell reckoned that by 1820 'one in three Lowland Scots had left the national church alto-gether'.[4]

In the latter years of his life Duncan continued to engage in a wide range of activities – not least in the savings bank movement. But he also became embroiled in the religious controversy which split the Church of Scotland in 1843. He came out in the Disruption, joined the new Free Church of Scotland, lost his parish and his manse and lived the last few years of his life in very modest circumstances. Yet he remained active and erected a new church and manse where he set about building up a new congregation. It was an emotional time for him and he was not always in control of his emotions. Yet he lived out his days as he had always lived his life – active, vigorous and seeking to serve others.

Chapter 2
Birth and Boyhood

When Henry Duncan was fifteen – and already a year into his under-graduate career – he was gifted a nightingale. Although he did his best to care for the young bird, it soon died, whereupon he built for it a mausoleum with bricks and mortar.

In front of this construction Henry chiselled the face of a grieving man, with small holes bored through the eyes, directing the path of an adjacent stream so that it appeared to cry. The stream was further directed through the necks of bottles to produce a sound similar to a mourning wail. And, to cap it all, Henry chiselled two Latin verses, which he later translated:

Stay traveller: if a tale of real woe
To gentle pity e'er subdued thy breast,
O stay! And whilst my tears do ever flow,
Let not thy rising sorrow be supprest.

For, ere mature her youthful blossom glow'd,
Stern death did lovely Philomel destroy:
No more her pleasing plaints, which sweetly flow'd,
Shall melt to love, or animate to joy.

The construction and its associated verses became something of a local curiosity and, although certainly unusual, it encapsulated Henry in his youth: both emotional and practical, and even as a teenager a whirlwind of activity, determined to fill his life with activity. The young Henry Duncan was a muse and a mason.

He was born on 8 October 1774 and originally called Hary, only adopting the name Henry when he was on the cusp of manhood. He emerged into the world in Lochrutton Manse, Kirkcudbrightshire, a parish in the south-west of Scotland where his father was the local minister. It was a rural parish four miles south-west of the town of Dumfries and close to the border with England. The military road to Portpatrick, the port that gave access to Ireland, ran through the village. The whole parish measured thirteen square miles, mostly of mixed farming land, and due to its relatively high elevation enjoyed largely cool weather.

The Duncan family had been in the area for a long time. Henry's father, George, had been minister there since 1766 and had succeeded his own father, also George, following the elder man's death by drowning in a loch.

The Duncans were a close-knit family with extensive kinship links. And, in the practice of the time, the manse door was always open to receive visitors – among whom was Robert Burns, Scotland's national bard.

When Henry's father, George, became the minister he sought a wife and found her in Ann McMurdo, the daughter of a Dumfries merchant and grand-daughter of a local minister.

Henry had two older brothers and was soon joined by a younger brother, Thomas Tudor Duncan, who became his best friend, then by another brother and two sisters, the younger of whom died in infancy. There was a particularly close bond formed between Henry's father and James Currie, minister at nearby Middlebie and, as we shall see, the two families became linked in a myriad of ways.

While life in the manse would include an expectation of high standards of behaviour from the Duncan children it would also involve a large degree of freedom, and we know that Henry took particular joy in wandering the fields, hills and woods around the nearby loch, often in the company of his brother Thomas.

It was the custom in many of Scotland's manses for the children to receive their early education from a tutor who operated under the strict supervision of the father, and this describes the early education of the Duncan children. Often the tutor would be a candidate for the ministry who had not yet been ordained.

As their education advanced Henry and Thomas were sent to school in Dumfries, where they lodged with a kindly but 'somewhat eccentric aunt'.[1] Henry was very fond of poetry and was especially keen on verse or prose which recounted the stories of heroes of yesteryear, be they kings, conquerors or Covenanters. Mr Wait, the classics teacher, was a 'profound scholar and severe disciplinarian',[2] but the brothers were good and attentive students who came out at, or near, the top of their class. Henry was not much interested in the rougher playground pursuits enjoyed by many boys; in addition to his poetry writing he was also keen on making models and mechanical devices. His abilities therefore were literary and practical, perhaps somewhat unusual in a young boy, but they were to shape his life in the years to come.

In later life his brother, Thomas, described Henry as a thoughtful and intelligent boy with good manners and a kindly disposition. He had a good complexion, curly hair and a self-assured and confident bearing. It was a combination that made him a favourite among his extensive network of family and friends.

It was the tradition of these times for boys to be sent to university at a young age and in 1788, at just fourteen, he was sent to the University of St Andrews, while Thomas went to the University of Edinburgh. While at university Henry lived with his relative Mrs Spens, widow of Dr Hary Spens, who had been Professor of Divinity.

The curriculum during Henry's second year at St Andrews, this time in the company of Thomas, included further language studies and an additional class in logic. A letter to his mother, dated 2 February 1790, reveals much about the character and emotions of the young Henry shortly after he had constructed a shrine to his pet nightingale.

Apparently, some disobedience had taken place that involved his brother Thomas, and the letter is both an apology and an explanation: 'Indeed I was to blame for not obeying you, but there was some excuse for it, I think,' wrote Henry.

Forgive my presumption, dear mother, if I try to vindicate myself, which I could not do when I was at home, because my heart was full, and the tear stood in my eye whenever I attempted to speak about it, and even when I thought about it – not from any consciousness of guilt, but from vexation that you should think me disobedient.[3]

There would be many occasions in his life when the tear stood in his eye.

Chapter 3
Banking in Liverpool

When Henry Duncan left St Andrews University he was still a teenager, and thus had to decide upon a career at – by today's standards – an astonishingly young age. At this stage, there was no suggestion he might follow his father and his mother's antecedents into the ministry, indeed Henry's father appears to have resisted the temptation to direct his son's path.

Help, however, was at hand. Dr James Currie of Liverpool, son of Rev. George Duncan's old friend, Rev. James Currie of Middlebie, suggested that an opening for Henry could be found in Heywood's Bank in Liverpool and, after due discussion, the young man agreed that this would be an appropriate career upon which to embark.

The few years that Henry spent in Liverpool, and the influence that Currie brought to bear in his life, were hugely formative and might be said to have provided directions for much of what engaged and concerned Henry in the years to come. There were three dimensions to his time in Liverpool – his personal development, his religion and his work in the bank.

Currie was a step-cousin to Henry Duncan through his mother's side of the family, and was beholden to the Duncans. As a young man, his aspirations to be a doctor were temporarily thwarted for lack of funds and he went to the American colonies to serve a commercial apprenticeship with a firm of Glasgow tobacco lords. It was a useful training but his presence there, and later in the West Indies, involved his tacit approval of the slave trade although, in his heart and mind, he was opposed to it. His father died in 1773 when he was still in America and, as the eldest male in the family, he became responsible for the welfare and upkeep of his sisters. The Duncan family at Lochrutton took them in and brought them up as their own children.

Henry's older brothers, George and William, were already working in mercantile houses in Liverpool and were there to welcome him when he arrived by merchant ship in the River Mersey from the River Nith in Dumfries. Furthermore, the three brothers formed part of a substantial community of Scots already in business there. Duncan would not be lonely and his gregarious nature soon led him into friendships with local people as well as with the Scottish diaspora. The occasion of his leaving Scotland was the spur to the writing of more poetry, about friends left behind and his arrival in a new place. It was written in the style of Ossian:

> *But where are the other friends of my love?*
> *A cloud of grief has darkened my soul.*
> *Why did I leave the house of my fathers,*
> *And the careful eye of my friends?*
>
> *The house of my fathers I have left.*
> *But the careful eye of friendship is still upon me*
> *The parents of my infancy are not here:*
> *But ye, O Cuthullin and Clatho[1]*
> *Ye are the generous parents of my youth.*

Surprisingly, Henry did not reside with his brothers during his time in Liverpool but with Currie, and it was there that he entered fully into city life. Currie was already well established in Liverpool's medical world (he was in charge of its infirmary), and also had a wide circle of friends there and in Manchester and Birmingham, among whom was the scientist Joseph Priestley.

Despite his own poor health (he suffered from consumption and melancholia), Currie led a very active life and there were regular meetings of like-minded men in all three cities at which papers were presented on matters of topical interest. These were often very convivial evenings and this was the milieu into which Henry Duncan was introduced.

On one occasion in December 1791 Robert Riddell read a paper on the 'Ancient Carved Stone Monuments of Scotland', and on another occasion Currie and his friends 'advanced the idea of a bank to protect the savings of labourers'.[2] Both topics, especially the latter, would consume Henry Duncan's attention for many years and both would become the contributions to society for which he is best remembered.

The range of interests discussed at these events was considerable. Currie's biographer, R. D.Thornton, explained how they managed it. 'Only by careful and unremitting use of leisure could they find time for their ordering, reading, discussing and writing books, and for the astonishing variety of other activities to which their studies led.'[3] Currie and his friends, who were of a liberal disposition, also served on many public bodies. They supported schemes for poor relief and for the establishment of a lunatic asylum, while Currie was the first biographer of Robert Burns. Again, these were subjects that would engage Henry Duncan in later life.

Other subjects under discussion were abolition of the slave trade, freedom of worship, municipal reform, relief for Ireland, monopoly breaking and peace with France. It was a vibrant, interesting and challenging milieu into which the youthful Henry Duncan had entered.

It was not long before Henry, who was still a teenager, had established his own 'salon' and begun to copy his older cousin's activities. Years later his son, George, had access to the records of this association and maintained that Duncan was 'the chief mover in their proceedings, and the presiding genius at their meetings'.[4]

One outcome of this was the production in 1791 of a pamphlet on the subject of the day 'Socinianism'. Religious matters were high on the agenda of public debate and a major topic at that time, in Britain and America, was the doctrine of the Trinity: God the Father, Son and Holy Spirit. The adherents of Socinianism, or to give it its more recognisable title, 'Unitarianism', believed there was no scriptural justification for the Trinity. Currie left the Presbyterian chapel where he had been worshipping in Kay Street and moved with its minister, Rev. John Yates, to the new Unitarian chapel in Paradise St.[5]

Regrettably, no copy of Duncan's pamphlet on the subject (which was published anonymously) has survived. His son, George, maintained that it was entirely orthodox and that many of its arguments were based upon Henry's correspondence with his father in Lochrutton.

The pamphlet produced responses, both in print and in public debate, and Duncan sometimes found himself in situations where the subject was under discussion and where his writings were being considered. It must have been a heady experience for the young man who surely came to realise just how influential the written word could be.

There is no doubt, notwithstanding what he had written, that his beliefs were shaken and he veered in the direction that Currie had taken. It was not until some time later, when he had time to study the matter more fully, that he was restored to his Presbyterian Christianity. Indeed, he came to the view that if the doctrine of the Trinity was untrue then it followed that Scripture could no longer be relied upon as the Word of God. Thereafter, his preaching and writing were entirely orthodox although, as we shall see, not without controversy in some respects.

The third element of Duncan's Liverpool experience was the reason that he had gone there in the first place, to embark on a banking career. In some senses, this turned out to be a useful part of his life, but was probably less important than his personal development or religious activities.

Henry's work in Heywood's Bank was mostly routine, requiring him to be punctual and diligent in his bookwork and polite with customers. Heywood's was one of the premier private banks, with connections in all of the city's major activities, including the slave trade. Indeed, it was in Liverpool that Duncan was first exposed to the trade in human beings, a trade to which Currie, in light of his experience in America, was implacably opposed. So hostile was he that he had even corresponded with William Wilberforce, the great reformer, on the subject. Inevitably it was the subject of much discussion and the public campaign to abolish the trade really got under way in 1788, two years before Duncan arrived in the city. It was almost inevitable, therefore, that he too would develop an aversion to slavery, but many years were to pass before he became an active campaigner.

In later years Duncan liked to tell stories about his days as a bank clerk and was especially fond of recounting how, one day, he was sent with a bag of coins (several hundred pounds in gold) to Warrington, a town about twenty miles outside Liverpool. He hired a horse, wrapped the money in paper and placed it in saddlebags which were then slung over the horse. When he set out the weather was fair and he was looking forward to a pleasant journey, but it soon began to rain and became very stormy. The water penetrated the saddlebags and destroyed the paper, whereupon the coins began to spill from the bags and fall into the mud. He dismounted, tied his horse to a tree, and began to look for the money. An old woman approached him and began to search with him, but Duncan, suspecting her motives, told her that her services were not required. When he had searched some more, he went to a nearby house to count the recovered money. Discovering that he was still missing some coins, he returned to the spot to discover a group of people engaged in a search. They remonstrated with him and took umbrage at how he had treated the old woman. He retreated to the house to consider what to do, whereupon six coins were brought to him which the finders handed over in return for modest rewards which Duncan was only too happy to pay. In the end he had lost five guineas, which was the only loss that he ever suffered on these journeys. Errors in the bank, however, were not unknown and on one occasion, when Duncan was employed there, the sum of £30 had to be written off to 'rectifications'.

Events such as this might have provided a little excitement in Henry's life, but otherwise his banking career was full of tedium:

> In the old days of the Bank it was the custom for those in its service to spend their entire banking life doing one particular job, there being little or no opportunity to have experience in other work. The nature of the work performed did not affect the remuneration, which increased as the years went by, even though a clerk performed the same duties as on the day of first entry to the service.[6]

So Duncan would arrive at work each morning knowing exactly what he would have to do during the day. It was not the kind of work that would stimulate his active imagination. It was also a strict regime, and the 'handwriting in the old ledgers shows that copperplate was the rule rather than the exception'.[7]

It was not the career for a young man with such a mind as Henry Duncan's. Nevertheless, it did bring the disciplines of working in an office and the opportunity to learn a great deal about business and people and how they handled their finances. Successful bankers had to be good judges of character. These were lessons that would be useful in later life.

Currie, who had been keeping a close watch on Duncan, wrote to Lochrutton to say that he was 'pained' to detect a certain carelessness in business matters and that Henry displayed a 'want of ambition'. This provoked a letter from George Duncan to his son to which Henry replied on 4 September 1793. Of his banking career, he told his father he had

> no actual dislike to it, but I do not feel interested enough in the business to derive any pleasure from it, and to discharge my duties as I ought to do [. . .] Besides, the continual cares and anxieties which a mercantile life is exposed to, would be to me by no means compensated by whatever fortune I might in a length of years amass [. . .] I feel that I could return to my studies with tenfold ardour; indeed I feel within myself a great desire for knowledge.[8]

Henry went on to suggest that he should study for the ministry, and even included a sample sermon he had written for his father's approval. But there is nothing to suggest he had received a 'call' to the ministry; rather it seems he felt a minister's life would afford him the time to pursue a literary career.[9] Thomas Chalmers, who was to become Duncan's friend and a leader in the church, said of his own early life as a minister that, 'after the satisfactory discharge of his parish duties, a minister may enjoy five days in the week of uninterrupted leisure, for the prosecution of any science in which his taste may dispose him to engage'.[10] As their careers developed, however, neither Chalmers nor Duncan found time to enjoy very much 'uninterrupted leisure'.

Despite what Duncan had said about his banking career, there is an altogether more prosaic reason why it was not a success. Good penmanship was the hallmark of a good bank clerk, and Henry's handwriting simply was not good enough.

Chapter 4
University Education

Henry Duncan got his wish. The next five years of his life were spent at university; he studied for a year at Edinburgh University, two years at Glasgow University and then another two years back in Edinburgh. Duncan's time in these cities was well spent and his thinking came to reflect the main elements of the Enlightenment, including

> rational approaches to the natural world, the regulation and disciplining of the passions, the promotion of toleration, and the practical emphases on social improvement.[1]

Many of these ideas stood in stark contrast to the mind-sets with which the young Duncan was raised and would have required considerable mental adjustment on his part.

Despite having been brought up in the country, Henry's years in Liverpool ensured that city living was not unfamiliar to him and he soon settled into the life of a student. Both universities had considerable histories, Glasgow having been founded in 1451 and Edinburgh in 1583. Both had come through the vicissitudes of the Reformation in the sixteenth century, Covenanting times in the seventeenth century and Jacobite risings in the eighteenth century. Moreover, Scottish scholars had a long tradition of productive contacts with European colleagues, particularly in France and the Netherlands.

It is perhaps no surprise, therefore, that many of the great thinkers of the Enlightenment were Scottish and that their work was expressed in those universities.

Central to the mind-set that the Enlightenment encouraged were curiosity and scepticism. Duncan had already been exposed to this way of thinking in the various clubs and societies to which Currie had introduced him in Liverpool and Manchester. It encouraged people to take an interest in a wide range of subjects and issues; the driving dynamic was improvement.

Just as importantly, it was possible for people to write and speak about those interests without fear of physical retribution. Almost a century had passed since a minister had been executed for heresy; toleration, even in the church, permeated society, except for Roman Catholics, who still suffered some legal restrictions and disadvantages. In every other respect, tolerance was seen as a social virtue. That does not mean to say, however, that Scotland was free of bigotry.

Nor was it sufficient merely to debate and write about the issues of the day. The kind of civic humanism that Duncan imbibed at university required participation and he, as we shall see, was not slow to take an active part. His was not to be a life filled just with observation; he would become an active participant and, in many cases, a leader.

Freedom of thought and freedom of association ensured that people could meet, exchange ideas, challenge their friends and colleagues and even challenge the authorities. By the time that Duncan attended university, however, the wars with revolutionary France had brought forth legislation that placed limits on freedom of association – at least for working-class people. The middle classes were little troubled by the legislation of the 1790s that had been introduced to ensure national security and to inhibit the spread of revolutionary ideas from writers such as Thomas Paine.

The leaders of the Scottish Enlightenment, the leading lights of which were David Hume and Adam Smith, saw themselves as internationalists and they were just as likely to engage in discourse with contacts overseas as they were with their fellow Britons. 'Citizenship depended not on place of birth, but solely on the writings with which a person put his thoughts before the public for discussion, dispute and improvement.'[2]

Clearly traditional boundaries were being broken down and new thought patterns were emerging, including the need to read and think about ideas that were being developed outside the British Isles.

This was the kind of environment into which Henry Duncan entered in 1793. War had just been declared with France but apart from student debates on war, peace and revolution the hostilities did nothing to diminish the intellectual ferment at the universities of Glasgow and Edinburgh.

The lecturer who made the greatest impact on Henry Duncan was John Millar, Regius Professor of Civil Law at the University of Glasgow. Millar, who was close to many of the leading figures of the Enlightenment, including Smith, Hume and Kames, taught his students that all human relationships were based on economics. It followed from this that if society was to be improved then alterations had to be made to the way in which the economic system operated. Henry Duncan's son later claimed that this thought process, more than any other that he learned at university, greatly influenced his father's life. To this idea 'he used to trace the earliest development in his mind of some of those principles of action, by which, in after life, he was habitually governed'.[3]

But if changes were needed then they had to be made with great care:

It was a commonplace of Scottish Enlightenment thought, expressed for instance by Adam Ferguson, that society was so complex a mechanism that any attempt to change it was liable to have unforeseen and possibly disastrous consequences. Change should therefore be undertaken only when clearly necessary and after very careful consideration.[4]

There was therefore a cautionary note to the ferment of ideas that were circulating in these times. And it was one to which Duncan paid particular attention.

At Edinburgh, Duncan was greatly influenced by Professor Dugald Stewart, and for years after he left the city he kept up a friendly correspondence with him and his wife. Stewart had been a student of Thomas Reid during the time that he spent in Glasgow and then of Adam Ferguson in Edinburgh. He had succeeded his father in the mathematics chair in 1775 and then followed Ferguson in the chair of moral philosophy a decade later. By the time that Henry Duncan became his student, Stewart had an international reputation and was attracting students from Europe and America.

Stewart belonged to the 'Scottish Common Sense School' of philosophy that became popular in the United States. Perhaps not the most original of thinkers, Stewart nevertheless had much to draw upon from the writings of his contemporaries and friends in the Enlightenment. He also made extensive use of the French philosophers in his work and was sympathetic to the French Revolution, a sympathy that drew suspicion from the authorities. He was a very popular lecturer and his book *Outlines of Moral Philosophy* went through several editions, compulsory reading for generations of students.

The Scottish Common Sense School of thought was essentially a rebuttal of Hume's scepticism. The originator of this school was none other than Dugald Stewart's teacher, Thomas Reid. He was determined to challenge Hume's theories on the grounds that '[i]t destroys the science of a philosopher, it undermines the faith of a Christian, and it renders nugatory the prudence of a man of common understanding'.[5] This then was the underpinning of the teaching that Henry Duncan received while at university. It encouraged him in scientific enquiry, nurtured his growing Christian faith and supported him in addressing serious problems in society.

Just as important as the education he received in Glasgow and Edinburgh were the friendships Henry made during his time as a student. Duncan was obviously a very sociable man with a gift both for making and retaining friendships. Many of the people he met and befriended as a young man remained his friends for life and many also played important roles within his numerous interests and projects.

The friendship that Duncan formed with Professor and Mrs Stewart has already been mentioned. And of all his other close personal relationships, those with Henry Brougham and Robert Lundie were the most significant and the longest lasting. Brougham was a man of prodigious talent who rose to become Lord Chancellor in 1830 and, like Duncan, his mind ranged widely. The two men were often to be found working together on projects as diverse as the anti-slavery campaign and a proposed university for Dumfries. Lundie, meanwhile, was heading for the ministry of the Church of Scotland and, following his good friend's example, set up one of the first savings banks in Kelso, where he had become the local minister.

Among Henry's many other friends and contemporaries were John Leyden, the oriental scholar, the poet William Gillespie, Francis Horner and Lord Henry Petty (who later became Home Secretary as Lord Lansdowne). When Leyden died in Batavia (modern-day Jakarta) at the age of thirty-five, Duncan and Lundie were responsible for persuading the trustees of India House to provide a sum of money to the Leyden family as the price for Leyden's research papers.[6]

The only student society that we are certain Duncan joined was the somewhat select Speculative Society, although he did not become a member until the final year of his studies. Membership was by invitation only, so a student had to build a reputation before one would be forthcoming. After serving three years as an 'ordinary' member, however, those in the 'Spec' could progress to 'extraordinary' privileges, in other words membership for life.

Henry joined at the same time as his friend Brougham, who went on to become its president.[7] Currie had also been a member, as had Walter Scott. The Society would have been a place in which Duncan was perfectly comfortable; he knew the people, his experiences in Currie's salons in Liverpool were similar in nature, and the issues under discussion had not changed greatly. Religious matters, slavery and the French Revolution were often the subjects of debate and essays.

Duncan clearly enjoyed his time as a student in Edinburgh and Glasgow. He read widely, took an interest in university affairs, made friends and still found time to write, mostly for his own amusement, a range of 'poetical epistles, satires and epigrams'.[8] Nothing was revealed by either of the family members who wrote biographies, about his studies for the ministry. Nothing was revealed about his theological studies but he undoubtedly imbibed many of the ideas that were part of discourse at the time, including civic humanism, which included the veneration of disinterested virtue, the ideal of the armed citizen, the duty of participation in public life, a stoic emphasis on moderating the passions, the rejection of luxuries, the belief in gradual improvement, and the elevation of individual independence and a love of freedom.[9]

And Henry must also have read enough theology and history to satisfy the church. In the summer of 1798 he returned to Lochrutton and prepared to become a minister.

Chapter 5
Early Years in Ministry

The Church of Scotland – or the 'Kirk' – was in Henry Duncan's blood. George Duncan, his father, was minister at Lochrutton and although his son felt no immediate inclination to follow in his footsteps, Henry's own religious career would provide the basis for a remarkably varied life.

Duncan was licensed in 1798 and soon 'taken on trial' by the Church of Scotland's Dumfries Presbytery and, after passing a series of rigorous tests, was admitted as a probationer minister of the 'Kirk' in 1798. This, in effect, gave him a licence to preach and it opened up the possibility that he might be called to be a parish minister, although this was unlikely to happen for some time.

It was often the case that newly-licensed ministers would have to wait, sometimes for years, before they could find a patron who would present them to a parish where they could be ordained and inducted. Meanwhile, they could accept invitations to preach where a pulpit was vacant either as a result of the illness or death of the minister or because the settled minister was away on some other business.

Many took on the role of private tutor to a gentleman's family in order to provide an income, and Duncan was no exception, becoming tutor to Colonel Erskine of Mar's two sons, residing in his home at Dalhonzie, near Crieff in central Scotland.

It was evident from Henry's activities, meanwhile, that he had not left behind the high spiritedness of his student days. At that time, it was feared the French would soon invade Great Britain and Duncan busied himself in raising the local people to prepare themselves for self-defence, a role he would fill more than once. It is said he even donned Highland dress and lost no opportunity to address the local people on the dangers they faced and the need to be prepared. It is doubtful, however, if he took himself very seriously. Verse was still pouring from his pen and he described himself as '[t]he young Lowland Highlander – / The merry grave soldier divine'.[1]

Doubtless Henry took himself a little more seriously when he was summoned to the house of some old ladies in his Highland district to perform an exorcism, a task at which he apparently achieved considerable success.

Duncan, however, did not remain long in Perthshire. In the spring of 1799 the parishes of Lochmaben and Ruthwell in Dumfriesshire became vacant, and in both cases the charge was in the gift of the local patron, the Earl of Mansfield. Duncan's family and friends probably would have brought his candidacy to the notice of the Earl's agents, and Duncan was asked to make a choice. There was also an interest in him from a Northern Irish church, again in the gift of Lord Mansfield, but he soon dismissed the idea of crossing the Irish Sea.

Both Lochmaben and Ruthwell were in the Presbytery of Annan and therefore not very far from Henry's home village of Lochrutton. In many ways Lochmaben was the more attractive prospect. Its population was twice the size of Ruthwell's, the stipend was larger and the wool and linen industries had helped make it a prosperous place. It was also an attractive town in a beautiful setting, a place where a man with ambition could make progress. Nevertheless, Duncan turned it down in favour of the much less salubrious parish of Ruthwell, situated several miles south-east of the county town of Dumfries.

At its meeting on 3 July 1799 the Presbytery of Annan dealt with the admission of a new minister to the parish of Ruthwell. The Earl of Mansfield had presented Henry Duncan; the presbyters agreed that the papers were in order and Henry, who had been waiting outside, was invited in. As the minutes recorded, he

> produced an extract of his licence and was desired to preach before the Presbytery which he did. The Presbytery, considering that the Parish of Ruthwell has been so long deprived of the

stated labours of a minister among them, in consequence of the long continued indisposition of the late incumbent, resolve to proceed to the settlement of Mr Henry Duncan with all convenient speed.

At the next meeting Duncan was asked to preach a sermon on 1 John 5:3. Having done so, he was then required to prepare an exegesis and to be examined on Church history and on the Bible.[2] His ordination then followed.

The parish of Ruthwell had a population of only 996, most of whom lived on its twenty-six farms. The villages of Ruthwell and adjacent Clarencefield were very small; the adjoining parish of Cummertrees, to the south, was slightly larger with a population of 1,300, while Mouswald, to the north, had only 705 people.[3] There were only fifty-two people in Ruthwell parish making a living from various trades, including salt panning which was an ancient tradition in the area, situated as it was on the Solway Firth.

It is tempting to think of Ruthwell as a quiet rural backwater which, in some ways, it was. But there were major changes in progress, that impacted greatly on the people of the district. As two historians later observed,

> over the course of two generations, from 1760 to 1830, the very structures of Lowland society were ripped apart; thousands of people were forced from their lands; hundreds of tiny settlements were abandoned or destroyed; an entire social stratum was eradicated and Scotland changed forever.[4]

At the same time, new towns and villages were springing up as landlords sought to benefit from the growing array of commercial opportunities that were emerging, most notably in textiles.[5]

The cash economy penetrated agriculture in new ways. It had been the tradition for people to burn peat in their fires and this they cut themselves, but it was arduous and time-consuming work so they stared to burn coal instead, often transporting it for miles. Better husbandry, land enclosures, manuring and James Small's invention of a new type of plough all added to the changes that were taking place. The opening of a lime quarry in Clarencefield may also have contributed to the general improvement in agriculture in the area. The Old Statistical Account records that there

> was not a single pig, fed in the parish, 40 years ago. Now almost every cottager feeds one. Pork or bacon is all the butcher meat the poor use in their families; and the breeding and feeding of swine is now carried on by the farmers to a considerable extent for sale, mostly for the English market.[6]

It is clear from all this that while some people were benefiting from modernisation others were suffering. It is also clear that the shift to a market economy was not always a beneficial influence on this part of the country. Shortages of commodities were commonplace, meal riots were not uncommon and these were 'rooted in the social dislocation caused by the displacement of communities'.[7] In 1796 Robert Burns recorded that, 'Here we have actual famine [. . .] Many days my family and hundreds of other families, are absolutely without one grain of meal; as money cannot purchase it.'[8] There were meal riots in Dumfries that year and many landlords established planned villages to provide employment and housing for those displaced as a result. Although there were some poor harvests, the main cause of shortages were provision agents buying up food stocks for transportation to new industrial centres of Glasgow and the west of Scotland.

Ruthwell seems to have been less seriously affected than other communities as its population continued to increase for some years after Duncan's arrival there in 1799, but it too eventually entered an inexorable decline. There were also problems created by a wartime economy to contend with, chiefly high prices and shortages. In such a situation people needed strategies to cope with the changes they faced. No sooner had Duncan arrived in the parish than he set about helping to devise institutions and plans that would assist them.

Six years after leaving Liverpool, full of doubts and confusions about his Christian faith, Henry Duncan was ordained and inducted as a minister of the Church of Scotland with responsibility for the spiritual welfare of the people of his parish. His son and biographer, George Duncan, implied that he was looking for a quiet life in which he could pursue his literary interests. He certainly used his pen to good effect but it was anything but a tranquil life. He subscribed to the view that his people's spiritual welfare would be enhanced if they did not have to worry so much about their economic welfare. And that simple thought directed his thinking and his work for the rest of his life.

Before he could begin what would become his life's work there were a few formalities with which he had to deal. Even before Henry left Dalhonzie for Ruthwell he wrote to the widow of his predecessor about the crop in the glebe. This was a large piece of land, about fifty acres, that a minister could farm to supplement his stipend. It was clear to Duncan that he had no claim to the crop that would be in the field that year and he wrote to Mrs Craig to say so. The style of the letter marks out his increasing maturity:

> Madam,
> You have probably heard that Lord Mansfield has presented me to the Church at Ruthwell. I take this opportunity of assuring you, that it will be my business to make you feel as lightly as possible the melancholy change which a fatal event has occasioned in your situation; and although I have not the happiness of being personally acquainted with you, I hope one day to prove myself worthy of your friendship.[9]

He went on to note that Church law said that he was entitled to the crop but assured Mrs Craig that he would not exercise that right and was happy for Mrs Craig to retain it and to dispose of it at her will. Mrs Craig, who would become Duncan's mother-in-law, replied that she was pleased to accept this kind offer and expressed her heartfelt appreciation.

Duncan was ordained by the Presbytery of Annan on 19 September

1799 and introduced to his parishioners the following Sunday. As was the tradition the sermon that day was preached by the senior minister of the Presbytery. The text was 1 Timothy 4:12: 'Let no man despise thy youth.' Henry Duncan was twenty-five but his fresh complexion and slender build made him look younger.

Doubtless there was much speculation among the parishioners about what kind of minister this young man was going to be. Dr Craig had been unwell for many years so it is doubtful he had served the parish as energetically as the new young minister would.

As a son of the manse, Duncan would be well aware of what was expected of him: two services, with sermons, on Sundays, administration of the Sacraments (only baptism and communion in the Church of Scotland), visits to parishioners (especially the sick), supervision of the parish, and moderation (chairing) of the Kirk Session were the major duties associated with his post. In reality ministers in the Church of Scotland had almost complete freedom in deciding how they would organise their work; as a Presbyterian Church there were no bishops to direct their paths. There was no prayer book to specify a liturgy. The local Presbytery and the regional Synod could be looked to for brotherly support and the local heritor (landlord) or, more likely, his agent, could usually be relied upon to keep the church and manse in reasonable repair.

Duncan's stipend of just less than £100 a year, in cash and kind, may seem modest, but when the new Dumfries Academy was established in 1802 the rector was paid £64 per annum. A tailor in the town earned £10 per annum.[10] Duncan also had the acreage of his glebe which, if farmed well, was more than enough to feed a family and produce a surplus for sale in local markets. Ministers were also provided with a manse (house) for their accommodation and, with the exception of the Earl of Mansfield's Comlongan Castle in nearby Clarencefield, this would be one of the larger houses in the parish. Duncan's situation, therefore, provided him with a very comfortable living and his income was sufficient for him to employ a servant.

Right from the start it was clear that Duncan was not going to be the kind of minister who would fulfil his duties in a day or two every week.[11] Moreover, he was a very sociable man and entered freely and enthusiastically into many of the events and societies in the parish and in Dumfries. He also became a freemason and joined the local lodge St Ruth No 191, serving for many years as the lodge chaplain.

When Napoleonic France again threatened to invade Great Britain, the Church of Scotland encouraged people to rise up in defence of their families. In August 1803 the Presbytery of Dumfries published a strongly-worded call to arms that was to be read in churches. It seems clear that all the presbyteries did the same. It read:

> Now brethren, now is the time to prepare for that resistance. But if the population be long delayed the impending storm may burst and your doom be completely sealed.

Several pages referred to former battles against the French – to Crécy, Agincourt and Poitier – and concluded with the call: 'We fight Brethren for our Lives, our Liberties and our Religion.' The sum of £100 was provided from presbytery funds. Clergymen were, of course, to be excluded from active service.[12]

This was not acceptable to Henry Duncan. He was prepared to fight, conscious perhaps of the example set by his maternal great grandfather, Rev. John Macmurdo, in the Jacobite rising of 1715, when he had raised a body of volunteers. Duncan had already evinced his military preparedness while still tutoring the boys at Dalhonzie. His sermon on the subject at Ruthwell included the words:

> Rouse then my brethren and gird on your armour. When the enemy arrives let him find you at your posts [. . .] Know that the security of your country depends not more on the efforts of its fleet and armies than upon the valour and public spirit of its people [. . .] I recommend a duty I am resolved myself to perform. I could plead the sanctity of my profession as a minister of the gospel of peace. It has been my happiness to live with you and should God and my country demand the sacrifice-it would be my glory to die with you.

On leaving the pulpit Henry called on his parishioners to follow him and sign up for active service, thus the Ruthwell Volunteers came into being, led by their minister.[13] Nor was this the full extent of Duncan's military exertions; he wrote letters to the local newspaper to encourage the people to action and, of course, he wrote a poem, which, like the above sermon, bears the date of August 1803:

Hark! The martial drums resound;
Valiant brothers, welcome all;
Crowd the royal standard round,
'Tis your injured country's call.

He whom dastard fears abash,
He was born to be a slave;
Let him feel the tyrant's lash
And sink inglorious to the grave.

He who spurns a coward's life,
He whose bosom freedom warms,
Let him share the glorious strife –
We'll take the hero to our arms.

Similarities to Burn's 'Scots Wha Hae' (which was written in 1793) may be entirely coincidental but the poem can be sung, with minor modification, to the same traditional tune 'Hae Tuttie Tatie'.

Duncan's endeavours to create a local volunteer force were successful. He later addressed the men, saying:

The first in the country, and among the first in the kingdom who made an offer to Government of voluntary service against the enemies of your country, you have set an example of zeal and alacrity, in the public cause, which reflects honour upon the parish to which you belong, and must endear you to all who have at heart the interests of liberty and religion. To convince you that I am desirous of declining no service, however arduous, in which it may be your duty to engage, I have at your earnest request, accepted of an appointment which will place me foremost in the hour of danger.

They had made him their captain and Duncan had accepted the position. It was, to say the least, a highly unusual thing for a minister to do and there were those who thought it inappropriate. Henry's son, writing his father's biography more than forty years later, recorded this episode with ill-concealed embarrassment.[14] Nevertheless, what Duncan was doing was 'living out the idea of civic humanism as a modest clerical landholder, an armed citizen, and an ardent champion of virtue and freedom'.[15]

Duncan maintained his position on the right to defend against attack until the end of his life. In 1840 he declined an invitation from the Peace Society to write an article on the grounds that he did not subscribe to non-resistance. 'We are bound to defend our lives, the chastity of our wives and daughters and, under certain circumstances, our property itself,' he reasoned, 'not only at the risk of our own lives but also at the hazard of depriving the aggressors of their lives.'[16]

The invasion, however, did not take place and the volunteers were never called to active service, although it is possible they became part of the Dumfries, Roxburgh and Selkirk militia who were designated the 7th Regiment of Militia in 1803 and who, on occasion, could be 'mustered, trained and exercised'.[17]

There could also be a lighter side to volunteering. On one occasion Duncan had been on guard duty in Dumfries but was due to preach in one of the Dumfries churches the following morning. Colonel de Peyser met him in the street as he struggled to divest himself of his red military uniform and don his black clerical robes, greeting him with the line: 'You reverse the couplet of Hudibras, "So like the lobster boil'd the morn / From black to red began to turn."'[18]

The young bachelor minister was often in Dumfries where he attended the assembly room and took part, according to his son, 'in the thoughtless amusements'.[19] Henry was clearly a man who enjoyed the company of others but there was certainly a rather serious side to him.

Shortly after this an event occurred which amply demonstrates Duncan's growing strength of character, a real test of his principles. A young member of his congregation had, due to an error, been called up for service in the military. He was under age and sought to have his name struck from the roll. However, this would mean that another man from Ruthwell would have to serve in his place. This was stoutly resisted by the parishioners, and when Duncan sought to assist the young man, the local people turned against him. Duncan sought to explain himself and the situation, but feelings were running high, notwithstanding that the young man was in the right. When the matter was brought before the authorities in Annan it was resolved in his favour. Friends advised Duncan, who had attended and spoken at the hearing, that his words and actions had raised considerable ire in the community and that he might not be safe on the road home. He ignored the warnings and returned home unharmed. The next morning, he visited a woman 'famous for both the violence of her tongue and the prowess of her arm' who had been threatening harm to Duncan. He managed to talk her round and she soon became his advocate. The episode eventually blew over but it must have illustrated to Duncan how delicate the good relationship between a minister and his parishioners could be. He might also have taken some satisfaction from having done the right thing and been vindicated.

Duncan was responsible for the spiritual welfare of his parishioners but, as we have already observed, their economic and physical well-being also occupied much of his thinking. Three years before his arrival in Ruthwell local people had established a friendly society to provide for members' needs in times of illness and unemployment or their families' needs in times of bereavement. In 1799, however, there was only £81 in the fund. It was not a success although sufficient funds had been laid aside for the management committee to purchase such items as a staff, flag, gloves, sashes and drink. There was a quasi-masonic nature to many friendly societies and, of course, it is highly likely that members of the local masonic lodge, with its emphasis on brotherly love and mutual support, were also members. The masonic lodge later formed its own friendly society.

Like many such bodies, however, it was not well regulated and Duncan, having been elected its president on 1 July 1800, took it upon himself to introduce some reforms. His immediate priority was the society's rules, which were deemed to be 'inadequate for the purpose for which they were intended'. The duties of office bearers were ill defined and some of the laws were so obscure that 'they served to promote a contentious disposition' to such an extent that they did not promote 'that spirit of order and harmony, which is the only means of securing respectability and contributing to the success of the institution'.[20] New rules and regulations were drawn up, approved in general meeting on 20 October 1800, and confirmed by the Quarter Sessions on 3 March 1801.

Duncan went on to become, in effect, the society's actuary when he worked out tables of mortality based upon the parish registers, of which he was the keeper, so that levies and benefits could be calculated more accurately. His input clearly made a difference, for by 1804 the fund's balance was £284 and six years later, when he set up the savings bank, it was £522, proof indeed that working people were able to save.

The Treaty of Amiens (1802), which brought peace between France and her enemies, lasted little more than a year, meaning Britain was at war almost continually between 1793 and 1815. The requirements of wartime added greatly to the distorting effects that were also taking place in the economy. Revolutions in agriculture, transport, industry and the urban environment all made heavy demands and produced changes that seriously disrupted more traditional ways of living and working. Prices of basic commodities rose, but an even more serious problem, especially in the south-west of the country, was that supplies were often inadequate. Bad harvests and the increasing commercialisation of agriculture were at the heart of the problem. Agents and speculators bought up supplies of foodstuffs and transported them to the growing urban areas where they could be sold for higher prices. This ran counter to traditional ways of thinking which said that supplies should not leave their local area until local needs had been met. Something had to be done if the meal riots of earlier years were not to be repeated.

It was not unknown for magistrates, landlords, kirk sessions, friendly societies and factory owners to address this problem by providing foodstuffs, often at discounted prices, to their tenants, workers, members or other local people.[21] David Dale, the proprietor of the New Lanark cotton works and agent for the Royal Bank of Scotland in Glasgow, did this in 1783 for the people of his home village of Stewarton in Ayrshire.[22] But a legal decision in the Court of Session in 1801 called into question the rights of magistrates to interfere in the markets by regulating the price of grain or determining to whom it could be sold. Market economics were clearly overcoming traditional ways of thinking.[23]

The practice of subsidising food became the norm for the Ruthwell friendly society but, in reality, it was Duncan who organised most of it. At a meeting of the society on 10 December 1800, he reported that a gathering of friendly societies in Dumfries had agreed to co-operate in importing meal from Rotterdam. At that same meeting the friendly society delegates argued that exporting grain to England was illegal. C. A. Whatley's research revealed that

in the time-honoured belief that local needs should be accommodated first, they asserted that the 'inhabitants of every country' were entitled to 'the produce of their native soil'. Denial of this was a 'violation of the rights of nature' and in opposition to the Will of Providence.[24]

Later that month it was reported to the Ruthwell members that the strategy of importing grain from Rotterdam had proved abortive, whereupon two members were deputed to try to buy meal locally at not more than 4 shillings (20p) per stone. This injunction was treated liberally and they were able to purchase meal at 5s (25p), which was then sold to local people for 4s 6d (22.5p). Transactions of this kind became commonplace, with the society absorbing the losses.

In January 1801, meanwhile, the minute book reveals that

Mr Duncan reported that he had heard from his brothers in Liverpool respecting Indian corn who inform him that it sells at Liverpool for 10 shillings per bushel and the committee direct him to order the amount of £40 for them to be shipped for them as soon as possible.[25]

Shortly thereafter the crisis was addressed by the factor to the major landowner, the Earl of Mansfield, who had been in conversation with Duncan and had agreed to provide a room for the society, and also with furniture to be made from timber from Comlongan wood. He further provided a village store to complement what the friendly society was doing and, at that point, the society decided thenceforth to cater only for its own members.

Human nature being what it is some members were soon declaring that the allocation of meal was not working well; some were receiving nothing while others were getting more than their fair share. Duncan's common sense response was to set up a rationing system with anyone found to be undermining the rules expelled from the society.

The problem of supply, however, persisted through 1801, which was certainly a crisis year, and in the spring one of the members, Mr Mundell, was asked to plough, sow and harrow the garden attached to the society room. As the year progressed prices began to fall and by January 1802, as peace was approaching, the remaining flour had to be sold at public auction as it was beginning to spoil. That was not the end of the matter and, as the war restarted, the meal supply system devised in 1800 continued and was still working in 1808. This suggests that the system was working well and at quite a high level.

All this was achieved through the mechanisms provided by the friendly society, its accounts revealing that the subsidy was borne by that organisation. However Duncan's biographers, his son and his great grand-daughter, seemed unaware of this fact and assumed the losses fell on Henry.[26] While it remains possible that he provided some other subsidy, perhaps by paying transport costs on the corn from Liverpool, there can be no doubt that the costs of this scheme were borne collectively. However, it is not a matter of dispute that Duncan was the organiser of the scheme and that it cost him a great deal in time and energy.

Nor was this the only mechanism that Duncan used to address the village's economic problems. He is known to have supplied flax for spinning by the unemployed women of the village, and when the potato crop was really poor he acquired a supply of seed potatoes so that a better crop could be grown. He also employed men, who would otherwise have had no work, to labour on the glebe in draining and ditching so that this area soon became a model farm. Finally, Duncan rose to the defence of local salt panners when their livelihoods were also threatened.

There was another part of the dynamic of the minster/people relationship that was vital in all this activity. It helped Duncan to get to know his people in their daily lives and went far beyond what happened in church each Sunday.

At this time the ministry of the Church of Scotland fell into two groups. An evangelical revival was showing signs of growth but most ministers were moderates whose zeal for the Gospel was lukewarm and, it may be said that, certainly in his early years in the ministry, Henry Duncan fell into this latter group: '[F]or some years after his ordination the peculiar doctrines of Christianity had held but a subordinate place instead of their due pre-eminence in his pulpit addresses'.[27] The Enlightenment had done much to introduce scepticism into people's minds, and first the universities and then the church had been affected. Duncan's education had steeped him in this intellectual melting pot and he had come out with a Christian faith that set him in the moderate group of ministers.

Duncan preached about things that interested him; the beauties of nature, the need for people to be independent and more practical matters. There was little of the Holy Spirit in any of this, but he did care about the people. Henry set up a library for their use and many of his own books were lent. He went on to hold classes on a Sunday afternoon on such subjects as history, science and astronomy, but the response of his parishioners was lukewarm and some thought that it was inappropriate to conduct such classes on the Sabbath. Some of them even thought that he was spending altogether too much time in the convivial atmosphere of the assembly rooms in Dumfries where the upper classes would gather for social occasions or just to take tea and play cards.

So Duncan's early years of ministry were not entirely as he might have wished. He had his critics, as all ministers do, but he had achieved some notable successes, especially through the friendly society, and he had demonstrated to his people that he was willing to work hard on their behalf. Duncan's personal life was also changing, in two important respects.

In the summer of 1804, while attending a Presbytery meeting in Annan, Henry learnt that three Quakers were to hold a public meeting that evening: Solomon Chapman, Deborah Darby and Rebecca Byrd, who travelled the English-speaking world impressing people with their modesty and sincerity.

Duncan, too, was struck by their spirituality and simplicity and, having heard them speak, he invited them to his manse in Ruthwell, which they would pass on their way to Dumfries. They came the following day and dined with Henry, his parents and his sister Christian, who was then keeping house for her brother. She recorded the event many years later; after dinner Deborah Darby turned to Duncan

and addressed him for some minutes in the friendliest and affecting way, saying that she could not leave his hospitable roof without expressing the interest she felt in him, and the assurance she entertained that he would be a blessing to those among whom he lived, and whom he was engaged in teaching the glorious gospel of Jesus Christ.

When she concluded Duncan attempted to reply, 'but was so overcome that he could only say a few words of thanks, and burst into tears. Indeed there was not a dry eye in the room'.[28]

All assembled sank to their knees and Deborah Darby led them in prayer.[29] Duncan was so taken with what was said that he followed the trio to Dumfries and heard them speak a second time. Lasting friendships were formed that day and correspondence was still passing between the Duncan and Darby families thirty years later. This experience undoubtedly strengthened Duncan's faith and prepared him for his life of service. He recorded his feelings and his renewed sense of faith in a diary dated 25 August 1804:

So far as I am acquainted with my own heart, I have reason to believe it is open to virtuous and pious impressions; but I have to lament an imbecility of mind and an indolence of disposition which have too often prevented me from resisting, with that firmness which becomes a Christian, the corruptions of the world, and from adhering with steady principle and unwearied diligence to the path of duty. When I would do good, evil has still been present within me; and my life has been little else than a series of broken resolutions, feeble efforts and misguided conduct. I have felt at times a pious ardour leading me to disinterested exertions in the cause of religion and virtue; but when I came to reduce to practice the resolutions which my better judgement had formed, an unworthy fear of the 'world's dread laugh,' or an exaggerated view of the difficulties I had to encounter, prevented me from performing what I knew to be my duty. The motives suggested in the gospel of Christ ought, I am well convinced, to have sufficient influence upon my mind in inducing me to hold fast my integrity, and to glorify in the truth; but I do not perceive, in fact, that the impressions which they make are so favourable as I could wish. I have not hitherto allowed them to dwell long enough upon my heart, and to enter minutely into the common transactions of life. The path of religion is not always distinctly seen through the false medium of prejudice and passion. There are so many methods of self-deception that the particulars of our duty require to be clearly understood, frequently reflected upon, and deeply impressed upon the mind.

Under the influence of these considerations I have thought it my duty coolly and deliberately to reflect upon the failures of my past conduct, and from a knowledge of the temptations by which I am most liable to be overcome, to lay down rules for my future behaviour, which, by the blessing of God, may be the means of enabling me to walk more worthy of the vocation wherewith I am called.

Gracious God! Without whom all my efforts are vain do thou grant me strength and grace to perform the resolutions which I now make!

1. The duties I owe to God.
I do solemnly resolve to impress upon my heart the obligations under which I lie to my heavenly father as my Creator, Preserver and Lawgiver, and in Jesus Christ my never-failing Benefactor and Friend – morning and evening to kneel before him and pour out my soul in gratitude and love – on all occasions to remember that He is present with me, and to bow submissive and resigned to his holy will

[. . .]

2. The duties I owe to my fellow creatures.
I do solemnly resolve to consider all mankind as my brethren, and to do to others as I would that they should do to me.

[. . .]

3. The duties which I owe to myself
I do solemnly resolve to preserve a continual guard upon the appetites and passions of my nature, and to keep myself unspotted from the world.

Under each of these headings, Duncan further expanded his thoughts to list the methods by which he would seek to live up to these undertakings. These included the regular reading of scripture, being charitable and regular self-examination.

At the end of this lengthy document Henry undertook:

to follow the example of the very respectable sect of Christians known by the name of Quakers, whose principles and conduct in many particulars I think worthy of being adopted – the suppression of pride and inordinate self-esteem – the mortification of every improper desire and irregular affection, and the resistance of every tendency to indulge too freely in the pleasures of the table.[30]

Duncan concluded his document with a prayer and the promise to read it every day until he had committed the life rules to memory. It was a seminal moment and evinced a renewed commitment to his calling and a determination to change his lifestyle. The promise to be a little more disciplined at the table was particularly revealing and may be an acknowledgement that he had been too often in the assembly rooms in Dumfries; as a single man it must have been difficult to resist the temptations to dine in male company, but that was about to change.

Shortly after the visit of the Quakers, Duncan got married. In November 1804 he wed Agnes Craig, the surviving daughter of his predecessor Rev. John Craig. The Craigs were a well-connected family – Agnes's uncle was James Craig, architect of Edinburgh's New Town. Also related to the Duncans was James Hogg (the Ettrick Shepherd), a poet and novelist who would become a regular visitor to the manse at Ruthwell.

Agnes was born in 1776 and her father had become minister at Ruthwell in 1780, so almost her entire life had been spent in the village. She was well known and well liked, and made a good match for Duncan: he trusted her judgement and consulted her on most matters, while their manse soon became a place where people with problems went for good advice. Their first-born son, George, described it as

the parish dispensary – the resort of the widow, the fatherless and the friendless – where the circumstantial story of real distress, the verbose complaints of imbecile depression, or the appeal of perplexity for advice, were sure to meet with kindly attention.[31]

Agnes's manners were quiet but self assured and she often, in reading what Henry had written, would counsel him to moderate his tone or spend a little more time in reflection before sending off a letter to a newspaper. She also encouraged his practical talents. He remodelled the manse in the years to come, created a marvellous garden and transformed the glebe into a productive farm.[32] Despite the very many claims on his time, Duncan continued to write extensively, also drawing pictures of local scenery and building models. His beeswax model of the Ruthwell Cross is a prominent artefact in the Savings Bank Museum.

The marriage produced three children: George John Craig in 1806, William Wallace three years later, and Barbara Ann, who followed in 1811. But this period was also marked by the deaths of James Currie (in 1805) and Henry's father. It is clear from the minutes of Dumfries Presbytery that Duncan senior was ailing, as he was clerk to the Presbytery and his handwriting was becoming very shaky. Consequently, his son Thomas Tudor who, despite having a medical degree, had chosen to enter the ministry and was by then minister at the New Church (Greyfriars) in Dumfries, was appointed assistant clerk. George Duncan died soon afterwards and was interred in Lochrutton cemetery on 7 April 1807.[33] Thereafter, with some help from his brothers in Liverpool, Duncan erected a cottage on his glebe in Ruthwell to house his mother.[34]

Although Thomas and Henry were in different presbyteries, they were living only a few miles apart and this afforded them the opportunity to renew their childhood fellowship and to become helpmates to one another in the years to come.

As Henry approached the tenth anniversary of his induction to the parish of Ruthwell he must have reflected on what he had achieved and on the condition of his people. He always maintained that the people of Ruthwell were industrious, regularly attending church, and thrifty in their habits. The existence of the friendly society undoubtedly brought benefits, not least in subsidising the cost of grain through the difficult years of the French wars (Agnes Duncan had also established a second friendly society, for women). But new farming methods in the area meant that employment for labourers was irregular and continuing high prices for grain, together with unreliable supplies, caused hardship.

As the local minister, Duncan would have been in charge of the dispensation of poor relief. Funds that were raised locally from heritors and parishioners were available to relieve cases of hardship and it was the role of the local minister to assess need and to dispense monies to relieve poverty. There are no records to tell us how much he had to distribute or how he went about it, but the Old Statistical Account of Scotland reveals that in the mid-1790s Duncan's predecessor had £25 per annum, a sum he considered sufficient for the purpose. It seems likely that in wartime Ruthwell the need for poor relief would rise.

Nevertheless, Duncan was averse to the kind of poor relief system that operated in England, which, he believed, led to dependency and reluctance to work among those in receipt of benefits. He believed that people should be encouraged to be – and remain – independent, and his thinking began to turn to ways in which this might be achieved.

One of Henry's great passions was education. As mentioned earlier, prior to entering the ministry he had served as a tutor to the sons of Colonel Erskine of Mar. And when he was settled in his own manse at Ruthwell, and his children were getting older, he established a small school at the manse in which to teach not just his own children but the children of other local people.

Although Duncan did some of the teaching himself he also hired tutors. One of these young men was Robert Mitchell, who remained in post for seven years before going to Kirkcaldy as rector in 1821 and then to the new Edinburgh Academy as classics master two years later. Duncan was known to all as 'Uncle Henry', and as his own son avowed, 'none could have told by the treatment of the boys, which of the group around him were his own, and which the children of strangers'.[35]

Duncan had firm views on the education of children. On one occasion he was consulted by a duchess, almost certainly the Duchess of Roxburghe, on the upbringing of her son. His advice to her was:

Indulgence, judiciously bestowed, will not injure a child, while undue severity is one of the worst bars to successful training. Indulge a young man in things not absolutely hurtful as much as your inclination prompts, only be firm and decided and unbending, whenever the laws of God and his own interest require it; and you will thus establish a sentiment in his mind, of mingled love and reverence, without which education can never be hopefully prosecuted.[36]

The existence of the school clearly gave Duncan great pleasure. Among the pupils in the school, aside from the Duncan children, were James Frederick Ferrier, who went on to become Professor of Moral Philosophy and Political Economy in the University of Edinburgh, and who described his time in the Ruthwell school as 'the golden age of our existence'.[37] Another pupil was James Dodds from nearby Cummertrees, who went on to be tutor in the house school before becoming a minister and then marrying Duncan's daughter, Barbara, in 1843. Dodds came out of the Church of Scotland with Duncan and his sons in the Disruption of that year.

A frequent visitor to Duncan was the young Thomas Carlyle, historian and philosopher, who was a close friend of the tutor Robert Mitchell. Carlyle and Mitchell corresponded for many years, especially after Carlyle left the area. Duncan soon became a mentor to the young man and provided him with letters of introduction to a variety of his associates in Edinburgh, including David Brewster. Carlyle deemed this kind act to be 'a favour which I reckon among the few acts of disinterested kindness that have been conferred upon me in this world'.[38] In a letter to Mitchell, he described Duncan as possessing 'the rare talent of conferring obligations without wounding the vanity of him who receives them, – and the still rarer disposition to exercise that talent'.[39] The relationship between Duncan and Carlyle was evidently very warm as Carlyle described Duncan as 'an intelligent pleasing man. Indeed the characteristic of every member of the family, seems to be a wish to make all about them happy'.[40] Carlyle also became a regular contributor to the newspaper established by Duncan to promote the bank.

Some years later the relationship was put under great strain when Carlyle asked Duncan to provide a reference for him as he applied for a professorship in the new University of London, which was then being established by Duncan's old friend Henry Brougham. By this time Carlyle had undergone a crisis of faith and Duncan told him that he would be happy to recommend him provided he could be assured that the moral philosophy that Carlyle would teach would be Christian. Duncan described Carlyle's reply as 'heart moving and embarrassing', and wrote to Carlyle saying 'your Christianity is not the Christianity of the Bible, nor, I trust of the 19th century'. Duncan was clearly moved by this situation and went on to say: 'I have been endeavouring to persuade myself that I might still conscientiously recommend you to Mr Brougham – a sore struggle I have had in my own mind – but it will not do – you yourself see this.'[41]

This is a clear indication that Duncan was not prepared to allow friendship to cloud his judgement when matters of his religious convictions were at stake. It was not, however, the end of the friendship and Carlyle continued to call at the Ruthwell manse whenever the opportunity arose.

Duncan's son George later said of his father that 'every scheme of benevolence, or piety, or of philanthropy, in which he found an opening for exertion or co-operation, was eagerly and heartily advocated by him'.[42] This was evidenced by his involvement in the British and Foreign Bible Society. A regional branch of the organisation was established in Dumfries in February 1810 and notwithstanding that Duncan was busy establishing his newspaper and bank he became the secretary. He went on to establish sub-branches in Bridekirk, Annan, Mouswald and Castle Douglas, and when the society began to produce bibles with commentary and the Apocrypha he cancelled the Dumfries membership and joined the Edinburgh Bible Society from where bibles were obtained with no additions and no commentaries.

By this stage Duncan's own preaching had evolved, almost certainly as a result of his meeting with the Quakers. His son recorded that

Disquisitions on Natural Theology, Virtue and Morality, first began to yield to discourses more directly founded on Scripture. Sentiment gave place to truth; at length evangelical doctrine, illustration and appeal came to take the prominence which poetry and fancy had once usurped; and, in the end, the affectionate and fervent spirit of a Christian pastor, yearning over lost souls, was apparent in every address he uttered.[43]

Ten years after arriving in Ruthwell, Duncan also added another outlet for his myriad of activities, by establishing a newspaper, *The Dumfries and Galloway Courier*. In doing so he had some financial help from his brothers in Liverpool and it seems there were some people, closer to Ruthwell and Dumfries, who also had a financial stake. Duncan felt the only local newspaper at that time lacked integrity and interest, so the success of his venture proved there was a market but, in this, Duncan had a second interest and ambition. He used it to publicise his ideas for establishing savings banks or, as he called them, 'parish banks', and he remained its editor until 1816.[44]

Duncan must also have been conscious of the influence that his editorship of a newspaper would bring. His position as minister in a small village was hardly likely to carry much social weight but being editor of a newspaper would bring his name to the attention of powerful and influential people in a wider area. It would open their doors to him. He also used his position as editor to promote subjects in which he was personally interested, such as the Bible Society, Sabbath schools and the evangelical work of Thomas Chalmers and Andrew Thomson.

By this stage in his life and ministry Duncan was involved with his young family, his parish, the Bible Society, the volunteers, the friendly society, the freemasons, the Presbytery, and he was now a newspaper proprietor. It was a busy life and about to become even more so with his most significant act as a social reformer, the creation and promotion of savings banks.

Chapter 6
The Bank

_____

Lighting the Fire

Savings banks originated in Europe during the eighteenth century
with the goal of providing access to interest-paying accounts to as
large a section of the population as possible. Social reform was often
an overt goal, institutions being designed to encourage less affluent
members of society to save money and have access to banking services.

In Scotland, as the first decade of the nineteenth century drew to
a close, there was a possibility that poor rates might be introduced to
address the growing problem of poverty, but Henry Duncan was
already convinced that a better way to deal with poverty was to help
people to maintain their own independence.

Aid for the really poor was provided by a poor relief system administered by the churches into which local heritors (landowners) and
others contributed regular sums. It was the responsibility of the local
minister, in this case Duncan, to dispense the funds.

There was a popular feeling that to be in receipt of these charitable
funds was a disgrace. That is what Robert Burns was talking about
when he wrote 'Epistle to a Young Friend', the poem that was to
become the leitmotif for the savings bank movement. This is stanza
vii:

To catch Dame fortune's golden smile,
Assiduous wait upon her;
And gather gear by ev'ry wile,
That's justified by Honour,

Not for to hide it in a hedge,
Nor for a train-attendant;
But for the glorious privilege
Of being independent.

Burns was criticised for becoming an excise-man in 1789 and he wrote at the time that 'people may talk as they please about the ignominy of the Excise, but what will support my family and keep me independent of the world is to me a very important matter'.[1] This sentiment was widely shared and well understood by Duncan, whose objective was, as Burns had said, to help people remain independent of the charity box. *The Courier*, therefore, became the major channel for promulgating Duncan's ideas about thrift and the importance of self-sufficiency.

Regrettably, copies of the first few years of the newspaper have not survived, but we know that, despite being its editor, Duncan was a frequent contributor of articles and letters on the idea that working people were able to save, and should be encouraged to do so, in institutions specifically designed for the purpose of encouraging thrift. However, the first letter that he published in the newspaper has survived. It was from Duncan himself and in it he set out his ideas:

The poor rates are well characterised, when they are said to be a tax on industry for the support of idleness: but we might perhaps have a still more accurate view of their evil tendency, were we to consider them as a bribe to the industrious to become idle, – My chief design in addressing you at present is, to lay before the public a scheme which cannot fail, I should hope, to produce an effect the very reverse of this, and to operate as a bribe to the idle to become industrious.

Benefits
1st That it leaves the members at liberty to consult their own convenience with respect to the amount of their payments and the time of making them.

2nd That it exempts them from all fines and forfeitures, which have been found necessary to the existence of friendly societies.
3rd That it provides a fund for enabling young persons to begin life, and particularly to enter into the married state with comfort and advantage.
4th That it affords a provision for old age to the servant, tradesman and labourer, in exact proportion to their industry and frugality during the season of youthful vigour.
5th That it enables the charitable to bestow their benefactions in such a manner as they are certain will be an encouragement to industry, and as is likely to diminish, if not entirely to remove, the necessity of poor rates and of public begging.[2]

It was one thing to have ideas about the need to encourage working people to save for their futures, but it was quite another thing to do something about it. Over the years many others had considered the idea of setting up some kind of organisation to gather and protect the savings of poor people, so Duncan could not claim – and never did – to be the originator of the idea, but he did develop a plan to put it into effect. It is clear that Duncan was not prepared to wait for someone else to take up his ideas and do something with them. The only way to know if such a scheme would work was to make a trial of it, and this is what he set out to do.

In preparing his letters for the newspaper Duncan had almost certainly not forgotten the discussion on the subject that had taken place in Currie's company in Liverpool. He also consulted some publications that had been sent to him by his old employer, Colonel Erskine of Mar.

One of these publications, by John Bone of London, was called *Tranquillity*, and was an elaborate scheme for gradually abolishing the poor rates in England. This scheme had been tried but given up for want of money to pay the management expenses. Duncan was in correspondence with a number of people, including Principal Baird of Edinburgh University, who was in possession of a letter from Bone to the Highland Society about his ideas. It is clear from this that

Duncan was not working alone and that a considerable correspondence was taking place all over the country. Contemporary writers like the economist Thomas Malthus had also canvassed the idea in his book on population.

It was clear that the commercial banks in Scotland, although more highly developed than in England, were not likely to be interested in running savings schemes for poor people but, as it transpired, they were interested in helping Duncan to develop his ideas.

Notwithstanding that the idea was being talked and written about, Duncan was firmly of the view that nothing would happen unless it could be demonstrated, in a practical way, that the scheme would actually work, thus he set about establishing his bank in Ruthwell. He was very conscious, however, that there were two factors in his parish that could well make it very difficult for his bank to succeed. The first was that none of the local heritors, i.e. the people of influence and power, was actually resident in the area. The second was that the local people who were to be the members of the bank were very poor and Duncan knew from first hand experience what difficulties they faced in making their contributions to the friendly society. Some 300 of the 1,100 parishioners were members of this society and Duncan, as its president, was well aware that many of them had to 'strain every nerve for a bare subsistence, and, so far from being able to lay up any additional savings, found at times extreme difficulty in fulfilling their engagements to the established societies'.[3]

These difficulties, however, did not deter him from making a trial of his scheme as he was aware, from his own experience, that he was dealing with a 'sober, virtuous and well-informed population'.[4] The Ruthwell Bank for Savings, therefore, opened in May 1810, meeting in what had become known as the society room, the building provided by the major heritor, the Earl of Mansfield, for the friendly society.

From the outset Duncan intended that this bank should be a model for others to follow, so he took great care to ensure that it appeared to be a highly respectable institution. His strategy was to invite the Lord Lieutenant of the county, the Vice-Lieutenant, the Sheriff and the local Members of Parliament to become honorary members. The fact that these men allowed their names to appear in this way as supporters of the bank is a measure of the influence that Duncan was already able to exercise in the region. Their names, appearing as supporters of the bank, would ensure that it was widely considered to be an organisation deserving of public support.

Duncan was also concerned that the bank should have the protection of the law, so the rules were framed in such a way that recently-passed friendly societies legislation would protect the bank and that it would therefore be recognised in the courts.

The third strand in Duncan's thinking was publicity. Consequently, he wrote about the bank from time to time in the *Courier*. The editors of other newspapers began to take note of what was happening in Ruthwell and to report to their own readers. Duncan also entered into correspondence with 'public-spirited individuals' in various parts of the country:

> Almost every post brought letters [. . .] making enquiries and asking advice as to the formation of such banks, and all these requisitions on his time and thoughts he willingly met by borrowing from the hours usually devoted to rest. In not a few instances he travelled to distant parts to give his personal aid.[5]

The expenses of all this travel and correspondence Duncan bore himself.

One of the heritors of the parish, who became an honorary member of the bank, was James Farquhar Gordon. He was a Writer to the Signet (lawyer) in Edinburgh and a member of the Edinburgh Society for the Suppression of Mendicity. Gordon received copies of the rules of the Ruthwell Bank together with regular reports of its progress. In 1813, by which time Duncan's bank had begun to make rapid progress, the Edinburgh Society decided to add a savings bank to its various schemes for the reduction of poverty and begging.

Both Duncan and the members of the Edinburgh Society were aware that in various places employers held back some part of their labourers' wages which they could then access in hard times, while in other places local ministers were 'in the habit of collecting the little earnings of their parishioners, and placing them in situations of security and profit'.[6] Indeed, Duncan went on to acknowledge that Rev. John Muckersey in West Calder had established a savings bank in 1807 (he had only recently learned of this from an Edinburgh Society report that mentioned it in passing). Muckersey apparently did not intend for his savings scheme to be a model for others, as he never printed the rules and no publicity was sought for its existence. In a footnote to his 1815 pamphlet, Duncan acknowledged that this gave Muckersey a 'claim of priority', a point that was of some importance when a rather acrimonious correspondence subsequently developed between Duncan and the Edinburgh Society.

Meanwhile Duncan was able to celebrate the success of the Ruthwell Bank and the fact that there were a number of savings banks springing up in other places. He was not at all concerned that some of them were not slavish copies of the Ruthwell model, which he continued to think of as an experiment.

Duncan's old friend from university days, Robert Lundie, was minister in the Borders town of Kelso and had taken a great interest in the savings bank. In 1814 Duncan paid him a visit and the 'Kelso Friendly Bank' was soon under way. A public meeting, chaired by the Duke of Roxburghe, introduced the scheme to the local residents.

From there the number of new savings banks grew rapidly, and not just in Scotland. Duncan even spoke of a committee in Dublin charged with disseminating the benefits of savings banks throughout Ireland.

Henry was hopeful that his ideas would spread throughout the United Kingdom, but he believed there were factors in England and Ireland that might militate against the successful development of savings banks. The habits of the people and the nature of the ecclesiastical establishment were two of these issues that, he thought, made the creation of savings banks an easier proposition in Scotland. There was also the fact that poor rates were already well established in England and, for Duncan, this was equated with 'idleness, meanness and profligacy'.

In the event, these reservations of Duncan's proved to be unfounded and the savings bank movement proceeded with as much speed and enthusiasm in the rest of the United Kingdom as it did in Scotland. The savings banks also began to appear overseas and the first in the United States was founded in Boston in 1816, from where the idea spread rapidly up and down the East Coast.[7] At that time Salem in Massachusetts was the United States' largest port and when the Salem Bank for Savings was established in 1818 the notice of its formation said that its purpose

> is to afford every industrious person the great advantage of public security and interest for small sums of money, and to enable them, without much expence of time, or trouble, to obtain that personal comfort and independence which arise from prudent conduct.[8]

This was almost an exact copy of what Duncan had written.

Duncan did not act alone and he was especially appreciative of the support provided by Principal Baird of Edinburgh University, whose tribute to Duncan was fulsome:

> the very remarkable impulse which during the currency of the past year (1815), was given to the system – an impulse which has already diffused it over every quarter of Scotland, and carried it successfully into the less accessible regions of England and Ireland, was in a great measure owing to that gentleman's individual exertions and influence.[9]

Driving Duncan's endeavours was the thought that savings banks would produce advantages that were of a moral, as well as of a political and economic nature. Foremost among these was temperance. He was also aware that the growth of the savings bank movement would not produce any 'striking incidents' but rather their impact would be 'more in the gradual amelioration of the habits of the people'.

In the pamphlet written to promote his ideas about savings banks,

Duncan gave some examples of changes that had taken place in the lives of his parishioners as a result of the availability of somewhere to save safely. One example related to a local mechanic and his apprentice who had performed some service for Duncan but had refused payment. As a token of his appreciation Duncan had opened accounts in the bank for both men in which he had deposited trifling amounts, sending them copies of their accounts together with the rules of the bank. Both had become steady savers and had amassed not inconsiderable amounts. When the apprentice became a journeyman and set up business on his own account he was able to purchase a full set of tools with the money he had saved in the bank.

In an example from his brother's bank in Dumfries, Duncan recorded how an employer lodged 5s in an account for each of his employees on the day that the bank first opened for business. The eight young men then began to vie with one another to see who could save the most. The savings habit had been instilled.

From a range of such stories it is clear that Duncan took some personal satisfaction and quiet pride in what he had begun. He recorded that

> a considerable part of the funds of the Ruthwell Bank consists of money lodged by the depositors in single payments, being the little store which they had accumulated by the efforts of their industry in the former period of their lives, or acquired by some other means. It is known to me, that in almost every instance, the sums thus deposited were, before the Institution of the Parish Bank, either lying in the houses of the owners without ever having been placed at interest, or entrusted to the care of private individuals, some of them of doubtful credit, without any proper security for their repayment. Those who happen to have observed how often people in the lower classes are under such circumstances deprived of their little all by fraud, violence, or the failure of those who are indebted to them, may have some idea of the value which such persons ought to attach to a Parish Bank.[10]

Spreading the Word

There can be no doubt that Duncan was persuaded that his 'experiment' had been successful and that he was keen to spread the concept to other places. He may not have been the originator of the idea but, as a result of the energy that he expended in promoting the savings bank model, first among his friends, family and other personal contacts, then more widely, he can justly lay claim to being the father of the savings bank movement.

The first vehicle that he used to spread the word about savings banks was the newspaper that he founded, the *Dumfries and Galloway Courier*. The circulation of this newspaper was largely confined to the south-west of Scotland but, in the way that newspapers worked in the nineteenth century, editors from far and wide were always looking for things they could copy from other newspapers and the *Courier* was known to be a fruitful source of material.

Duncan, however, knew that if the idea was to develop then he must do more. As news of the bank began to spread he received correspondence, most of it looking for advice, from many parts of the United Kingdom and from overseas. Rather than write lengthy letters to all of his correspondents he published his pamphlet in 1815 in which he outlined his ideas. A more highly developed pamphlet followed in 1816, published in Edinburgh and available from booksellers in Dumfries, Glasgow, London and Belfast. Interestingly it was also in this year that he gave up his editorship of the *Courier*, doubtless so he could devote more of his time and energy to the development of the savings bank movement. He had come to regard the newspaper as 'a great moral engine, of such power over the sentiments and feelings of the community that the conductor of it incurs no small responsibility'.[11]

Even before the first edition of the pamphlet appeared, news of its imminent publication was circulating. In January 1815 Henry Home Drummond, a circuit court judge who lived in Stirlingshire, wrote to his friend Thomas Duncan: 'Your brother's scheme for the Parish of Ruthwell has attracted great and deserved notice. I heard an account of it was to be published. When it is, I wish to get it, that I may set something of the kind a-going about us.'[12]

In the introduction to the 1816 edition Duncan made clear that the movement was gaining momentum and that, since the first edition of the pamphlet had been published at the start of 1815, savings banks had

> acquired a popularity and importance, which its most sanguine friends could scarcely have anticipated. With a rapidity which, in the history of institutions with a similar tendency, is without example, it has extended itself, in that short period, over every part of Scotland, and found zealous supporters in the sister kingdoms of England and Ireland.[13]

What Duncan did not add was that this had happened without any central organisation to direct its path.

Surprisingly the savings bank model that he chose to publicise in the 1816 pamphlet was not the Ruthwell model but that of the savings bank established by his brother, Rev. Dr Thomas Tudor Duncan, minister in the New Church (Greyfriars) in Dumfries. It seems clear from this that he did not regard the Ruthwell bank as having been perfectly formed. Rather he viewed it as an experiment which might well be capable of further improvement, and he acknowledged that circumstances might vary in other parts of the country, so that what might suit a small rural parish like Ruthwell might not be suitable in a county town like Dumfries, notwithstanding that they were only a few miles apart. Indeed, in the introduction to the pamphlet Duncan stated clearly that he considered the Dumfries regulations to be 'more perfect' than those of Ruthwell. He went on to suggest to anyone contemplating the establishment of a parish bank that they might profitably consult the rules and regulations of a number of such organisations and then distil a model suited to the area of the country in which their new bank was to be formed. It is evident from this that Duncan was not at all precious about his creation, just keen to see it developed and expanded.

The 1816 pamphlet was titled *An Essay on the Nature and Advantages of Parish Banks: For the Savings of the Industrious*. Yet Duncan was also clear that the ultimate benefits of a parish bank would be for the whole community and not just for the industrious poor, provided that it was well understood that the purpose of these banks was to enable poor people 'to provide for their own support and comfort – to cherish in them the spirit of independence, which is the parent of so many virtues'. Duncan went on to say that some organisations, such as friendly societies, had been set up with financial help from the better off classes, i.e. with a subsidy. Duncan clearly had some knowledge of a range of these organisations and was convinced that any element of subsidy would likely encourage them to offer advantages to the members that could not, in the longer term, be justified by the state of their finances. Therefore, they were likely to fail.

Duncan was generally supportive of friendly societies but felt, as we have seen, that they were confined to a narrow range of benefits and many people could not afford the regular contributions required. Consequently, something was needed that would assist people to provide for the difficult times in their lives caused by unemployment, under-employment, illness or by unexpected events. He firmly believed that most people could afford to save something from their income even if they could not do it on a regular, i.e. weekly, monthly or quarterly basis. Yet there were many circumstances that inhibited people from saving. Foremost among these was the lack of somewhere safe to keep the money. It might be stolen or wasted.

> It is distressing to think, how much money is thrown away by young women on dress unsuitable to their station, and by young men at the alehouse, and in other extravagances, for no other reason, than that they have no safe place for laying up their surplus earnings.[14]

This was a sentiment echoed by other ministers of the same era.[15]

The success of the friendly society movement, especially since it had been given legal standing by legislation in 1793, was remarkable and proved the point that many poor people could afford to save and that they would save, given the opportunity to do it safely. Duncan believed that 'This is evinced in many ways; and in none more than by the anxiety which they show to become members of Friendly Societies, and the efforts they make to pay their quarterly contributions.'[16]

The substance of this very long pamphlet (it runs to 93 pages) dealt with the practicalities of how to set up and run a 'parish bank for savings'. But that was not all. Duncan used this pamphlet to address and answer some of the criticisms that he had encountered and to emphasise the sound reasons he had for tackling some of the difficulties that were likely to be met along the way.

The number one priority, as it should be in all financial systems, was security.

> As it is of the utmost consequence that the depositors should feel perfect confidence, not only in the honesty, but the pecuniary responsibility of those entrusted with the administration of their funds, every provision, in this respect, ought to be attended to with the most scrupulous minuteness.[17]

Despite this very clear statement, Duncan again allowed for some flexibility in devising rules for new institutions because of regional variations. He thought that the nature of people varied from place to place and that there were particular differences between people in industrial and agricultural areas. The latter, in Duncan's view were inhabited by people who were 'more sober and judicious' than town dwellers.

Drawing upon the experience of friendly societies, Henry firmly believed that it was vital to involve the depositors in the management of the schemes rather than have them run by the middle classes, which was the case with the Edinburgh Savings Bank and with which Duncan had a long running battle.

> Hence it happens, that a great number of active and zealous supporters of the Institution are always to be found amongst

the members of a Friendly Society, who do more for the success of the establishment, than can be effected by the benevolent exertions of individuals in a higher station.[18]

His own experience in setting up the bank in Ruthwell had confirmed this view in his thinking, as there had been plenty of people there who imagined that the new bank was merely a device for parting them from their savings. Even Duncan himself was suspected of having some private end to serve. The minds of most were put at rest by the involvement of depositors on the management board.

Duncan drove the point home by making a comparison between the savings banks in Edinburgh and Dumfries arguing that, when the differences in population were taken into account, the Dumfries bank was the more successful and that the reason for its success was 'the popular form of its constitution'. Duncan went on to draw on all his skills of diplomatic language by taking exception to the claim emanating from Edinburgh that its scheme had been proposed as the 'only perfect model'.

Duncan drew this part of the pamphlet to a close by returning to the subject of security. He argued that, to encourage public trust in the institutions of savings banks it would be necessary to provide depositors with a copy of their account, the forerunner of the bank passbook. He went on to develop this point by saying that there should be an annual statement from the committee of management that set out the balance sheet and the accounts. Commercial banks did not begin to publish their balance sheets for another fifty years. To protect the privacy of depositors their names should not be printed in the statement but the folio numbers of their ledger page should appear and this would also appear on the copy of the account held by the depositor. This would enable depositors to check that their accounts were in order without revealing the level of their savings to anyone else. The practice of having account numbers evolved from this, and indeed these ideas were far ahead of anything being done at this time by the commercial banks.

The next part of the pamphlet dealt with the need for profit. Duncan was worried that many people of modest means were soon separated from their savings by people who offered high rates of interest but no security, and whose real motives in gathering savings were highly suspect. There were many cases, known to Duncan, where savers were parted from their savings permanently. Consequently, if savings banks were to be successful, then they had to offer a high rate of interest to attract people away from these disreputable people. He also reckoned that, in order to discourage people from withdrawing their money for frivolous reasons, a higher rate of interest should be paid on accounts on which there were no withdrawals in the year.

Other ideas considered by Duncan included the payment of an extra rate of interest to depositors who had been saving for three years, and a dividend to depositors, out of accumulated profits, such as had been proposed by the banks in Hawick and Kelso. The Dumfries bank had also introduced a scheme to reward people who saved regularly out of their earnings. No fewer than forty-one depositors had earned the extra reward in the first year of that bank, something Duncan considered a great success. Conversely he was opposed to the idea that when a depositor's savings amounted to £10 they should be transferred to an account in a public (i.e. commercial) bank. This is what happened in Edinburgh but depositors in Dumfries had rejected the idea. The idea had been canvassed as a protection for the trustees as it would diminish their responsibility when particular savings became too large, but Duncan saw the real danger in it, the creation of a distance between a saver and his money. He also saw it as highly unlikely that commercial banks would be so generous with the rate of interest as they had afforded to the savings banks.

Duncan went on to lend his support to the idea of having a rule that made it compulsory for depositors to make at least one payment a year into their account. This idea was conceived to encourage thrifty habits among depositors and behind this thinking was Duncan's hope that friendly societies, where regular payments were compulsory, and savings banks could be run in tandem. He returned to this theme later in the pamphlet, but the idea was never fully developed and did not come to fruition.

He then discussed how, and on what balances, interest should be paid and how savings banks might accumulate surpluses with which to pay the expenses of running the organisation. It seems clear, from the generous interest rates allowed to savings banks by the commercial banks, when balanced against the rates of interest paid to savings bank depositors, that a small surplus could be achieved. However, seemingly in contradiction of what he had written earlier about charitable donations, Duncan countenanced the possibility that rich patrons might bestow their benevolence on their local bank and enable it to build up an 'auxiliary' (or reserve) fund, out of which some expenses might be paid. He justified this position with the words:

> The common methods of bestowing charity, however well intended, frequently operate as a premium to idleness and dissipation; whilst the pittance given in aid of Banks for Savings, cannot fail to have a tendency directly the reverse; and it must be delightful to every enlightened mind to be assured, that a method is at last found of uniting liberality to the poor, with the certainty of promoting the best interests of society.[19]

In a footnote, Duncan even suggested that the poor rates in England might be used to support local savings banks.

From all this it seems clear that Duncan still had an open mind when it came to the organisational development of savings banks. He was also prepared to countenance regional variations in the ways that they were run, indeed he encouraged it. Yet he was resolute in his opposition to the Edinburgh model, at least so far as its governance was organised, and this was the subject to which he turned later in the pamphlet.

Before doing so Duncan addressed some other practicalities. He saw one possible obstacle to the erection of a network of savings banks: 'the difficulty of finding individuals in the different parishes willing to undertake the labour and responsibility of conducting the business in all its details'.[20] His solution was simple: have the savings bank in the chief town of every district to act as a central bank and have local collecting agencies in the smaller towns. What he was describing, of course, was a branch banking system. The commercial banks in Scotland had pioneered branch banking and there were several branches of national banks in Dumfries. What he neglected to mention in this part of his analysis was that the Edinburgh savings bank had already opened sub-branches.

The advantage of operating this model was that local organisation could be kept to a minimum. A cash-book was all the accounting record required and it would be the responsibility of the central office to calculate interest and do all the other necessary book keeping. This was the model upon which Germany's savings banks were developing.

Duncan was clearly looking forward and anticipating how the savings bank system might evolve, and was suggesting possible solutions to problems and issues that might arise. He even went on to contemplate the possibility of a national organisation in Edinburgh that would act as a central bank for all Scottish savings banks. This had been suggested to him by, among others, Principal Baird of the University of Edinburgh, a noted supporter of the savings bank movement.

At the outset the commercial banks had generously allowed 5 per cent interest on all savings bank deposits and this had enabled savers to be well rewarded for their thrift. But Duncan was worried that, as the system developed and became nationwide, the commercial banks might limit their generosity. It was a prudent consideration and was just what happened in the early 1820s. Duncan hoped that by bringing all the funds in a district into one central savings bank that the commercial banks might continue their generous position, but he acknowledged that this might not happen and that some other outlet might have to be sought for the savings. If the commercial banks were unwilling to continue to offer such a high interest rate, then savings banks money would have to be invested in government funds or in some 'unexceptionable landed security'. It is possible that Duncan was looking forward to the parliamentary bill that he would eventually bring forward, for these were the solutions proposed in the legislation enacted three years later.

In the conclusion to this section of the pamphlet Duncan returned to the need for security. He envisaged a situation where office bearers in the banks would need to provide security for their intromissions, normally via a bond of fidelity underpinned by an insurance policy. He also suggested that, if the idea of central banks was to be developed then there would be a need to appoint a senior officer whose salary might be paid by the local heritors:

> I am convinced they would not hesitate to do so, were they to consider the good which the scheme [. . .] could not fail to accomplish; not to mention the eventual advantage they might themselves derive from it by removing the necessity of poor rates.[21]

None of these wider developments happened in Duncan's lifetime. While the movement grew strongly it was dominated by small local banks.

Fighting the Fight

Relations with the Edinburgh Society were never very good. Quite what initially aroused the animosity is not clear, but any chance that the relationship might be a healthy one was dashed when John Forbes, one of the trustees and a senior Edinburgh advocate, published a pamphlet and sent a letter to the editor of the *Quarterly Review*.[22] These documents were not only critical of the Ruthwell model but claimed for the Edinburgh Society the parenthood of the savings bank movement. Duncan was incensed, and his friends encouraged him to make a robust reply. Among these allies was Principal Baird of Edinburgh University who, although a director of the Edinburgh Society, nevertheless felt strongly that Forbes had misrepresented the situation and that a strong rebuttal was required. The reality was that the Edinburgh savings bank had not been established until three and a half years after the Ruthwell bank.

Henry Duncan's response was both polite and trenchant, and was again published as a pamphlet. Apparently being part owner of a newspaper gave Duncan easy access to print facilities and he made good use of them. His pamphlet was published and made available in Dumfries, Glasgow, London, Dublin and Belfast, but not Edinburgh. Nevertheless, he made sure that Forbes received a copy. It began:

> You will not, I think, be surprised to see, from my pen, an answer to some passages in your pamphlet, entitled 'Observations on Banks for Savings;' as it contains statements and reasonings which you must be sensible cannot fail to appear to me both unfounded in themselves, and injurious to those institutions in which we feel a mutual interest.

The tone was moderate but it was obvious that Duncan was unhappy. Forbes seemed unaware of some of the finer points of the management of the Ruthwell system, but this had not prevented him from offering critical comments. For example, he had decreed that the annual meeting of depositors in Ruthwell was a waste of time. Duncan took the view that it was only once a year and served to produce good feelings and greater public knowledge while, in Edinburgh, the relationship between bank and depositor was conducted in 'profound silence':

> The Ruthwell scheme, on the contrary, creates a strong and salutary bond of union among all the depositors; they are members of a common establishment, instituted for their mutual benefit; some of the office bearers are taken from among their own number, and keep alive the spirit of the association by the zeal and ardour their office inspires; their yearly meetings give still greater publicity to the society, and a stronger interest in its concerns; the gentlemen who manage the institution, as well as the committee of superintendence, are then elected by the free choice of the members, the advantages of the establishment are discussed, the progressive improvement of the funds is stated, and remarkable instances of industry and frugality are mentioned with approbation. It is easy to perceive the powerful influence which all these circumstances must produce on the prosperity of the institution.

Duncan went on to demolish Forbes's points one by one. He made particular reference to the use of folio numbers on the accounts as a way of maintaining privacy and security. All this led Duncan to the view that Forbes had not done his homework and did not really understand the Ruthwell situation.

Duncan moved to a conclusion and added that he had entered this controversy reluctantly:

> Add to this, an extreme unwillingness to enter the lists of controversy with any person, and particularly with you, sir, whose judicious and unremitting efforts in the cause of the poor, I have long had reason to admire, and whose talents and virtues have established a claim to high consideration and universal esteem. On the other hand, I was too deeply impressed with the importance of the subject, to be deterred even by formidable obstacles, or to yield readily to personal considerations.

He noted too, in a sharp barb, that affluent people were often reluctant to associate themselves in any way with the poor, and that might dispose them to prefer the Edinburgh model.

The question of which was the parent bank was resolved, at least to Duncan's satisfaction, when he pointed out that when the Edinburgh bank was established it was in possession of papers provided by J. Farquhar Gordon WS, who was both a heritor in Ruthwell and an Edinburgh lawyer. Gordon was a trustee of the Edinburgh bank and Duncan had provided him with information on how Ruthwell was organised and run. At the same time Duncan was in possession of letters from as far away as Ashford, in the south of England, requesting information about how to set up and run a savings bank.

All this was an unsavoury incident through which Duncan managed, with some apparent difficulty, to contain his anger. It was not the end of the matter and the relationship between Duncan and the Edinburgh bank remained strained.

Duncan was in the habit of referring to the Ruthwell bank as the 'parent' institution and it was this claim that had produced the ire of the Edinburgh establishment.

Duncan's son was in no doubt where the honour of being the parent institution lay:

> To withhold from Mr Duncan the merit of originating this movement, would be no less unjust and ungenerous, than to deny to Watt or Arkwright their high claims as mechanical inventors, or to Galileo and Newton their still loftier titles as the fathers of modern science.[23]

Forbes eventually withdrew his claims, but not before the matter had been settled in the pages of the *Quarterly Review*, a journal which had published several articles on the subject of savings banks in 1816 and which, in a subsequent edition commented:

> We are warranted on the whole to conclude, that, though some institutions, similar both in principles and details, had been formed before the parish bank of Ruthwell, yet it was the first of the kind which was regularly and minutely organised and brought before the public; and farther, that as that society gave the impulse which is fast spreading through the kingdom, it is in all fairness entitled to the appellation of the *Parent Society*.

The article went on to praise Duncan by saying that

> Justice leads us to say that we have seldom heard of a private individual in a retired sphere, with numerous avocations and a narrow income, who has sacrificed so much ease, expense and time for an object purely disinterested, as Mr Duncan has done.[24]

Thomas Carlyle, who was then teaching in Kirkcaldy, took note of this and, in a letter to his friend Robert Mitchell in Ruthwell, wrote: 'I was happy to see that due credit is at length given to Mr Duncan for his valuable institution.'[25] Duncan's friend Rev. Andrew Thomson was also glad to see the matter settled in Duncan's favour. 'My heart is gladdened to see truth victorious,' he wrote, 'and in that great victory to see the high tory tone of your opponent laid so completely prostrate.'[26]

Duncan's old university friend Robert Lundie had established a savings bank in his parish at Kelso, and in a lengthy letter to him on the subject Duncan explained why he had structured his pamphlet in the way that it appeared. Lundie had apparently offered some criticism, and in a telling concluding paragraph he wrote: 'What does your excellent spouse say to all this rout about savings banks? I fear she will think we are forgetting the more needful occupation of saving souls.'[27]

Running the Bank

That Duncan's experiment was successful there can be no doubt. And that success came at three levels – local, national (i.e. the United Kingdom) and international. Within a few years of the Ruthwell Parish Bank having been established there were savings banks all across the UK and in other parts of the world.

At the end of the first year the annual meeting of depositors convened in the church at Ruthwell for the 'election of office bearers, auditing the accounts etc.' (the society room where deposits were gathered was too small). Attendance at the meeting was compulsory for all depositors and they gathered to hear about what had been achieved. There are no surviving records of the meeting but we know that total deposits were £151. It was a small beginning but by year four they had risen to £922, almost £1 for every resident. Not everyone in the parish was a depositor, but this balance added to what was in the friendly society gave the lie to those critics who maintained that poor people did not have the capacity or ability to save. By 1822 deposits totalled £2,042.

The rules of the bank were quite strict. The statement of account, in effect her passbook, for Janet Dinwiddie from Murraythwaite for the period 1817–25 shows her folio number and it is signed by 'Henry

Duncan, Governor'. The rules of the bank are printed on one side of the statement: every depositor was required to lodge a minimum of 4s (20p) per annum; failure to do so incurred a penalty of 1s (5p); and depositors had to give a week's notice of making a withdrawal. The statement of account, meanwhile, had to be 'produced every time any transaction is made with the Bank', ensuring the bank's records tallied with the customer's account.[28]

In the light of subsequent practice these rules might seem a little draconian, but they were well counter-balanced by the interest that savers would earn on their deposits, which was at the rate of 5 per cent so long as they kept the account, and kept saving for three years. Interest was allowed only on whole pounds. If there had been withdrawals from the account then the rate of interest was reduced to 4 per cent. These were very generous rates of interest and were made possible only because the British Linen Bank branch in Dumfries, where the deposits were lodged, was prepared to pay a higher rate of interest for the savings banks deposits than it paid to its other customers. This has been depicted as a charitable act by the commercial banks, which it undoubtedly was, but it was not entirely disinterested as the advantage for the British Linen was that the savings bank monies would be in coins of small denominations. These were necessary for commercial banks in their daily transactions and, if they did not come from local sources such as the savings bank, then they would have to be brought, at some expense, from the bank's head office in Edinburgh.

As in every well-run bank routine ensured that all was regular, that the funds were protected, that the depositors had confidence in the safety of the bank, and that the office bearers were honest. One way to ensure this last point was to keep the monies that were not deposited in the British Linen Bank safely locked in a chest with three locks. Each of the office bearers had a key and the attendance of all three key-holders was necessary to transact business. This ensured that no single office bearer, and no two acting in concert, could steal the cash. Duncan eventually had a steel lined wrought iron safe installed.

By 1822 the total deposits of the bank had risen to £2,042 19s 5d

and the surplus fund held £35 17s 7d. Duncan must have felt that
the enormous amount of work that he had put into making the bank
a success had been worthwhile. He was, however, aware that his
experiment had not solved the problem of poverty in the parish,
although it had certainly helped to alleviate it, while showing relatively
poor people that self-help could keep them independent and assist
them to avoid the deeply felt stigma of having to accept parish relief.
There were 158 accounts in 1822, of which ten had been opened that
year.

The list of office bearers read:[29]

Trustees
Henry Duncan, Governor
William Richardson, Deputy Governor
William Muir, Secretary
Thomas Ewart
David Sinclair

Treasurer
Thomas Ferguson, Schoolmaster

Ordinary Members of the Committee
Andrew Boyd
William Dunbar
Gabriel Chalmers
John G Underwood
John Hastie
Christopher Dickson
Joseph Wilson

The task of being treasurer seems to have been an obligatory task for
whoever was the local schoolmaster. The report also gives a list of
depositors by folio number; only the names of organisations that were
depositors are identified. They were:

Ruthwell Savings Bank Organisations	Balance
Female Association	£12 16s 10d
Militia Club	£2 14s 1d
Male Friendly Society	£198 11s 5d
Female Friendly Society	£120 13s 6d
Parish Store	£1 8s 1d
School Book Society	£3 19s 6d
St Ruth's Masonic Lodge	£0 5s 0d
New Militia Club	£1 7s 3d
Bible Association	£9 9s 6d

What is remarkable about this table is that Henry Duncan, sometimes acting with his wife Agnes, had an interest, often a controlling one, in every one of these organisations. This is a measure of how influential a parish minister could be, but it is unlikely that many parish ministers had the range of interests and the determination to exercise the necessary energies as Duncan.

The 'experiment', as Duncan described it, was watched closely by many people, not least by his friends and his brother Thomas and, as has been said, it was not long before they too set up savings banks in their home towns. Thomas was petitioned by members of his congregation to establish a bank in Dumfries and promptly did so. It met at first in the church session house[30] and then in a small room in the treasurer's house in Chapel Street where 'the counter consisted of two planks placed over a couple of barrels, lighted by dip candles'.[31] Even before Thomas got his bank in operation savings banks were established in the border towns of Hawick and Kelso, the latter by Duncan's old friend from his university days, Robert Lundie.

In 1818, perhaps at Duncan's instigation, the General Assembly of the Church of Scotland conducted an investigation into the state of the poor in Scotland. There was little doubt that the problems of the poor were worsening following the end of the Napoleonic Wars and the church set about finding out what was happening throughout the country. Ministers were required to submit their assessments of their own parishes and were required to state if there was a savings bank in their parish. The response probably surprised Duncan. There were 132 parish banks in the list, which was clustered by presbytery, but the number is certainly understated as a number of presbyteries were missing including Duncan's own, that of Annan. So the Ruthwell bank is not on the list.

There was a similar tale to be told in other parts of the United Kingdom. Savings banks sprang up throughout the country. Nor was the movement confined to these shores. As we have said the first savings bank in the United States was established in Boston in 1816, from where the movement spread rapidly.

The reforming King William I of Wurttemberg sent an emissary to Ruthwell to learn what was happening, as did the King of Sweden, although it is not clear whether the order was given by the elderly King Charles XIII or by his successor Jean Baptiste Bernadotte, who was one of Napoleon's generals and who reigned as King Charles XIV. The emissary from Sweden may well have been Carl David Skogman who, more than any other, was the man who established the movement in his homeland. One of the papers that he wrote on the subject compared poor relief systems in England and Scotland:

> He claimed that English laws on social welfare encouraged vagrancy and harmed the working class interests. In Scotland, however, the first savings banks showed the positive effects of organised saving.[32]

Gaining the Act

When Duncan established the Ruthwell bank in 1810 he gave some thought to how his creation would exist in relation to the law. At that time, he believed the protections afforded by the friendly societies legislation would be adequate but he, nevertheless, contemplated that legislation might eventually be required for savings banks if their numbers grew and if their activities diverged from those of friendly societies to such an extent that the Friendly Societies Act of 1793 no longer sufficed.

The main issue was that trustees and managers might find themselves dragged into courts to settle legal disputes and discover that they were personally responsible for whatever had happened. There was also the need to protect the banks' funds from criminal mismanagement. By mid-1815, when the movement was growing apace, Duncan began to receive legal advice that suggested that the Friendly Societies Act would not protect savings banks and their personnel. Local courts run by Justices of the Peace might make decisions on issues relating to them, but there was no appeal process from there to a higher court. Duncan decided that something had to be done and turned his mind to what was required. He was not alone in his thinking.

The possibility of legal protection for savings banks first arose in England where George Rose MP, having published a pamphlet on the subject in 1816, introduced a Bill into parliament that year which passed into law in May 1817. This Act provided some legal protections and, at the same time, required savings banks to invest their funds in government securities. It was not unusual for particular Scottish interests to be ignored when legislation was being prepared in the British parliament and this was no exception. Duncan was aware that, if Scottish savings banks were required to subscribe to this legislation then the rate of interest that could be offered to depositors would be lowered, as the rate of return on government securities was a full 1 per cent lower than was allowed by the Scottish commercial banks on savings bank deposits at that time. Moreover, investing in government securities was a lot less flexible a medium than bank deposits as, when funds were required by the bank, the securities would have to be sold. This was clearly a lot less convenient than bank deposits, especially for savings banks in the more remote parts of the country.

When the tenor of Rose's bill became public knowledge opposition to it came from unexpected quarters. Nor was the opposition just to the legislation; some of it was to the very idea of savings banks. William

Cobbett was a newspaper proprietor and an MP and was bitterly opposed to any state support for savings banks. He referred to Rose's bill as the 'Savings Bank Bubble', as he saw it as a way of extending the national debt to which he was violently opposed.

Rose had proposed that savings bank funds should be invested in government securities, thus becoming part of the national debt. It was also his intention that the government would pay a higher rate of interest on them than it paid on the rest of the national debt. The reason why this avenue for investing savings was proposed rather than the banking system, as happened in Scotland, was simply that the English banking system, compared with that in Scotland, was underdeveloped. Banks were local, with a small number of partners and low levels of capital. There were few branches and many banks did not offer depositing as a service. So, if the savings bank system was to grow in England it required the kind of legislation that Rose had introduced.

Cobbett took the view that the national debt existed because governments over many years had squandered resources, and that corruption and venality had exacerbated the problem. He viewed the proposed legislation as a means of bringing working people and their savings into this essentially corrupt system:

Now then, in order to enlist great numbers of labourers on their side, the Borough-mongers have taken up the scheme of coaxing them to put small sums into what they called banks. These sums they pay large interest upon, and suffer the parties to take them out whenever they please. By this scheme they bind great numbers to their tyranny. They think that great numbers of labourers and artizans, seeing their little sums increase, as they will imagine, will begin to conceive the hopes of becoming rich by such means; and, as these persons are to be told that their money is in the funds, they will soon imbibe the spirit of fund-holders, and will not care who suffers, or whether freedom or slavery prevail, so that the funds be but safe.

Such is the scheme, and such the motives. It will fail of this object, though not un-worthy of the inventive power of the servile knaves of Edinburgh [. . .] The parsons seem to be the main tools in this coaxing scheme.[33]

A more measured, and more influential, opposition came from *The Times*, which maintained its hostility for many years. Faced with this resistance, Rose and Duncan agreed that separate legislation would be presented for Scotland and the rest of the UK. As Duncan's scheme did not involve investing the money in government securities he must have entertained the idea that his Bill would have a smoother passage through parliament than the one promoted by Rose. If he entertained this notion, he could not have been more wrong.

Before Rose's bill was introduced Duncan had written to his local MP, W. R. K. Douglas, on this very subject. Douglas became Duncan's friend and collaborator on a number of his projects in years to come, and his contribution in helping Duncan get appropriate legislation passed for savings banks in Scotland was substantial. Their initial intention was simply to have a piece of legislation which clarified the friendly society position and stated, for the avoidance of doubt, that the 1793 Friendly Societies Act did apply to Scotland and its savings banks. The introduction of Rose's Bill, however, required a more considered response. The immediate necessity was to take steps to ensure that when it was passed it applied only to England and Wales. This was achieved after some friendly correspondence between Duncan and Rose. The way was then left open for Duncan to devise a Bill that would suit the particular needs of Scotland.

This was not a task for which Duncan had any experience, but he set about it with assistance from Douglas. He also had the good sense not simply to write a proposal and then get it introduced in parliament. Before then he circulated drafts of what was being proposed around the Scottish savings banks, and other interested parties, asking for comments and criticisms. Duncan's son and biographer gave the impression that there was widespread support for legislation, apart from Edinburgh, but this was not entirely the case.[34] It took two years of hard work before an Act was passed.

Douglas wrote to Duncan on the subject in June 1817. He had consulted with those involved in running the Glasgow savings bank and with Kirkman Finlay the Glasgow MP. 'The general feeling is adverse to any legislative enactment whatever – they consider it premature to attempt to legislate when no practical inconvenience has yet occurred.' The Glasgow people also advised that popular sentiment was strongly hostile to any legislative interference with savings banks. Finlay advised delay and further suggested that Duncan should consult Principal Baird of Edinburgh University on the subject.[35] Duncan had already done so and received a reply confirming Baird's views as being similar to those of Douglas.[36] Over the ensuing winter Duncan continued to receive letters which urged caution in this matter. Sir R. C. Ferguson, Lord Rosslyn, Rev. James Thomson and William Munnochie all advised Duncan to hold fire and for broadly similar reasons. Indeed, Munnochie, who was Lord Advocate (Scotland's senior law officer), wrote to Douglas in March 1818 to say: 'I read Mr Duncan's bill, which appeared to me cumbersome and I have much doubt if any bill at all be necessary.'[37] Popular opinion, especially among the working classes, was against any government involvement with their savings. Rev. James Thomson in Dundee wrote to say that

the democratic press in this country, ever ready to misrepresent every act of government [. . .] may take advantage of the proposed enactment to alarm the contributors (the depositors), as if the whole was a plan to enable Government more easily to possess themselves of the wealth of the country, or at least to avail themselves of it, for supporting not the credit of the country but that of the Minister.[38]

Moreover, there was nothing broken in the system so there was no need to fix it. Duncan held his ground. He believed in anticipating problems rather than waiting for them to occur. He had in mind the huge expansion of friendly societies after legislation had been passed for them in 1793 and thought that the same thing would happen to savings banks. Duncan was also somewhat dismissive of Munnochie's response as he was the Lord Advocate and Duncan believed that he was under the influence of the Edinburgh bank whose directors, with one exception, were hostile to the proposed legislation.

Hay Donaldson, an old friend of Duncan's, was polite but ultimately dismissive. He went through the Bill clause by clause and argued with almost every point. The main elements concerned the right to sue and be sued, protection of deposits and freedom from stamp duty. He pointed out that Duncan's original ambition for savings banks was that local conditions would produce banks that were different, depending on their locality, and this was what had happened. But legislation would bring them all under one protective Act and this would damage their individuality.[39] However Donaldson, who had founded a savings bank himself, also acknowledged that Duncan deserved the 'just respect and affection of every friend of humanity'.[40]

Just as Hay Donaldson was writing his cautionary letter, however, the tide began to turn. The Glasgow bank changed its mind and came out in support. The *Scotsman* newspaper found the proposed Bill to be 'unexceptionable' but did not oppose it. In April 1818 Duncan decided to go to Edinburgh to meet as many of the interested parties as possible. He also intended to consult his lawyer John Henderson and take his advice.

While he was in Edinburgh he received a letter from H. W. Smith in London, a friend of Douglas's. Smith was well versed in the affairs of savings banks and encouraged Duncan to proceed with his plans for legislation while offering him advice on the drafting of the Bill. He told Duncan that good progress was being made by the English savings banks: 'It is become a disgrace to any town or village that it should not have its own savings bank.' But progress in Ireland had been slower. He also noted that as more and more people adopted the savings habit 'the Publicans and Dispensers of Drams are beginning to find a diminution in their custom'.

Smith's letter concluded: 'The principles we are disseminating indicate throughout the labouring community, by the medium of our Depositors, are operating with wholesome effect and *must* produce in the end great common good.'[41] He also suggested that the banks should be called 'savings banks' rather than 'banks for savings'. If Duncan needed some encouragement for what was to follow, then Smith's letter surely provided it. Meetings with the Edinburgh savings bank board had already proved abortive.

Prior to his trip to Edinburgh Duncan had circulated his proposal as widely as possible. Many of the replies were certainly more supportive than the feedback he had received during the winter. No reply was received from Edinburgh due to the recipient of the draft failing to pass it on to his fellow directors. When it became generally known that a Bill was proposed the other Edinburgh directors imagined some slight and relations with the Edinburgh Society, already rather poor after the Forbes affair, were further undermined.

The Edinburgh directors met to discuss the proposal and voted against any involvement. They went further and endeavoured to get the Glasgow savings bank to join them in opposing the Bill, but the Glasgow men had already voted in its favour and refused to change their minds.

Duncan then sought a meeting with the Edinburgh board which took place on 9 April 1818, and although some of the its members, such as Principal Baird, were in favour of Duncan's proposal a majority, led by Forbes, were not. The meeting was adjourned until the next day when Duncan with a substantial number of leading Edinburgh men, many of whom were advocates or bankers, met with the Edinburgh board. Despite the distinction of his party, Duncan's efforts to persuade the Edinburgh board into a change of mind were unsuccessful. The Edinburgh Society then conveyed its views to every Scottish MP and to some members of the House of Lords.

Duncan remained in Edinburgh for some time and, with his friends and supporters, formed a committee which called itself 'Friends of Parliamentary Protection for Savings Banks in Scotland'. This included a range of senior people from the law, the church and the university. They considered the Bill again, made some alterations and then gave it back to Duncan to have it printed. A second scrutiny followed and it was printed a second time. This was the version that Douglas eventually presented to the House of Commons.[42] The main provisions were to provide legal protection for trustees and managers, to exempt savings banks from stamp duty and to make arrangements for some of the tricky situations that could arise, for example when a depositor died and there was uncertainty as to who was entitled to the money. Duncan referred to this as 'propinquity'.

Before anything else could happen Duncan made a visit to Liverpool at the beginning of May, where his brother George's wife was very seriously ill, leaving Thomas Duncan in charge of his affairs.

On his return to Ruthwell, Duncan became aware that the Edinburgh board were putting it about that there was no support for Duncan's Bill and, in a letter to Douglas he told him that he was collecting a dossier of all the letters of support that he had received.[43] In July 1818 he received another encouraging letter from H. W. Smith, who was acquainted with the man who had established a savings bank in Hamburg. Also in this letter was the news that the King of Wurttemberg had established a savings bank in Stuttgart and that the savings banks in America were 'rivalling ours'.[44] Smith was more than ever convinced of the need for savings banks and other instruments that would help maintain social stability in the years after the Napoleonic wars.

The early days of January 1819 found Duncan preparing for a trip to London. The Bill had been printed and Duncan and his lawyer, Henderson, had drawn up a circulation list. They did not include Forbes in Edinburgh on the list and took the view that if he wanted one he could go to the bookseller and buy it. Before he left home Duncan wrote letters for the *Dumfries Courier* and sent copies to other newspapers, in the hope that they would publish them. He also acquired, from his friends, several letters of introduction addressed to people of influence in London. Notwithstanding all this work Duncan remained committed to his role as a parish minister. As he prepared to leave for London he was still busy with parish and presbytery affairs.

Duncan mounted his horse on Monday 8 February 1819 and set off for London, arriving there on Saturday of that week. Quite why he chose to ride the 300 miles or so rather than take the coach is unclear.[45] It may simply have been a matter of economics, as he was meeting the expenses of this trip from his own pocket and may even have had to pay for someone to preach in Ruthwell Church in his absence. It proved to be a longer trip than he had imagined and he was away from home for just over six weeks.

While in London Duncan resided at The Albany in Piccadilly, also the residence of his friends William Douglas, Henry Brougham and some other Members of Parliament. He presented his letters of introduction in various places and met many of the leading politicians. He also visited William Wilberforce at his home and was introduced to the gentlemen who were breakfasting with him as 'the founder of Savings Banks'. Wilberforce promised his support. George Canning, president of the Board of Control,[46] also received him. Kirkman Finlay, the Glasgow MP, likewise offered support. There was a meeting in a solicitor's office where the draft of the Bill was considered clause by clause by a group of interested MPs.

Duncan went on to meet with a number of the leading Scottish politicians in London: Lord Minto, Sir George Clerk and the Marquess of Lansdowne. Where there was doubt in the minds of these men he spoke with them and gave them a copy of the pamphlet that responded to the Edinburgh criticism. All save Clerk were convinced by his arguments. The biggest challenges were not with the Bill itself but with getting a sufficient number of people interested in getting it approved and in overcoming any residual opposition. Douglas was busy with other parliamentary work and the task of campaigning fell largely on Duncan's shoulders. The Lord Advocate, who was then in Scotland, was still opposed.

Although H. W. Smith was not an MP he was a man of influence and the son of a director of the Bank of England. He held a dinner to which Duncan was invited and where the main topic of conversation was the proposed legislation for Scottish savings banks.

Duncan worked hard. In letters to his wife and to Robert Lundie in Kelso he described what was going on, who he had met, who needed to be persuaded about the necessity and efficacy of the Bill, and conditions in London.

Nor did he forget that he was a minister during his time in London. In a letter to his wife he wrote: 'I have been very successful since I came to town in making converts to my savings bank views. I wish I could flatter myself with being as successful in making converts to *saving* in a spiritual sense.' He was invited to preach 'for the benefit of the Caledonian Asylum which supports a school'. Wilberforce and all his fellow Christian philanthropists – 'the Saints' – were expected to attend. He also met with James Stephen, brother-in-law to Wilberforce and another noted anti-slavery campaigner. It is highly likely that savings banks were not the only topic of conversation and that what was said about slavery influenced Duncan's later writings on the subject.

It is clear from the letters home that Duncan felt that his trip to London had been necessary,

> though I have met with more difficulties and prejudices than I anticipated, and found it quite necessary to have come to London, yet everything goes on as well as possible, and there is not now a doubt of success. I must, however, stay in London till the bill is not only introduced, but read a second time, and carried through a committee.[47]

It is also clear that he did not like London very much. He wrote to Lundie that,

> This is a very bustling town, and people pay greatly for their greatness. I would not live such a life for all the wealth and honours the world can bestow. I begin to feel that I have too much of the latter commodity already. Pray for me that I should be humbled if I should forget myself.[48]

Duncan told his wife he was looking forward to returning home:

> With what pleasure do I look forward to the time when I shall have reaped laurels, and have turned my back on this great city,

with all its vanities and vexations of spirit! [. . .] O, for my own quiet, or rather *noisy* fireside, with my wife and bairns about me, and a metaphysical controversy with Mr Mitchell and Walter Phillips and then 'Cato is himself again!'[49]

The poet Shelley was also in London at that time and described it with the words: 'Hell is a city much like London – a populous and smoky city.'[50]

It may seem from this that Duncan's task was done and that he was getting ready to return home, but this was far from the case. A further round of meetings took place and he was even introduced to the Prince Regent, soon to become King George IV. The meetings with the Scottish MPs took place in the British Coffeehouse. Duncan produced a shorter version of his pamphlet as 'M.P's have neither time nor inclination to read *long* statements'.[51]

The following day his spirits were up and he wrote to Lundie:

I cannot go to sleep without informing you that, after a tough, and at one time a doubtful battle, I have at last carried the day triumphantly. On Thursday last week there was a meeting of Scotch members, at which not more than eighteen or twenty attended, and of those it was evident scarcely half a dozen had taken the trouble to read my pamphlet. It had evidently excited no general interest; and although I had a few zealous friends, among whom Mr Elliot Lockhart was one of the most zealous, yet their voice was nearly overpowered by that of William Dundas, seconded by the general ignorance and indifference on the subject. All that my friends could effect was to get the meeting adjourned till to-day. In the meantime, I printed and circulated an abridged statement of the case in a letter to the members, and this, with the interest excited by the previous meetings, had the desired effect. I had neutralised Sir John Marjoribanks and Sir James Montgomery, and had Kirkman Finlay, Lord Rosslyn and Mr Gladstone for my firm friends. I knew also that several others were friendly and that my only determined opponents were Mr William Dundas, Mr Kennedy of Dunure [. . .] and perhaps one or two more. I went, however, to the meeting with fear and trembling.[52]

Duncan returned from London heartened by the support that he had gathered and by the fact that he had been successful in persuading a number of leading people to change their minds on the subject. He had taken on the establishments of Edinburgh and London and carried the day, and his resulting exhilaration and exhaustion are clear from his letters. He was back home by the end of March and wrote to Lundie on 1 April, evidently pleased to be home and referring to his time in London as a dream that he hoped would never return: 'Once is quite enough for the head of a quiet Presbyterian minister.'[53] It would not, however, be the last occasion on which he had cause to make the journey south.

Sir George Clerk and the Lord Advocate, in a meeting with Douglas, reversed their earlier opposition and the Bill was passed in the House of Lords on 2 July 1819. All the clauses that Duncan had included were passed into law with only minor amendments.

While in London Duncan also had the opportunity to develop his broader ideas on poverty and poor relief. He was invited to give evidence to the Parliamentary Committee on the Poor Laws and, in doing so, he

had the privilege of furnishing the committee with the leading questions, which gave me an opportunity of developing the whole of our Scotch system of management, including even our parochial schools, as one means of elevating the character of the lower orders, and raising them above the meanness of depending on charity, as well as of giving them an enterprising spirit, which leads them to seek the means of subsistence abroad, and thus to free their mother country from a superabundant population under which England groans. This led to the consideration of emigration as the means of freeing England from her extra population, a subject which I conceive to be of great importance.[54]

Notwithstanding this last comment, emigration was not a subject to which Duncan's energies were devoted. He did nevertheless continue his work to help working people to remain independent.

Of course Duncan was not the only person in the land who was thinking about how best to deal with issues concerning poverty. Thomas Kennedy of Dunure, whom Duncan had met in London, had introduced to parliament a poor law bill for Scotland that gave more power to kirk sessions and took power away from heritors. Duncan was opposed to this. In a letter to Douglas he wrote:

> The more I reflect on it the more doubtful the propriety of the measure in the extent to which he would carry it appears, and I am confirmed in my opinion by conversing with my brethren on the subject, who all deprecate it as likely to be the means of introducing greater evils than it will cure. I spoke to your brother the Marquis on this business, who entered into my views and begged that I would put in writing my ideas regarding it, that he might be prepared to speak to Mr Kennedy.[55]

He went on to say that the matter of poor rates was not well understood in Scotland: 'If Parliament [. . .] puts into the hands of the Kirk Sessions (or in other words the clergy) the dangerous power of assessing their heritors without control [. . .] I foresee very hurtful consequences.'

Duncan conceded that the poor were, if anything, becoming poorer in the current economic climate. Savings banks certainly helped people deal with difficult circumstances, but they were obviously not the complete answer to the more general problem of poverty caused by adverse economic conditions. The question of what parliament would do about Scotland's poor remained unanswered for many more years.

Nevertheless, wherever savings banks had been established they seemed to be working well and serving the interests of the people. In the spring of 1819 the minister at Fordoun in Aberdeenshire wrote to Duncan:

> You, we consider, as the Father of Parish Banks: and they will

hand down your memory with well merited respect and affection to Posterity. The persons who are now reaping benefit from them have good cause to bless you; and by the institution of them you have conferred an essential benefit on your country. They have done much already to arrest the progress that was rapidly making among the lower orders in this country to Pauperism; and they will, I trust, ere long restore throughout Scotland that Independence of Character, and that economy among the lower orders, which were our boast but a few years ago. The interests of Morality and Religion will also be benefited by them. May you be spared for many years to witness their farther spread, and their increasing benefits.[56]

Duncan, by this stage, was getting worried about the slowness of the progress of the Bill through the House of Commons. He wrote again to Douglas asking for a progress report. Douglas replied immediately with words of reassurance and Duncan expressed his relief. It was not, however, a time to rest, as Duncan was already thinking and planning for the next stage.

He planned, with Henderson's assistance, to draw up 'something like a universal code founded on the provisions of the act and adapted to the general circumstances of our institutions'.[57]

This was soon in print and was circulated to all the banks in Scotland. Even the Edinburgh bank availed itself of the terms of the Act. Duncan was satisfied that 'heirs will at once be enabled to decide for themselves on the validity of their pretensions, and managers will feel confidence in making payment to them, without the intervention of a legal adviser'. It seems there had been numerous problems around the question of who was entitled to money in an account when the saver had died. There had been 'many doubtful questions [. . .] from the informality of testamentary deeds, and numerous evils and vexations among the lower classes' had arisen as a result.

There had also been concerns about the legal position of office bearers in the savings banks and the necessity to have a division of responsibilities between the treasurer and the trustee(s):

It was obviously desirable that certain office-bearers of the institution should be invested with a legal character, and should acquire power over the funds by virtue of their mere appointment and acceptance, having these funds so vested in themselves, as to enable them, if necessary, to appear in a court of law in defence of the rights of their constituents.

Duncan's paper went on:

the character of treasurer and trustee should not be vested in the same person. Some provision of this kind appears to be necessary under all possible circumstances, and ought to form a fundamental rule of every Bank for Savings. Should this be neglected, and any defalcation take place (the impossibility of which must never be pre-supposed) the prosecutor pointed out by the act might happen to be the same individual as the person against whom the prosecution was to be instituted; a circumstance which would, at all events occasion manifest embarrassments even though it should not entirely defeat the ends of justice.[58]

Duncan must have been well satisfied that his foresight and the exertions that he had spent in conceiving the Bill and then getting it through parliament were well worthwhile.

That, however, was not the end of the matter. Savings banks, especially in England, were not established without controversy and opposition and there were many Acts of Parliament dealing with the issues that arose. Given that the English commercial banks were somewhat less well developed than those in Scotland, and, as has been said, many were not in the habit of paying interest on deposits, the legislation that had been passed for the English savings banks insisted that funds be deposited in government securities. This was not the Scottish way, where commercial banks paid interest on deposits and most were prepared to support the savings bank movement by paying interest sufficient to allow savers to receive 5 per cent interest on their deposits.

In 1824 a Bill was before parliament that would have required savings banks in Scotland to deposit their funds in the Bank of England. Duncan helped organise a chorus of protest and the Scottish clause was left out.[59]

But in his circular letter to the managers of savings banks in 1820, Duncan foresaw the possibility that the commercial banks might, at some future date, be unable or unwilling to continue with their generous treatment of the savings banks. In this he was far-sighted and legislation was eventually required in 1835 that gave savings banks in Scotland the option to invest in government securities. Any bank founded after 1835 was compelled to do so. Most took advantage of this legislation. The Ruthwell savings bank did not.

It was Duncan's decision, but it meant he was then obliged to find alternative investment opportunities for the funds that would return a sufficiently high rate of interest to allow him to continue to pay a reasonable rate to depositors. He, and the few other banks that did not register, chose to invest in heritable securities. This, in turn, placed on his shoulders the responsibility of finding suitable properties on which to lend and in ensuring that these properties were well built and well insured. It was not a minor task.

Nevertheless, within a decade Duncan had established his bank, proved its soundness, promoted the idea through his correspondence, newspaper and the pamphlet, defended it in public, promoted an Act of Parliament, and he had done all this while serving his parish as a minister and pursuing, as we shall see, a myriad of other activities.

Chapter 7
Presbytery and Politics

Right from the outset of his ministry, Duncan involved himself in the day-to-day calls upon his time for work in his parish. But he also made time for the courts of the church. As an ordained parish minister he was automatically a member of his local presbytery, in this case the Presbytery of Annan, which was a grouping of eight parishes. He was also a member of the Synod of Dumfries, which was a grouping of several presbyteries.

The presbytery meetings took place in the town of Annan on market days, although this was later changed to allow the ministers to meet in less noisy circumstances. In theory, there was supposed to be the same number of elders as ministers in presbytery, but as most elders were working men the meetings were dominated by the ministers.

It was not long before Duncan was given positions of responsibility. In October 1800, shortly after his induction to Ruthwell, he became the pro tem presbytery clerk and a month later the presbyters elected him to be their moderator for six months. The position of moderator, or chairman, rotated in this way to ensure that no one minister could exercise any undue influence over the presbytery. In such a small presbytery it was inevitable that a minister would fill the role several times during his ministry. A few months later the post of clerk was declared vacant, as the office holder was inconsistent and had made promises that he did not keep. Indeed the Synod inspection of the records detailed items that had not been minuted.[1] Duncan was given the role and he held this position until the Disruption in 1843.

This was a position of great influence. Not only did the clerk keep the minutes he was also the treasurer, the caller of meetings and the arranger of business. It was also mildly lucrative as there were some functions for which the clerk could charge a fee.

Most of the business of presbytery was routine but occasionally it could become complex. Presbyteries dealt with the admission of new ministers, repairs to churches and manses, and the appointment of schoolmasters. They also dealt with violations of the Sabbath. Fishing was the most common breach. At that time kirk sessions and presbyteries still saw part of their role as being to maintain moral order in the country and this meant investigating cases of illegitimate babies, cohabitation and anything else that might disturb that moral order. More often, however, their concern was with who would become financially responsible for the upkeep of the illegitimate child – a concern that was mixed, with a desire that the child should be cared for and a worry that this responsibility should not fall upon the parish.

Very early on in Duncan's ministry one of his parishioners was discovered to be pregnant out of wedlock, and the young woman named someone from another parish as the father. She had already been questioned by the Ruthwell kirk session but now the case came to the presbytery. As clerk Duncan had to write to the parish where the father was resident and ask the minister there to investigate further. The presbytery minutes run to several pages on this case. There were many such cases, all of which added considerably to Duncan's workload. Presbyteries took their duties very seriously and were prepared to invest large amounts of their time and energy in investigating and dealing with the cases that were brought before them.

The meetings usually took place in Annan but it was a common occurrence for them to take place elsewhere, especially when repairs to a church or manse were on the agenda. Often these meetings took the form of a site meeting as when, in June 1801, presbytery met in Clarencefield to discuss repairs to Ruthwell Church, the graveyard dyke and the manse. An architect from Dalkeith was present, as was John Paterson, factor to the Earl of Mansfield, who would be required to pay a substantial portion of the costs. On this occasion it was agreed that substantial repairs to church and manse were required and these were estimated at £321 for the church and £254 for the manse. No figure was given for the seven-foot wall that Duncan wanted to erect around the graveyard – perhaps as a make-work scheme for the local unemployed. It seems that Mansfield's factor was reluctant to agree on this latter matter.

Occasionally Duncan made repairs himself without involving the Earl. On the eve of his marriage, Duncan sought agreement for further repairs to the manse. A new kitchen was approved but not the other changes that he wanted. There were more repairs in 1813. It was clear that Duncan was determined to maintain church property to a high standard.

Presbytery would also meet in parish schools, which were inspected on a regular basis. In April 1802 it was the turn of Ruthwell School to be examined. Presbyters were 'well satisfied with the abilities of the several teachers and the proficiency of the scholars'.

In April each year presbyteries around the country would nominate who of their number should attend the General Assembly of the Church of Scotland, which met annually in Edinburgh in the third week of May. Duncan first became a commissioner in 1801, and this was an early chance for him to gain experience of the highest court of the church, but also a great opportunity to visit friends from his student days. He met up with Andrew Thomson – the two men would later disagree on the emancipation of slaves in the British Empire. He also met up with Professor and Mrs Dugald Stewart in the university. He may even have attended a meeting of the Speculative Society, which he was entitled to do as an 'extraordinary' (or life) member.

For the most part Duncan's early years in the ministry and in the presbytery were spent in dealing with relatively mundane matters. There was some agitation in the summer of 1803 when it was widely expected that Napoleon would invade the British Isles. The Solway Firth, an extensive waterway, was viewed as a likely point of attack. Various documents were drawn up by churchmen that called for resistance. It is likely that Duncan, as clerk of presbytery and given his aforementioned military interests, was the author of the document read from pulpits in the parishes of Annan Presbytery. It called for parishioners to 'fight for your honour, your property, and your lives'.[2]

When he was appointed to be a commissioner to the General Assembly in 1805, Duncan decided that he would not just go to be an observer but would try to make his mark. He drew up a report on breaches of the Sabbath by people going fishing. This was circulated to the Assembly, which does not appear to have taken the matter too seriously. Its response was to tell Annan Presbytery 'to continue its diligence in endeavouring to suppress a practice so detrimental to the interests of religion and morality'.[3] It is possible to see in Duncan's action a desire to test the water and to learn how 'the system' worked so that he could make use of it in the years to come.

Thereafter Duncan grew in confidence. In 1813, by which time he had set up his newspaper and his bank, Duncan persuaded the presbytery to petition parliament on the subject of religion in India, a country which was then under the control of the East India Company. Both houses of parliament were petitioned in a document that expressed concern not just for the native people but for migrants from the United Kingdom. The native people were described as 'being subject to the same dominion as Britain' but 'fifty millions of whom are sunk in the lowest state of degradation and wickedness and groan under the debasing influence of a gloomy, cruel and licentious superstition'.

The charter of the East India Company was due for renewal and the petition asked for ministers and teachers from the Church of Scotland to be allowed to settle in India and to promote the gospel and Presbyterianism there (at that time only the Anglican Church was permitted to operate in India).[4] The petition was sent to the Duke of Buccleuch in the House of Lords and to W. R. K. Douglas at the House of Commons. This was Duncan's first flirtation with the world of politics and it certainly would not be his last. In fact it was a useful training ground for the political activity regarding the bank that was described in the last chapter. Nor did he lose sight of the Indian question, becoming instrumental in having the Church of Scotland's first missionary to India appointed more than twenty years later.

At a local level, meanwhile, Duncan established and became the first president of the Dumfries Missionary Society. This was less successful than many of his other ventures due to sectarian differences.[5]

A year later, when Napoleon had been defeated and before he escaped from Elba, Duncan drew up a petition for the presbytery to send to the Prince Regent which expressed the happiness of the people at the restoration of peace,

> but at the same time regretting that the treaty should have contained an article permitting France to renew for five years the infamous traffic in human flesh and expressing a hope that His Royal Highness would take such measures as would appear best calculated to put an immediate end of a system so disgraceful to the Christian world.[6]

This was the first time that Duncan had expressed his aversion to slavery in public.

Duncan was growing in confidence and had a clear view of the importance of the role of the church in national affairs. Nor was he prepared to allow that influence to be diminished. He understood that if the church was to maintain its position in the country then it would take the actions of men like him to ensure that its voice was heard.

This was all happening as Duncan was extremely busy with the bank and with the large body of correspondence that entailed. A difficult diversion at that time brought a huge amount of work and a row with his patron, the Earl of Mansfield. When presbytery met early in January 1815 it was to learn that the Earl had enclosed a piece of land that Duncan had always believed was part of his glebe. Landlords all over the United Kingdom were busy at this time in enclosing land which they believed belonged to them but which had, nevertheless, been used by local people for common grazing. It was an entirely different matter, however, for a landlord to enclose part of a minister's glebe. The glebe, after all, was part of the minister's stipend, and such action on the part of a landlord could not go unopposed.

Presbytery duly assembled at Ruthwell to investigate the matter with Joseph Smith and William Thompson, the Earl's factor and law agent respectively, in attendance. Duncan was angry and was not prepared to compromise. He cited a number of old men of the parish, all of whom testified that the land in dispute had been available for the minister's use and that it had been shared with parishioners, some of whom grazed their cattle there. Duncan had also grazed his own cattle and dug turfs on the land. The meeting was adjourned and Duncan was told to do nothing that would compromise the rights of the church.[7]

The matter had still not been resolved a year and a half later so Duncan took down part of the wall that had been erected by the land-lord's factor. This was to allow him to bring peats to the manse from land that he had traditionally used for this purpose. He described this whole affair as 'unpleasant business' but presbytery had inspected the property and approved of his actions. It was extremely unlikely that they would have thought otherwise as Duncan, at this time, was both clerk and moderator and therefore in a strong position to set the presbytery agenda. The minutes, which he wrote, told him to 'persevere in this firm and steady conduct that the property of the incumbent [Duncan] be not deteriorated'.[8]

A compromise was eventually reached with the landlord,[9] but the whole episode revealed Duncan to be a man of steely resolve who was prepared to stand up for his rights and to fight for what he believed to be right. It also revealed a man who was prepared to go to great lengths to fight his case and to put all his energy into the struggle. It was a trait of his character that would surface in the future.

By this time the war with Napoleonic France had come to an end and Duncan organised a collection for the benefit of the widows and children of those who had fallen at the Battle of Waterloo. Of the eight parishes in the presbytery the people of Ruthwell were the most generous and raised £14.

Economic conditions after the war, however, continued to deteriorate. It was estimated that the cost of living had increased by 50 per cent between 1790 and 1815.[10] The corn laws, introduced in 1815 to favour growers by keeping prices high, and the enclosure movement continued to put pressure on poor people, and agricultural labourers suffered the greatest hardships. Panaceas were two a penny as people from all walks of life tried to come up with ideas that would address these problems. The most prolific group were the radicals and political agitators. The clamour for political reform rose to a crescendo that culminated in the Peterloo massacre in Manchester in August 1819, when cavalry charged into a large crowd in an attempt to arrest the leaders of the demonstration. Several hundred people were injured and fifteen were killed.

Michael Fry made the point that

> With the peace economic differences and social problems earlier taken for granted suddenly appeared intolerable [. . .] Strident voices called for reform and radical reform at that. The first response from the ruling class was often panic and repression. Yet some also felt their way to a more positive response. They decided the task of leadership lay in looking to the character of the people and to the mutual obligations within their society: this was how to deal with the radicals.[11]

That was the year in which Duncan had visited London in an effort to have legislation enacted for the protection of savings banks. The experience had undoubtedly heightened his awareness of how the political system operated and, on reflection, it had made him think where his political loyalties lay. They did not lie with the agitators. Consequently, in December 1819 he led a discussion at presbytery the minute of which reads:

> The Presbytery taking into their consideration the present alarming state of the country resolve to send an address to the Prince Regent expressive of the dutiful and loyal sentiments of the Presbytery as a body as well as of the people under their charge and they also resolve to issue a pastoral address to their parishioners warning them against the seductive influence of these blasphemous and disloyal opinions which have gone abroad in the world and which have so unhappily gained ground in the manufacturing districts of the country.

Duncan had already written the loyal address to be sent to the Prince Regent and a pastoral address to be read in churches, both of which presbytery endorsed. The loyal address read:

> We view with sorrow and indignation the designs of those factious men who endeavour to raise commotions in the state by inflaming the minds of the people with false representations and by propagating opinions subversive of social order, and hostile to our most holy faith.

The pastoral address was even more pointed. It read:

> Ever since the awful period of that convulsion in a neighbouring land, which unsettled the opinions of men, and shook society to its foundations, the prevalence of revolutionary, and above all of infidel principles, had filled every friend of his country with alarm. By the industrious circulation of the most detestable publications; by frequent and insidious attacks on constituted authorities, and on the national councils; by dark insinuations against the credit and authenticity of the Sacred Scriptures; and by open calumny against those who conscientiously maintain the cause of religion and of social order, men practised in treasonable arts have been gradually undermining the safeguards of society, and preparing the way for the accomplishment of their unhallowed and ruinous designs.

It went on to call for ordinary people to rally in support of the throne. The argument was that government worked well, and people had liberty, including freedom of religion. It concluded:

> Dearly beloved! Our hearts desire and prayer to God is, that he may keep you in your most holy faith and disappoint the evil designs of the enemies of your peace, and of your salvation. While others blaspheme the name of the Supreme Being, and reject the domination of the Prince of Peace, may you be strength-

ened to stand fast in that liberty wherewith Christ has made you free; and deriving the knowledge of your duty from no earthly monitor, may you yield an unreserved obedience to that divine command, which requires you to 'fear God and honour the King'.[12]

In view of what happened in Duncan's later life, his loyalty to the Crown stands out in these passages. They demonstrate that, at this point in time, he saw a clear link between his faith and the political establishment. Despite the unreformed nature of parliament, and its venality, which he had seen at first hand earlier that year, he saw it as a bulwark against forces that were hostile to the reformed church. But this was a position that would be tested beyond breaking point in the years to come. When King George IV (whom he had met as Prince Regent) visited Scotland in 1822, Duncan was presented to him at the Palace of Holyroodhouse in Edinburgh.

By this time Duncan had been clerk to the presbytery for twenty years. He was trusted by his fellow ministers and was clearly in a position of leadership. His work in setting up the savings bank was well understood and had been copied in many places. He had become something of an expert on church law and in 1820 he used this knowledge to seek an increase in his stipend by raising a 'process of augmentation'. At that time his stipend was £56 13s 4d in cash plus five chalders (large measures varying with what was being measured) of victual, half wheat and half barley. His own recollection is that this was worth £100 per annum, but to this was added whatever he could grow in the glebe. He was successful in gaining an increase but it is not clear what this amounted to. His wife later maintained that his earnings from ministry never exceeded £296 per annum.[13]

Duncan's reputation was growing steadily, and he was often called upon to speak at public meetings. On one such occasion he was invited to Manchester where a new Presbyterian congregation was being established. He was there in the company of Andrew Thomson, his old friend from Edinburgh, and Rev. Ralph, the Presbyterian minister in Liverpool. He was invited to preach a sermon on the constitution of the Church of Scotland and chose to expound on the duties of ministers:

> There are private duties required of them on the faithful discharge of which the efficiency of their public labours depends. They are bound to a constant residence among their people. They are enjoined to institute, from year to year, a minute personal enquiry into the religious knowledge of every individual belonging to their flock, by means of catechising, – an exercise which, whilst to themselves it conveys information, calculated to increase their usefulness, teaches those who are the object of it, to give an answer of the faith that is in them. By frequent parochial visitations, they are expected to make themselves intimately acquainted with every family [. . .] and to perform the duty [. . .] of the success of which the Apostles left so remarkable an example – that of preaching Jesus Christ not only in the temple but in every house.[14]

Duncan went on to talk about a subject that would soon become of considerable importance in the work of the church – the relationship between church and state:

> It would nevertheless be extremely erroneous to say that no visible effects have been produced by the peculiar creed and constitution of our Scottish Church, even on the very highest ranks of our countrymen. As our establishment professes to renounce all direct dependence on the civil power, and as, in truth, its institutions are but ill calculated to be converted into an engine of state, it is less indebted, for its support to mere human policy, than those churches which form a constituent part of the political fabric; and, hence, its members are less tempted to regard it in a secular light, and are more forcibly reminded, that it holds out to themselves individually, as well as to others, infinitely higher inducements, and an unspeakably more noble ambition than this world can offer.[15]

This was a clear signal that he understood the dangers of government interference in church affairs but, for the time being, he was more concerned with the other dimension of this statement – the kirk's need to maintain a separation between church and state.

Occasionally the presbytery would consider matters of national importance, especially what was happening in parliament. As clerk, it was Duncan's job to bring these matters to the presbytery's attention. In 1828 parliament was considering the seventeenth-century Test and Corporation Acts, pieces of legislation that required candidates for public office to be communicant members of the Church of England. Duncan described these Acts as 'inexpedient' as they required communicant members of the Church of Scotland to take the sacrament in the Church of England before they could accept public or military office in England. The universities of Oxford and Cambridge were also covered by this legislation. A petition was duly drawn up and submitted to parliament, which repealed the legislation without much debate as it had been little enforced in the previous thirty years.

A far more serious, but related, consideration was the question of Catholic emancipation. Roman Catholics suffered even more restrictions than non-Anglicans, and in 1823 the Irish reformer, Daniel O'Connell, began a campaign to have these restrictions removed. An Act in 1778 to provide limited relief had led to rioting in Scotland in 1779 and in England the following year so politicians were wary of pursuing further legislation. The issues at stake were the preservation of peace in Ireland and the Protestant succession of the monarchy as well as the restrictions on public office for Roman Catholics. The matter was not discussed at Annan Presbytery but it was discussed in Dumfries where there was a majority against emancipation.[16]

Duncan, however, was very much in favour. He was aware that this was unlikely to be a universally popular position. Some of his parishioners had, apparently, prepared a petition to be sent to parliament, but Duncan refused to sign it; nor would he forward it to parliament on their behalf. Inevitably this created a rift. In his now time-honoured fashion he sought to address this upset in his relations with some of his parishioners by writing a pamphlet in which he expounded his ideas and sentiments. This pamphlet is an important and early indicator of the way in which his thinking was turning. It makes the critical distinction between civil and religious authority: 'That civil disabilities should be distinct from religious ones'. And in a phrase that is now long forgotten but has contemporary relevance he wrote: 'It is the curse of all measures adopted or retained in a worldly spirit, for strengthening the bulwarks of religion, that they not only defeat their own object, but are actually not seldom converted into barriers against it.' Duncan went on:

> It is an insult to Christianity to use carnal weapons for its support [. . .] You wonder that while all other classes of British subjects are rapidly advancing in civilisation the Irish Catholics should alone be excluded from the generous race – that they alone should be left centuries behind – but your wonder is misplaced, for how could it be otherwise when Protestant hands have placed such fetters on their souls.[17]

> Civil disabilities imposed purely for the purpose of influencing the judgement on the subject of religion, lay an unwarrantable burden on the conscience, and, if this worldly engine be productive of any effect in obtaining converts to the religion by which it is employed, it certainly could not accomplish this by rendering men true believers, but only by bringing them to become vile and hypocritical renegades.[18]

The letters in this pamphlet went on to sound warnings about the 'Church of Rome', especially about outward observances and deathbed services. So there was no sense in which Duncan was veering towards Rome. His concern was simply that he had to express his views about the restrictions under which Roman Catholics lived and, in the process, lend support to the Government in its endeavours to right a wrong.

This may seem a very liberal attitude to have adopted but it is entirely consistent with his Enlightenment education. It is also consistent with what Duncan wrote earlier that decade in support of free trade:

May commerce, released from her old swaddling bands,
Burst forth in her strength and with freedom join hands;
While science shall shed on the poorest her pleasures,
And faith, love and peace fill the world with her treasures.[19]

Artificial and government-imposed restrictions on peoples' lives were unlikely to serve a useful or helpful purpose. In reaching this position Duncan may well have been influenced, as many in the British debate were, by the American Constitution and the First Amendment, which guaranteed freedom of religion. It separated church from state but did not remove religion from public life. This was the basis on which Duncan's thinking, and, eventually, his activities would develop. A Catholic Emancipation Act was passed in 1829.

Much of the work in parish and presbytery, meanwhile, was routine but occasionally church affairs would throw up a particular difficulty. Edward Irving was a friend of Duncan, and a local man, whose licence to be a minister was registered with Annan Presbytery in 1822. He then went off to become a highly successful minister in the Caledonian Church in London. So successful was his ministry there that a new church had to be built to accommodate the growing congregation. He was a powerful preacher and had many admirers. George Duncan, Henry's son, who was taken on trials for ministry in 1827, spent some weeks in London with Irving before his own ordination.

Irving was, to say the least, an unusual minister, both in the style of his preaching and in his theology, which developed in ways that were increasingly inconsistent with mainstream thinking in the Church of Scotland. James Hogg, the Ettrick Shepherd, who was related to Duncan, heard Irving preach in 1832 and described his sermon as 'the ravings of enthusiastic madness'.[20] His unorthodoxy brought Irving to the attention of the church authorities and to the General Assembly in 1832, where he was invited to disavow some of the things that he had written. The matter was remitted to Annan Presbytery where he had been licensed.

It was with a heavy heart, in March 1833, that Henry Duncan led the proceedings against his old friend Irving, who refused to recant or to apologise for some of the intemperate things he had said about the General Assembly – he had referred to it as 'that synagogue of Satan'. A lengthy hearing in front of Annan Presbytery led to his licence to preach being revoked. He had been, in effect, excommunicated. Irving then founded the Holy Catholic Apostolic Church but did not live to see the fruits of his labours, dying in 1834.

There were happier times for Duncan when another local man and personal friend, Robert Murray McCheyne, was licensed to preach in 1835 and subsequently ordained. McCheyne's first sermons were delivered in Ruthwell Church and he went on to a highly successful ministry in Dundee, but died of typhus on the eve of the Disruption. Another local man, James Dodds, was taken on trials for ministry in 1838. He had been a pupil and then tutor in the manse at Ruthwell and went on to marry Duncan's daughter Barbara in 1843.

In many ways things were going well. In 1837 the Church of Scotland's first missionary to India, Mr Duff, visited the presbytery. Foreign missions had long been a favourite subject of Henry Duncan.

And in 1838 a decision was made that there should be a new church built at Kirtlebridge within the presbytery boundary. Duncan went to Glasgow to raise funds for the new building and eventually his efforts raised more than £100 (a smaller sum was raised in Edinburgh). He then went to Manchester where he raised £57 from its Scottish population. This proved to be useful experience for what was to come after the Disruption.

Around this time, Duncan learned that he was to be nominated to be Moderator of the General Assembly in 1839. He was, at first, reluctant to serve as he was worried about his health but he was soon prevailed upon to accept the position. There were big issues at stake and he, through knowledge and experience, was well placed to serve the church in this important role.

That same year the Synod of Dumfries asked Duncan to head an investigation into illegitimacy. The concern was that fathers of illegitimate babies were evading their responsibilities and the burden of supporting the children was falling on the parishes. Duncan went about the task with his customary thoroughness and even went so far as to consult the Lord Advocate on the legal position. The survey that he prepared had seven questions on fornication, adultery and support for illegitimate children. There were forty-nine responses from parish ministers. Doubtless his position as Moderator designate, then as Moderator of the General Assembly, persuaded other ministers that his survey could not be ignored.

Much of what followed in the presbytery minutes dealt with the increasing tensions between the church and the state but the routine business was not neglected, especially the protection of the Sabbath as a holy day. In May 1842 Duncan was asked by fellow presbyters to write to the trustees of the Edinburgh and Glasgow Railway Company to express their 'unanimous disapprobation' of the fact that trains were running on Sundays.[21]

On 5 April 1843 Duncan signed the presbytery minutes for the last time. He had been its clerk for forty-four years.

Chapter 8
Duncan's Other Interests

From early in his life, and particularly on becoming minister for Ruthwell, Henry Duncan was remarkable for the sheer breadth of his interests. Although his kirk, editing and banking responsibilities consumed much of his time, he still maintained and pursued an eclectic range of activities.

The Ruthwell Cross

When Duncan arrived in Ruthwell in 1799, he found pieces of a runic cross scattered around the churchyard. They had originally been inside the church, but when a flagstone floor replaced the earthen one in 1780 the stones were cast out into the yard. Being a man of unbounded curiosity, he set about discovering what it was and, having done so, he decided to erect it in the manse garden in 1802. It is possible that the lecture that he had heard on ancient Scottish monuments when he was a young man in Liverpool had piqued his interest.

The cross was seventeen feet and six inches tall (5.3 metres) and had characters and inscriptions carved on four sides. Some of the letters were in roman and some in runic script.

Duncan's investigations revealed that it was a teaching cross that preachers used to illustrate stories from the Bible. It was ornately carved, although some of the carvings had been damaged, apparently in the 1640s, when the General Assembly decreed that graven images were inconsistent with the Ten Commandments and should, therefore, be destroyed. Those tasked with the destruction did an imperfect job and many of the carvings and writings were still discernible. It was clear that it was a very ancient artefact and subsequent scholarship dated it to between 680 and 750 AD. *Baedeker's Guide* declared the inscriptions on the stone to be the 'Earliest piece of written English',[1] while an American scholar described it as 'undoubtedly the most important sculptural survival from Anglo-Saxon Britain, and arguably from early medieval Europe'.[2]

Duncan was fascinated by the cross and made models of it, one of which was presented to the Scottish Society of Antiquaries, of which he was a member, and to which he gave a talk on the subject.[3] Another, which he made out of beeswax, is now at the Savings Bank Museum in Ruthwell.

In his article for the Society of Antiquaries, Duncan described the

> manifest superiority of the work, both in elegance of design and skill of execution, on the sides described with Runic characters, when compared with those on which Roman letters are found. There is a boldness, a freedom and a beauty in the sculpture on the runic sides, which would not disgrace a classic age, and which the Christian figures on the other side are far from exhibiting in an equal degree. It is scarcely possible, indeed, that they could have been designed by the same artist, or executed by the same workman.[4]

When he had it put together and erected it in the garden the crosspiece was missing. This clearly posed a challenge and eventually he had a local stonemason carve a new piece that was added in 1823. It has been said, perhaps reflecting Duncan's active participation in freemasonry, that the piece that was added represented masonic signs, but this is highly questionable.[5]

Duncan's work in preserving the cross, which is now housed inside the church, has given great scope to scholars who have written extensively on the workmen who carved the original, the nature of the art work and whether or not the cross owed its origins to the Roman or Celtic church. Some have been quite critical of Duncan and the new cross piece that he had carved, on the grounds that Duncan had no expert knowledge of such monuments and the piece that he added bore little relationship to the rest of the edifice.[6]

Geology

At some point, probably around 1813, while walking in Corncockle Muir, near Lochmaben, local workmen drew Duncan's attention to strange formations in the stone. He persuaded himself that these were footprints made by some ancient animal. It took him some time and effort to persuade other people, but so convinced was he that he wrote to Dr William Buckland, then president of the Geological Society of London. The discipline of geology was then in its infancy and Buckland was sceptical, writing to say: '[T]ill I see your specimens, I can, of course, give no further opinion than a general one, against even the remote probability of the marks you mention being the impressions of feet.' But Duncan had support from his friend Sir David Brewster, then Scotland's leading scientist, and he also had casts made of the marks, which he sent south. When Buckland saw these he was persuaded, later writing to say he looked upon Duncan's

> discovery as one of the most curious and most important that
> has ever been made in geology and, as it is a discovery that will
> forever connect your name with the progress of the science, I
> am anxious that the entire evidence relating to it should be
> worked out and recorded by yourself.[7]

Duncan had already done this, as he had made a presentation to the Royal Society of Edinburgh in 1828, which was published in that society's transactions.[8] He had several slabs made, one of which measured more than five feet, and had them all with him in Edinburgh for the presentation. The imprints, which were thought to be of some ancient variety of tortoise, were given the scientific name *Testudo Duncani*. Duncan went on, in his article, to speculate as to how the sandstone layers in which the imprints had been found had been laid down.

Before concluding that some kind of tortoise had made these marks, Duncan experimented with live animals crossing soft dough and wet sand to see what kind of impression they made.

This is yet another example of Duncan's sense of the curious and of his growing self-belief and self-confidence. He had stood up to the scientific world and persuaded them of the rightness of his thinking. Speculating on his discovery he remarked:

This fact leads the mind into the remotest antiquity, and perplexes it in a maze of interminable conjecture as to the state of the earth's material when these living creatures walked on its surface, bathed in other waters and browzed on other pastures, and not less on the extraordinary changes and convulsions of nature which have since taken place, and which have broken up, over-turned and remodelled all things.[9]

From this point onwards geology was one of Duncan's passions, and was the subject of some of the talks that he gave in mechanics' institutes in Dumfries and Glasgow.

Nature and Life

Duncan's curiosity about nature was insatiable. With the assistance of James Veitch, his faithful gardener, he turned his glebe from an unproductive piece of land into an experimental farm, improving the soil and sowing new crops. And in the school that he ran at the manse there were scientific machines, studies of astronomy and how bees produced honey (to demonstrate this process a glass beehive was constructed).

Duncan's great grand-daughter described it thus:

His kitchen garden and orchard were his glory: his red streaked apples, his russets, his lavender bushes made the autumn garden an old fashioned paradise, while the spring flower border, with its endless succession of sweet Williams, snap dragons, anemones and wall flowers, was a blaze of colours.[10]

Duncan's ministerial colleague and friend Rev. Dr Thomas Chalmers described the acres around the manse as having been 'transformed from a moor into a very beautiful and gentlemanly pleasure ground consisting of gardens, lake and a number of well disposed trees'.[11]

Duncan also spent a lot of time and energy in improving the manse, as well as providing a cottage in which his aging mother could live.

Not content with admiring nature and writing about it, Duncan was also to be found on occasion with an easel. He drew local scenes including the nearby Brow Well, which Robert Burns had visited a few days before his death.

Many of Duncan's pursuits involved a sedentary lifestyle, with the exception of gardening. He did not seem to have been greatly interested in sports, unlike his relation James Hogg, who sponsored sporting events. The sole exception was that he was very keen on curling, providing a rink on the glebe and establishing the Ruthwell Curling Club in 1833, which was still in operation a century later. He also wrote a lengthy poem concerning the joy of playing and the conviviality to be enjoyed when the game was over (see appendices).

Poetry and Robert Burns

Duncan, as we have seen, was a poet of some talent, but he never considered himself the equal of Scotland's national bard, Robert Burns, who had died in Dumfries in 1796. Duncan had met Burns when he had visited his childhood home at Lochrutton, while the poet had also visited the manse at Ruthwell a few days before his death. Duncan was not yet the minister there but his future wife, Agnes, had met the bard and later recorded the event.

Burns's fame and popularity continued to grow after his death and in December 1813 a group of his admirers, including Duncan and his brother Thomas, met at the George Inn in Dumfries, 'for the purpose of taking into consideration the measure of opening a subscription for erecting a mausoleum over his remains in St Michael's Churchyard, Dumfries'.[12] Local nobles and notables were invited to join the committee, although in reality they were lending their names rather than their time to the project in an effort to ensure it would be perceived as a respectable project worthy of broad support.

Duncan and W. Grierson were appointed joint secretaries and treasurers although, judging by the handwriting, the latter must have kept the minutes. Subscriptions were to be sought locally, in the East and West Indies, in the rest of the British Empire and in America, while local magistrates were to be approached to lend their support. The project got off to a good start. Mrs Jordan, a local performer, gave a benefit concert that raised £33; Sir Walter Scott organised a benefit concert in Edinburgh that raised £39; a merchant in Lisbon sent £23; and Duncan's brother in Liverpool and Rathbone, his business partner, raised £133, so by February 1815 the sum of £515 had been raised, more than enough to provide the project with the necessary momentum.

Advertisements were placed in newspapers in Dumfries, Edinburgh, Liverpool and London requesting architects to design a mausoleum, with a prize promised to the winning artist. Matters moved quickly: by April 1815 fifty designs had been received and the winner was Thomas Hunt from St James' Place in London, who was asked to provide working drawings. A special request then went to the minister of St Michael's Church and to the Dumfries Presbytery as the plan, if executed, would intrude a little into the glebe.

Plans were made to lay the foundation stone in June 1815, a dinner was arranged and the local masonic lodges made arrangements to meet in Thomas Duncan's church before parading to the churchyard. Then, however, the project hit a snag. Mr Maitland of Eccles had decided to erect a wall around his father's grave and this interfered with the mausoleum project, so it was then decided to move Burns's body, with the consent of Mrs Burns, to a different part of the graveyard.

Thomas Hunt arrived for the laying of the foundation stone and the dinner took place as arranged. Discussions followed concerning the art work that was to be part of the project and a competition was held to decide what was best. Then the project hit another snag. There were problems over the supply of stone.

In December 1816 the organising committee decided to meet on the anniversary of Burns's birth on 25 January 1817, as it had often been 'recommended that the birth of Burns should be celebrated by his friends and admirers'. They were aware that this was happening in other parts of Scotland and decided to meet at the Kings' Arms Inn.

The organising committee met monthly and Duncan, despite all the other demands on his time, was a regular attender. Burns's body was moved to the mausoleum in September 1817, but the committee continued to raise money for the project. Thomas Hunt arrived in August 1818 to inspect the building and declared himself to be unhappy with it. The final minute was recorded on 20 January 1819 when money was still being gathered and it appeared that there might be a shortfall.[13]

Out of this emerged the Dumfries Burns Club although, despite their great fondness for his poetry, neither Duncan nor his brother appeared on the original list of members.[14]

Freemasonry

Closely allied to Duncan's interest in the poetry of Robert Burns was his attachment to freemasonry. Burns had been a noted freemason and Duncan was a long-standing member of Lodge St Ruth No 191 in Ruthwell, where he served as chaplain (the lodge actually met in nearby Clarencefield). In 1808 he became aware of a plan by the master of a lodge in Lochmaben to establish a new lodge in Mouswald, which was only two miles from Clarencefield. Duncan wrote a strongly worded letter to Lochmaben opposing the plan, explaining why a new lodge was unnecessary and declaring the 'multiplication of lodges' as being 'disreputable and injurious to the craft'.[15] Doubtless he felt that a lodge in Mouswald would result in a reduced number of members in Clarencefield. Quite why Duncan, rather than the master or secretary of Lodge St Ruth, wrote this letter is unclear, but it is certainly an indication of Duncan's close and concerned involvement in freemasonry.

In 1816 he was appointed clerk pro tem of the lodge's mutual aid society to enable him to introduce new rules and regulations in much the same way that he had sorted out the problems of the village friendly society some years earlier. Duncan does not seem to have sought any higher office in his lodge, probably seeing his membership as an extension of his ministry or perhaps as a way to maintain a closer relationship with local people. He was a convivial man and would have enjoyed the social aspects of masonic harmony.

Freemasonry was growing in popularity and at that time there were few towns, or even villages, that did not have at least one masonic lodge under the umbrella of the Grand Lodge of Scotland. New entrants to lodges would undergo three degrees, which raised them to the rank of master mason, and the rituals were loosely derived from the building of King Solomon's temple, as described in the Old Testament book of Chronicles.

Duncan does not seem to have ever written anything about his membership of the lodge, but it is unlikely he found anything in its rituals that was inconsistent with his Christian faith based, as they were, on the masonic principles of harmony, charity and brotherly love. Moreover, the masonic description of God as the Great Architect of the Universe was entirely in keeping with his view of the world and its creator.

It was also the case that the friendly society run by Duncan was based on quasi-masonic principles. The four elements of church membership, friendly society membership, freemasonry and having an account in the savings bank were what bound the people of Ruthwell into a tightly-knit community, and Henry Duncan was at the heart of all four.

Despite living in a small village, Duncan's view of the world was in no way limited by the remoteness of his location. At one stage, when he was busy with all these other activities, he decided that the world needed a universal language so he set about creating one. His notebook on the subject had the title 'Hints for the Formation of a new language on Philosophical Principles', although this was one project he would not pursue.

Chapter 9
Poet and Novelist

It was clear even before he became a minister that Henry Duncan would be an author. His early attempts at writing verse were well received and it's possible that his choice of the quiet parish of Ruthwell was contrived to allow him time to write. Writing poetry also ran in the family, and his great uncle was Dr Thomas Blacklock, the blind poet and friend of Robert Burns.

For more than forty years a pen was seldom out of Duncan's hand; whether it was in writing his sermons, preparing material for his newspaper or in correspondence about the savings bank, his lively brain and his way with words produced an oeuvre of substantial proportions. Sadly, neither his sermons nor early copies of the newspaper have survived, and his wife destroyed many of his letters after his death. But his published work has survived, and much of it is available electronically.

There is also no trace of the pamphlet that Duncan wrote on Socinianism when he was still in Liverpool, but most of the remainder of his published writings is available. His old university friend Andrew Thomson launched a journal called *The Christian Instructor* in 1810 and Duncan became a regular contributor and book reviewer. He also contributed an article on his great uncle (Thomas Blacklock) to David Brewster's *Edinburgh Encyclopaedia*.

The first pamphlet written by Duncan as a minister was entitled *Life and Character of Maitland Smith*. It was a true story of someone who was executed for murder and robbery in Dumfries on 21 October 1807. Duncan's brother Thomas had ministered to the man during his incarceration and at his execution. Duncan then wrote the story of his life, his crimes and his execution, and used the money that the pamphlet raised in support of the man's family. Despite the seriousness of the subject matter, it was an uplifting story of how the young man had acknowledged his crime and sought forgiveness and redemption.

The success of this pamphlet led to the creation of what can only be described as a writers' club. Duncan and his fellow ministers, including his brother Thomas, 'met at each other's houses in rotation, on the first Monday of every month, and critically examined the Tract intended next for publication'. The institution of this little association Duncan always considered as among the happiest incidents of his life.

The idea for this association arose out of the writings of Hannah More, whose *Moral Tales* had been a highly successful and influential publication:

> The intention of the authors was to adapt this captivating mode of instruction to the religious sentiments, as well as to the manners and habits, of the intelligent peasantry in this northern division of the United Kingdom; and particularly, by exciting local interest in the publication, to render it subservient to the moral and spiritual improvement of their own parishioners.[1]

The essays were originally published under the banner title *Scotch Cheap Repository Tracts by a Society of Clergymen*, and the outpourings from the pens of Duncan and his friends were eventually published as a book that went through many editions, and was still being published in New York in 1847.

Duncan's other contribution to the series was *The Cottage Fireside*.[2] This was more than a pamphlet and the second, enlarged, edition, published in Dumfries in 1815, ran to 251 pages. This edition was prepared at a time when Duncan was busy with the bank and was also writing the second edition of his pamphlet on that subject (*Cottage Fireside* was published separately from the later New York edition of the *Tales*). Copies of these publications found their way into many libraries and so went far beyond the stated intention of their authors. American universities including Princeton, perhaps not surprisingly given its Scottish and Presbyterian connections, had copies on their shelves.

Duncan's contributions to the series were, like the others, designed for the spiritual edification, rather than the doctrinal instruction, of readers. The fictional hero of the *Cottage Fireside* was a school teacher and the book opens, somewhat portentously, with the words:

> I am a country schoolmaster, and have, in that situation, had daily opportunity to observe, and occasion to lament, the ill-judged manner in which the families of tradesmen, labourers and small farmers, are commonly brought up at home: and as I feel a very warm interest in the welfare of the rising generation, I intend to point out the common errors in education, into which parents of this rank of life are apt to fall.[3]

The story goes on to recount how the schoolmaster went to stay with his brother who, as a tenant farmer, occupied a somewhat lowlier station in life. This brother was married and had a young family, and much of the first part of the book is about the problems of bringing up children; homilies about behaviour, lying, mischief making, disrespect and over indulgence. There is also an acknowledgement that religious instruction must be in language that children can understand. Despite the severity of the opening paragraph, many parts of the story are written in an engaging style that draws in the reader to a point where it is understood that this is not just about bringing up children – it is also about the general behaviour of adults:

> Were people to seriously reflect how much mischief may be occasioned to their children by a single word or look, tending to undermine the authority of their teacher, they would, undoubtedly, be more cautious in this respect than they usually are. This hint may be useful to people in every rank in life.[4]

In all of this Duncan reveals himself as a man who has a deep and abiding concern for the well being of the people, but he also comes across as a man who is not prepared to challenge the social order.

Henry Duncan (1774–1846) with his sons George and William.
(© Savings Bank Museum, Ruthwell / Bethan Thompson)

Mrs Mary Duncan, Henry Duncan's second wife, photographed by David Octavius Hill and Robert Adamson in the 1840s. (© Special Collections, Glasgow University Library. Licensor www.scran.ac.uk)

Lord Chancellor Henry Brougham (1778–1868), Scottish author and statesman, circa 1860s.
Brougham was a great friend of Henry Duncan. (Sean Sexton / Hulton Archive / Getty Images)

Portrait of Dugald Stewart by Sir Henry Raeburn, circa 1810. Stewart was professor of moral philosophy at the University of Edinburgh and a close friend of Henry Duncan.
(© National Galleries of Scotland. Licensor www.scran.ac.uk)

Henry Duncan's drawing of his manse and glebe. (© Savings Bank Museum, Ruthwell / Bethan Thompson)

Henry Duncan's drawing of the Brow Well, now on the Robert Burns Trail.
(© Savings Bank Museum, Ruthwell / Bethan Thompson)

Ruthwell Savings Bank, Ruthwell, Dumfriesshire, in the 1950s. It was the first of its kind in the world, founded by Henry Duncan in 1810. (© National Museums Scotland. Licensor www.scran.ac.uk)

Ruthwell Parish bank box. Each of the three trustees held a key.
(© Savings Bank Museum, Ruthwell / Bethan Thompson)

Ruthwell Cross in Ruthwell Church, Dumfries and Galloway. The new cross piece added by Henry Duncan can be seen. (© Savings Bank Museum, Ruthwell / Bethan Thompson)

Detail of the Ruthwell Cross. (© Savings Bank Museum, Ruthwell / Bethan Thompson)

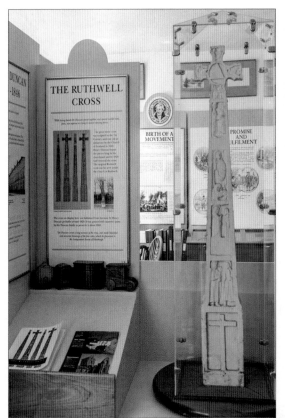

Left. Henry Duncan's beeswax model of the Ruthwell cross in the Savings Bank Museum, Ruthwell. (© Savings Bank Museum, Ruthwell / Bethan Thompson)

Below. 'The Stane Man' statue of Henry Duncan, commissioned by Thomas Tudor Duncan, on the outside of the building that housed the Dumfries Savings Bank.
(© Savings Bank Museum, Ruthwell / Bethan Thompson)

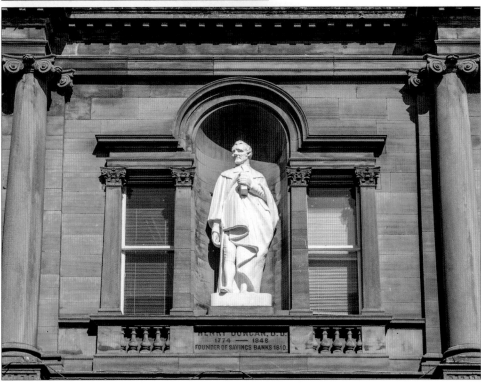

Memorial to Henry Duncan, erected by public subscription at Mount Kedar, Mouswald, Dumfries and Galloway. The inscription reads 'Rev Henry Duncan, Founder of Savings Banks. The righteous shall be in everlasting remembrance'. (© Savings Bank Museum, Ruthwell / Bethan Thompson)

The schoolmaster and the minister in the story are the clear leaders in the village. The local men may engage in some serious discussion from time to time while the women are more likely to go in for damaging gossip. Sabbath observance and good taste appear frequently as social norms that should be observed by everyone and it is the role of the minister and school teacher to ensure that they are.

Throughout the book Duncan used examples from his own life as a minister to illustrate what could be done to enhance the condition, and the behaviour, of the people. There is a mention of the minister in the story providing a lending library, which is something that Duncan did in Ruthwell.

Duncan had long been concerned about the expense that families incurred in providing food and drink at funerals, many taking on debt, so as not to appear to be stingy, and he wove his solution into the story. The school teacher enlarged upon what would happen as follows:

It had formerly been the practice [. . .] to give five or six services, as they were called, of spirits and wine, each accompanied by sweet biscuits, or other kinds of bread. This, besides being extremely ill-timed, and unbecoming the solemnity of such a meeting, was attended with other circumstances of a very hurtful nature. It occasioned a great waste of time, for the company were sometimes detained no less than four or five hours; it encouraged a habit of dram drinking before dinner; for it was no unusual thing to see many of the party actually *tipsy* with the bumpers they had swallowed; and what was another consideration of no small importance, it induced the poor labourer to vie with his richer neighbour in the expensiveness of the entertainment, and thus to bring a debt upon his head, which all his industry could scarcely enable him to discharge, and which sometimes deprived his family of the common necessaries of life.[5]

The solution was for the minister to get heads of families to sign an undertaking not to serve more than one glass at a family funeral. Needless to say there was some opposition to the proposal and Duncan wrote colourfully about those who refused to sign the undertaking and insisted upon having several drams according to the tradition of laying the head 'decently in the grave', among 'this number' being 'all the loose characters who liked idleness and drunkenness'.[6]

As an addendum to this part of the narrative Duncan allowed himself a footnote in which he claimed some credit for reforming this tradition:

> The abuses alluded to prevailed to a great extent, till lately, in the South of Scotland. They are now much reformed by means of funeral regulations. This reformation began in the parish of Ruthwell, and met at first with some opposition.[7]

Whether or not this idea originated with Duncan is uncertain, as the reformer Patrick Colquhoun had also taken it up, but whereas Colquhoun took the view that 'the manners of the lower orders had to be controlled and regulated for the public good',[8] Duncan, ever the paternalist, would have added that reform was also in the best interests of those involved.

One of Duncan's correspondents in London, H. W. Smith, wrote to him in July 1818 acknowledging the wisdom displayed in the work on how to raise children and asked Duncan to produce a version in 'English garb', i.e. 'by rendering the phraseology of your dialogues into homely English so that your work might be inculcated to advantage among the lower classes in the South'.[9] An 'English language' version of this work never appeared.

The practice of the writers' club seems to have died out after an early burst of enthusiasm, but Duncan's desire to write still burned brightly. Despite many claims on his time he wrote *The Young South Country Weaver; Or a Journey to Glasgow, a Tale for the Radicals*. The second edition, which quickly followed the first, was published in Edinburgh and London in 1821.

Duncan's purpose in writing this book (it ran to 192 pages) was similar to that in writing the *Cottage Fireside*. He maintained that the two books should be 'bound uniformly' as they had for their object 'to counteract some of the prejudices prevalent among the middle and lower classes, and to convey moral and religious instruction through the alluring medium of a tale'.[10]

The book was written at a time when radicalism was at its height, especially in the new urban and industrial areas of the country, where economic pressures had driven many people to seek relief from their troubles in, as Duncan would see it, extreme political action, including revolutionary activities. This new book was intended to be one of a series that would be written by a 'loyal society in Edinburgh'. As Duncan was a minister, a freemason and a member of the Speculative Society one can only speculate about the origins of this group. But whatever its provenance, it did not hold together and published only a few tracts. When Duncan's manuscript was submitted for publication it had already disbanded, but he was supported by a few friends to have the book published.

The hero of the story is a well brought up young weaver from the south-country Dumfries who, in order to develop his talents for weaving, decides to go to Glasgow to reside with his uncle. However, the uncle and the cousin are both far gone in radical tendencies; they try to persuade the young weaver round to their views but he stoutly resists their entreaties.

All is not well in the household. There is domestic violence and, on one occasion, the son attacks the father and our hero intervenes to prevent a murder. The young weaver then becomes acquainted with a radical orator from London who tries to recruit him to his cause but meets stout and well-argued resistance. Much violence ensues and our hero is wounded. The cousin is eventually killed but his father is redeemed when visiting his brother in Dumfriesshire.

Much of the discussion in the book concerns the issues of the day. Taxes were a major source of contention as was the national debt, while there was talk about equality, with references to the American and French revolutions. Clearly Duncan was well versed in these issues and wove them into the text with great skill.

The *New Edinburgh Review* devoted in excess of twenty pages to its review of the book, with lengthy excerpts to illustrate various points and to support its stance against the radicalisation that was taking place in some sections of Scottish society.[11] The review commenced with the words:

> The Excellent author of this little work will, we take it, be more surprised than any other person, to find the benevolent and unpretending labours, which he meant for the humbler and less informed classes of his countrymen, recommended in the pages of a quarterly review, to the attention of the most enlightened.

Yet again the influence of Duncan's pen went far beyond what he had anticipated. It is perhaps no surprise, therefore, that he was emboldened to attempt something on an altogether grander scale.

Duncan was an avid reader and Sir Walter Scott was busy writing novels, many of which were based upon stories from Scottish history. There is no record of Duncan and Scott ever having met but it is likely that they were acquainted with one another; they had friends and family in common – James Hogg for one – and both were members of the Speculative Society in Edinburgh. Both were also admirers of the poetry of Robert Burns and while Duncan was joint secretary of the project to build a mausoleum for the Bard, Scott was a contributor to the cause. Moreover, Scott lived at no great distance from Ruthwell.

It is certain that Duncan read Scott's 1815 novel *Old Mortality* and, while he may have admired it as a novel, he, and many other Presbyterians, did not care much for the story line which they regarded as too sympathetic to the Royalists and not sufficiently sympathetic to the Covenanters in this story about the maelstrom of seventeenth-century Scottish politics.

In 1826 Duncan's novel *William Douglas, or the Scottish Exiles*, was published by Oliver and Boyd in Edinburgh and Longman in London. It was very much in the tradition of romantic fiction of which Scott was the acknowledged master. Although Duncan had published short stories in the 'Cheap Repository' series this was his only attempt at a full-length novel. He did not spare himself in the writing and the finished product ran to three volumes and more than 900 pages. It was published anonymously as Duncan could not persuade himself that novel writing was a suitable pursuit for a minister of religion. He did not acknowledge his authorship, except to a few close friends, until, in a letter to George Sturge of the Peace Society in 1839, he wrote:

> I did not think it decorous in a Minister of the Gospel to give himself to the world as the author of a work of fiction [. . .] Not, indeed, that I had any misgivings in my own mind as to the employment of narrative [. . .] for the purpose of conveying important truth [. . .] for of such a practice our Saviour himself has left us a most eminent and effective example in his parables; but that I did shrink, and do still shrink from the character of a mere novel writer, which might have been maliciously laid to my charge and might have been employed by opponents as an instrument against the sacred profession to which I belong.[12]

The subject of Duncan's novel was the Covenanters of the seventeenth century, a story of religious persecution as Scottish Presbyterians struggled against a British king who was determined to establish Episcopacy as the way in which church government would operate. In effect he was concerned to have a common system of church government and worship throughout his kingdoms. The Scots resisted and were especially hostile to bishops and the common prayer book, viewing these as ways to reverse some of the achievements, as they saw it, of the Reformation. They viewed the king's policy not just as a cultural imposition but as a hostile act and historical anti-English mind-sets were revived.

In 1638, not for the first time, the Scots signed a 'National Covenant', in effect a contract with God, binding themselves to maintain Presbyterian doctrines and policy as the sole form of religion in Scotland. This was a direct challenge to the authoritarian government of King Charles I, a man of Scottish birth but who had been resident in England since his father King James VI of Scotland became King James I of England in 1603. Swords were sharpened and put to use and the matter was not settled until the Revolution of 1688 brought King William of Orange and Queen Mary to the throne.

This struggle and its 'killing times' became a rich vein of material for novelists. Duncan's idea was to write a book that would be more sympathetic to the Covenanters than Walter Scott had been in *Old Mortality*, published in 1816. The covenanting tradition had been strongest in the south-west of Scotland, i.e. in Duncan's part of the country, and his own ministerial forebears had probably been involved. Critics of Scott maintained that he had been too sympathetic to the Royalists, but before Duncan could get his novel written and published, his contemporary John Galt produced *Ringan Gilhaize*, a novel of the Reformation and covenanting times, in 1823. Duncan's relative James Hogg (the Ettrick Shepherd) published, anonymously, *The Private Memoirs and Confessions of a Justified Sinner* the following year. This was not about the Covenanters but it did deal with some of the more difficult aspects of theology. So by the time Duncan brought his book to the notice of the public, the market was already well served with books about religious extremism and persecution.

Duncan's plot was relatively simple. The first volume dealt with the cruelties and oppressions visited on those parts of Scotland that were known to be sympathetic to the covenanting cause. There is a certain amount of sermonising but there is also some humour and a well-drafted debate about the divine right of kings to govern. This was counterbalanced by what the Covenanters saw as their divine right to resist a king who denied them the right to worship God as they pleased – especially a king like Charles II who had promised to permit Presbyterianism but had then gone back on his word.

Duncan was careful to make the point that there were two groups of Covenanters, those who acknowledged the king as leader in temporal, but not spiritual matters and those who denied the right of the king to govern in any domain. The leader of the more extreme view, Richard Cameron, makes an appearance as one of the characters in the novel. The violence that ensues is anticipated in some of the early pages when Duncan puts inflammatory words into the mouth of the military commander in the south-east of Scotland, Sir John Davenport. He says of Covenanters that 'they only acknowledge the Sovereign as set over them in *temporal* things [. . .] they therefore by direct inference deny his authority over the church, which is downright treason'. He goes on to say that they have 'a malignant spirit, totally incompatible with regular government and with public welfare', before concluding that 'Coercion is absolutely necessary. It is true policy. It is true mercy – Scotland must be treated as a conquered province [. . .] We must set our feet on the neck of Presbytery.'[13]

Duncan never concealed his admiration for the Covenanters, either in this novel or in anything else that he wrote or said. But this novel was written at a time when his own views about the relationship between church and state were changing. Whether the writing of the novel encouraged him to change his views, or vice versa, it is impossible to tell, but from this point forward Duncan's life was set on a path that led to the Disruption of the Church of Scotland and the loss of his own church and manse.

The knowledge that Duncan gained as a leader of the Ruthwell Volunteers was used to good effect. Battle scenes, military movements and the topography of the area are described in great detail and the text moves from battlefield to religious dispute with great skill.

In the second volume the hero, who has fallen in love with a young lady, is banished on account of his religious beliefs to the West Indies, where he is shipwrecked and settles on an island populated by a mysterious group of people who speak English, are of British origin, dress in white clothes and are Christian. The crew and officers, one of whom is called Lieutenant Bembow, are also saved and they settle down to life in this Arcadia. However, in volume three, it becomes known that there are pirates, living in huts surrounded by a palisade, on the other side of the island (one wonders if Robert Louis Stevenson had read Duncan's novel). Our hero, and his Arcadian friend, are captured by the pirates, one escapes and a rescue mission sets out to rescue the other; but before this happens Duncan uses the opportunity to develop an argument about the right to defend oneself when attacked. It is a position consistent with his advocacy of resistance during the Napoleonic wars. Only this time his argument is tinged with a degree of caution:

> We must preserve our chastity, our integrity, our good name, our religious profession when these are invaded [. . .] I know not where you will find any Christian precept which forbids us to defend our lives, even though it be at the expense of those of our assailants; and, if there be no express command enjoining self-preservation, that is because the dictate of nature is suffi-cient.
>
> But if you once admit the lawfulness of defensive war, you will find it difficult to draw a practical line of distinction between that and a war of offence.[14]

The pirates are defeated and our hero, his friends and the crew, sail to Holland in the pirates' ship where they meet Prince William of Orange. On their return to London they meet King James and are imprisoned in the Tower of London. They are helped to escape by the young ensign that they knew at the beginning of the novel and, by the time they get back to Scotland, Prince William has succeeded King James on the throne. Presbyterianism is secure.

Duncan completed his novel with two simple but revealing state-ments. The first is an exchange between Ensign Forshaw and our hero:

> 'Would that I could possess such faith as yours!' said Forshaw. 'Clouds and darkness are round me whenever I turn my thoughts to the ways of the Eternal, and my mind is filled with doubt and dismay.'
>
> 'Alas my young friend!' returned the other, – 'think you I am exempt from this weakness of humanity? [. . .] Here below, the triumph of faith is seldom complete, and few of the children of mortality can utter a prayer of greater assurance than – Lord, I believe – help thou my unbelief.'[15]

It was a prayer that Duncan would have cause to use again.

The reviews of Duncan's novel were mixed. The *Scotsman* applauded 'the sincerity and earnestness of the principle which is displayed and sustained throughout', while the *Edinburgh Weekly Journal* recorded that it

> depicts, with much strength of colouring, the misery of the persecuted Covenanters, and sometimes with exquisite pathos and high ability, their constancy in suffering and exile; while the shifting of the scene to a transatlantic region gives variety to the entertainment, and affords the occasion of much fine moral as well as natural description.[16]

Meanwhile *La Belle Assemblée*, an English magazine for ladies, was sympathetic,[17] but the more serious *Monthly Review* scathing:

> The first page of this 'historical novel' told us what we had to dread – another imitation of Sir Walter Scott, and a new inundation of eloquent Presbyterians, ferocious covenanters, heroic young ladies and old gentlemen, generous officers in red coats, and a whole army of saints and martyrs [. . .]

The reviewer's concern was that Scott had occupied the territory of novels about the Covenanters and no more were necessary or wanted. He was, however, more complimentary about Duncan's writing style, which he acknowledged displayed 'considerable elegance and [. . .] energy'.[18] The *Scots Magazine* took a similar view, feeling that an

> impartial and comprehensive view of the character of the times is perhaps still a desideratum in literature. But, most assuredly, that task is not likely to be fulfilled by the author of this novel, who, with all his professions of impartiality, has adopted the same limited and party views with his predecessors.

It went on: 'The truth is, that, as a novel, as a series of events, connected together by any common bearing, containing any progressive interest, the book is utterly defective.' Despite this damning criticism the *Scots Magazine* went on to include a very large excerpt from one of the chapters.[19]

In modern parlance, Duncan had missed his market and never wrote another novel. Nevertheless, as we shall see, his pen was not idle.

Very shortly after the novel was published, Duncan's old friend Henry Brougham told him about his plan to establish the Society for the Diffusion of Useful Knowledge. The main aim of the society was to publish useful tracts on a wide range of subjects, mostly scientific and civil history, with the target audience of the working class and those who preferred self-education to attending classes. Duncan was asked to contribute, recruit other authors and establish a committee that would serve the south of Scotland and north of England; subjects involving 'party politics and controversial divinity' were to be avoided.[20] As was his wont, Duncan set about the task with alacrity, but he experienced some difficulty in setting up the committee and Brougham told him never to give up until the task seemed impossible.

His own initial contributions were on friendly societies and savings banks. Duncan recruited his brother Thomas and a range of friends, including Thomas Carlyle, to the task. Brougham also wanted him to provide a Christian exposition of popular science. It was a task that Duncan approached with great caution, fearing that some writers would introduce material that was not Christian or that would give those hostile to God some ammunition. Nevertheless, the challenge was almost certainly what persuaded him some years later to turn this thinking to his major life project.

The early 1830s saw Duncan without a writing project. His wife Agnes was unwell and she died in 1832. Whether it was her death or some other event that stirred him into writing his *magnum opus* is unclear; it may well be that he had this major project in mind for many years. *The Sacred Philosophy of the Seasons* was published in four volumes in 1836-7,[21] and more than anything else it justifies Duncan's claim to be considered a polymath. The sub-title of the work was 'The Perfections of God in the Phenomena of the Year', and one of his objectives in writing these volumes was to challenge a growing mind-set that separated science and religion. The scepticism, born of the Enlightenment, continued to grow as more and more people saw science, rather than religion, as providing answers to many of their questions. Duncan believed that there was no barrier between the two and that religious belief was in no way incompatible with scientific research.

Duncan had long been interested in scientific matters. He had, as we have already seen, contributed to the science of geology and counted leading scientists, including Sir David Brewster, among his closest friends. He did not see any dichotomy between science and religion, but he could see such a thing in the minds and writings of others, and *Sacred Philosophy* was his sincere attempt to re-establish harmony between faith in God and the realities of the world. There were many such exercises. William Buckland, dean of Westminster and Edward Hitchcock, principal of Amherst College in Massachusetts, both published books with similar objectives and both men, like Duncan, were geologists.

Beginning with the volume on 'Winter' in 1836, the book was published over the next year, with a volume for each season. This put Duncan under enormous pressure to meet the deadlines of publishers and he invited his close circle of family and friends to assist him. These included his sons, his wife and his daughter-in-law. However, there can be no doubt that the vast majority of what was written came from his own pen, and we know that he would rise from his bed at a very early hour to complete his writing commitments. Neither can there be any doubt that Duncan's own library must have been substantial. *Sacred Philosophy* draws upon the work of scientists, philosophers, poets and others from many ages and from many parts of the world. This cannot have been an easy book to write, as it would have required careful study and constant cross-referencing.

The four volumes were organised so that a sub-chapter could be read each day and the whole would be finished in a calendar year. Each chapter covered a week and each had seven sub-chapters.

The volume for 'Summer' reveals the scale and scope of Duncan's undertaking. It begins with a week's reading on what he describes as 'cosmical arrangements', with sub- chapters on 'Increased Heat', 'Internal Heat of the Earth', 'Increased Light', 'Electricity', 'Clouds' and 'Dew'. Readers were then treated to a week's reading on vegetables, with a further week on the non-food uses of plants. What followed were chapters and sub-chapters on insects, reptiles, birds, quadrupeds and man.

A great deal of what Duncan wrote dealt with technical matters and reveals a well-read man who had the ability to relay his knowledge in easily-understood terms. But he also recognised the limits of his own knowledge and was not afraid to say so. In the sub-chapter on electricity, for example, he paid homage to the work of Franklin and Galvani, giving short shrift to the claims of Bertholon who believed that electricity could be used to promote vegetable growth by using what today would be described as lightning rods. Duncan well understood about positive and negative charges, but was not afraid to admit that further knowledge on this subject was beyond him, as it would be beyond most people at that time.

It is clear that Duncan admired, and was fascinated by, nature in all its manifestations and although he does not say so it seems unlikely he believed in the literal truth of the Genesis story of creation. He did, however, see God as the creator of the universe. That was the whole point of this publication, although the religious messages were largely reserved for the Sunday readings:

> As we spring from our couch, therefore, on the bright summer morning, and walk joyfully forth into the fragrant fields, to breathe the inspiring air, feast our eyes upon the glowing mixture of colours in which all nature is arrayed, and listen to the sweet and various music that ascends from every grove, let us not fail to derive a high spiritual lesson from the dew that is so strictly strewn upon the grass beneath our feet. Distilled in the silent night by the reciprocal influences of heaven and earth, it bathes and refreshes each blade and flower with its stainless moisture. Let us regard it as the chosen image of God's choicest blessing,

the cleansing and sanctifying influence of His Spirit upon the heart of man.[22]

These were the words of a man who was confident in his faith and who had left the doubts of his youth firmly behind him. Indeed, when one of Duncan's friendly correspondents, the Scottish poet Joanna Baillie, sent him a book she had written from her home in Hampstead he responded critically, as she had written that the doctrine of the Trinity 'had no just foundation in scripture'.[23] He told her that the book had caused him pain; possibly it reminded him of his own flirtation with Unitarianism in Liverpool.

Duncan sent copies of the four volumes of *Sacred Philosophy* to various friends, including Alexander Duff, the Church of Scotland's first missionary to India, who replied:

These volumes constitute a perfect encyclopaedia of knowledge – knowledge in its right place and connection – knowledge consecrated to the highest and noblest of purposes. I do bless God our heavenly Father for having put it into your heart, and having conferred on you the ability to rear so goodly a temple sacred to religion and science, in happy and blessed union.[24]

It may, however, have been something of a concern to him that the American edition of *Sacred Philosophy* was prepared by a Unitarian, Rev. Francis William Pitt Greenwood, DD. Unitarians had gained a strong foothold in the United States, especially in Eastern Massachusetts where Harvard University was strongly under their influence. Nevertheless, *Sacred Philosophy* was recommended for use in schools in Massachusetts and, again, Duncan may have been surprised (but quietly delighted) that his work had found an unexpected audience.

Greenwood, who preached at King's Chapel in Boston, was, on the whole, very complimentary about the books, writing:

Another merit of this work, is its religious character and tendency. It develops, and often very happily, the *sacred* philosophy of the Seasons. Its main object, never lost sight of, is to show that the operations of Nature are the work of God's hand, the intimations of his presence and agency, the proofs of his wisdom, the manifestations of his love. It aims at constructing no cunning argument, at weaving no newly devised web of too ingenious thought, but steadily it points to some nice adaptation, some beautiful arrangement in this lower world, and then seriously up to the Great Designer.[25]

Another American reviewer, Rev. Dr Cheever of New York, wrote: 'There is one delightful production which we may mention with unmixed praise, adapted for all classes, and full of the lessons both of science and religion – it is the 'Sacred Philosophy of the Seasons', by Dr Duncan.'[26] He could have hoped for no better compliments. Edgar Allan Poe, writing for *Burton's Gentleman's Magazine*, also provided a favourable review:

In our last number we had barely room to acknowledge the reception of this valuable work, and to speak of it in general terms of commendation. A careful perusal has since assured us that we did not err in our opinion. The book will recommend itself wherever seen, as a well-arranged and well-digested compendium, embracing a vast amount of information upon the various topics of physical science, and especially well adapted to those educational purposes for which the volumes are designed [. . .]

The 'Philosophy of the Seasons' is a book of which every one must think well. Its great comprehensiveness, its general accuracy, its ingenious and luminous arrangement, render it, in every respect, a valuable work.[27]

In addition to the American imprint, there would be further editions in Great Britain, but it was the last major work Duncan would produce. The remainder of his active life was to be spent in the arcane world of church politics.

Chapter 10
A University for Dumfries

By the early nineteenth century, Scotland possessed four universities, later known as the 'ancients'. The University of St Andrews had been founded in 1413, with Glasgow following in 1451, Aberdeen in 1495 and Edinburgh the most recent in 1583. None had been formed since the end of the sixteenth century.

Education was another issue dear to Henry Duncan's heart. Some at that time believed that to educate poor people beyond the basics was not in their best interests; it would simply make them dissatisfied with their position in life, maybe even make them question some of the basic tenets of their religion.

Duncan set himself against these ideas and dedicated a large part of his life to ensuring education was accessible to all, even paying for peripatetic lecturers to come to Ruthwell to give talks on astronomy, natural science and history.[1] He was encouraged in this by Sir David Brewster, a man from the Scottish borders who was a frequent visitor to Ruthwell manse and who went on to become principal of Edinburgh University. Brewster also greatly assisted Duncan in some of his other endeavours.

Duncan's interests in education were a key part of his world view, believing as he did that education would help people to remain independent. This, therefore, was entirely consistent with his purpose in setting up the savings bank: a good education and thrifty habits would ensure that people were resilient in the face of economic and social pressures. But it had to be good-quality education, and Duncan took the view that teachers' pay was inadequate. Consequently he endeavoured to have their salaries increased.[2]

As minister Duncan was responsible for the parish school and, as we have seen in the chapter on church politics, he took his oversight of the school and schoolmaster very seriously. Moreover, surplus funds from the savings bank were used to build a school in one of the remoter parts of his parish. Many of his writings were also designed to educate and to help people to maintain high moral standards, but these were not the limits of his ambition in the education world.

Duncan believed there should be a university in Dumfries, and in 1814 he saw his chance to make that belief a reality. A rumour was circulating that St Andrews University, then languishing having failed to make much of a showing in the Scottish Enlightenment and facing stiff competition from Glasgow and Edinburgh, might be interested in moving. The rumour seems to have started in the *London Star* and Duncan, aided and abetted by his brother Thomas, lost no time in reprinting it in the *Courier* together with an appeal to local dignitaries to support a move from St Andrews to Dumfries.

Duncan believed that an institution of higher learning in Dumfries would attract students from Ireland and the north of England as well as from the south of Scotland. The local Commissioners of Supply were attracted by the idea and endeavoured to ascertain if there was any truth in the rumour.[3] The chancellor of St Andrews, Viscount Melville, and Dr Hill, principal of St Salvator's College, replied in the negative and said that the Senate had not even considered the matter. But Dr Playfair, principal of St Leonard's College, said that some members of the university *had* discussed the idea before deciding it was impractical.

That was not quite the end of the matter and other articles in the *Courier* tried, with increasing desperation, to keep the idea alive. There were articles about the buildings that would be needed in Dumfries and what might be done with the buildings in St Andrews. The library, for example, might make a fine masonic lodge. The writers, almost certainly the Duncan brothers, went on to assure the readers (and probably themselves) that the inhabitants of Dumfries would be liberal in their support for such an institution.[4]

Nothing came of the St Andrews move but the Duncan brothers

had greater success in their efforts to establish a mechanics institute in Dumfries. A public meeting, held on 15 March 1825 in the Trades' Hall, was convened for the purpose of establishing such an organisation, which was deemed to be 'a measure calculated to improve extensively [the tradesmen's] habits and condition, to advance the arts and sciences, and to add largely to the power, resources and prosperity of the country'. This has to be seen as part of a wider movement to enhance the education and training of working people and is entirely consistent with one of Duncan's other interests at the time, Henry Brougham's Society for the Diffusion of Useful Knowledge. But it might also have had a deeper purpose, an attempt to address and combat the rising tide of radical politics among the working classes. One of the rules about the management of the new institute was archetypal Duncan. The new organisation was 'likely to be most stable and useful, when entirely or chiefly supported by the Mechanics themselves'. This was exactly the kind of management structure he had introduced in the savings bank, and it had worked well. But it was also part of a wider effort to enhance working-class participation in society and counterbalance radical tendencies.

The movement to establish similar organisations in other places was not without controversy. Duncan wrote that

Truth cannot oppose truth. Intelligent men-though but half educated-in an age like ours *will* inquire into doubtful and difficult subjects, and no one has a right to prevent them, even were it possible. Surely then, it is but a duty-on the part of those who have the power-to afford them the aid they need, in cultivating their mental faculties, and in seeking to discover whatever is genuine in science. Any other course on the part of Christian professors naturally throws a suspicion on the claims of our holy faith, while it leaves the instruction of the people in hands to which it may be less safely confided. Let the Christian afford what assistance he can to all classes in the improvement of their minds; let him sympathise with the humbler orders in their laudable ambition to attain a greater measure of knowledge, and

he may thus wield an influence by which many may be led to
enquire into that infinitely nobler subject which involves the
eternal destiny of man.[5]

Duncan's son George put it succinctly when he wrote that his father's
objective was to guide the current rather than block it.

Within weeks a new management committee – mainly comprising
artisans – was elected. Thomas Duncan was elected as a trustee and
Henry, no longer a committee member, offered to give lectures and
to arrange for friends to speak at the meetings. Various talks on such
subjects as architectural drawing, mathematics, geography and
grammar were arranged and a library was established and housed,
at first, in a room at the Academy.

By 1828 the institute was going well and subscription prices were
reduced to encourage more people to join.[6] It went on to have a long
and successful life, eventually erecting its own building in which
Duncan continued to give guest lectures.

The same could not be said for the university project. The Duncan
brothers, with some help from Henry Brougham, were still pursuing
the idea of a university for Dumfries, the cause of this revived interest
being the will of Dr James Crichton, who had made a fortune as a
medical man and trader in the Far East. He died in 1823 leaving his
money in a trust fund to be allocated by his wife for charitable purposes.
The problem, as it arose, was that the money could only be disbursed
'with the approbation of his trustees'.

The Duncan brothers became advisers to Mrs Crichton. Henry
Duncan had been a neighbour of her father and was, presumably,
well acquainted with the widow. But the will was challenged by John
Crichton, brother of the deceased, who took his case all the way to
the House of Lords. This took years and, in the meantime, Henry and
Thomas Duncan hatched plans to use the money to establish a university. Mrs Crichton was, at first, amenable to this suggestion and devoted
a great deal of her time and energy to promote the idea to people of
influence.

Once again the idea was to bring the University of St Andrews to

Dumfries, and this time the Duncans were assisted by Dr John Lee, then Professor of Divinity and Church History at St Mary's College, St Andrews. It remains possible, even likely, that Lee was the instigator of the earlier proposal. Henry Duncan insisted on complete confidentiality in the correspondence and then set about recruiting backers. Among those pledging their support was the Rev. Professor Thomas Chalmers who, having just given up St John's Church in Glasgow where he had done much good work among the poor (including the establishment of a savings bank), had become Professor of Moral Philosophy at St Andrews.[7] Duncan's sons were then studying in Glasgow and often breakfasted with Chalmers, so Duncan felt bold enough to write to him in the strongest terms about his new post:

> The Moral Philosophy chair, as its business has hitherto usually been conducted, has been not useless merely, but positively noxious in its effects, and that to a fearful extent. It has sown the seeds of infidelity, or at least indifference to religion in that soil where it was of the utmost consequence that the mere principles of Christianity should have taken the deepest root. It has separated religion from the everyday affairs of human life and induced a belief that for all moral purposes the human mind is competent of itself-and what is perhaps scarcely less pernicious, it has introduced the young imagination into an ideal world of metaphysics and made it conversant with a jargon of words and phrases calculated rather to conceal ignorance than to promote truth and to make its pupils proud of their understandings at the very moment that they ought to be more distrustful and most humble.[8]

As events unfolded in the national church, Chalmers and Duncan would find common cause on a number of issues. Chalmers also became a source of good counsel to Duncan's sons, both of whom entered the ministry.

It was at this time, in 1823, that Henry Duncan was awarded the degree of Doctor of Divinity at St Andrews. The occasion was the arrival of Chalmers in St Andrews where Duncan's sons had followed. Duncan had gone to join in the celebrations and to see his sons settled there, but at a public dinner given by the University Senate the principal proposed a toast to Duncan and, in doing so, announced that the degree of Doctor of Divinity was to be conferred on him. It is possible that the events of that year and the honour bestowed were connected but it is impossible to say with any certainty.

The position of respect that Duncan held in the Church of Scotland and his work in establishing the savings bank movement were certainly enough in themselves to warrant the award. His thoughts are recorded in a letter to Robert Lundie in Kelso: 'I have not mentioned it to a single person but yourself, nor do I mean to do so-nor will I take the title unless it be forced on me.'[9] He later relented and seems to have taken satisfaction, if not pride, in being styled as 'Dr Duncan'. But it must have been a strange feeling to receive the highest academic honour from a university he was intent on moving to another part of Scotland.

Duncan and Mrs Crichton wanted Chalmers to accept the role of principal of the proposed university but he declined and, despite their persistence, held firm to his decision. He was well established in the academic world and in the church and his ambitions lay in other directions.

Some years later Henry Brougham, who was of some support to Duncan in this project, tried to get Chalmers to apply for a chair in moral philosophy in University College London, which he was then engaged in establishing, but again Chalmers declined. In 1828 he accepted the chair of theology at the University of Edinburgh and remained in that city for the rest of his life although not, as we shall see, at the University of Edinburgh.

Meanwhile the Dumfries university project was bogged down in the courts as John Crichton contested his brother's will. Until his challenge was settled there was little that could be done except to negotiate with St Andrews University. The major stumbling block seems to have been the fact that many of the professors also had church appointments in and around St Andrews and, if the university moved to Dumfries,

similar appointments would have to be found for them there. Before
1823 was out, however, the Duncan brothers were thinking that it
might be easier to bring King's College Aberdeen to Dumfries. In
December 1823 Duncan wrote to Chalmers: '[T]he more I think of
the Aberdeen plan and compare it with the St Andrews one, the more
I am convinced that the difficulties are much less formidable in the
removal of the former than of the latter.'[10]

In May 1826 the Court of Session in Edinburgh found against John
Crichton. He then appealed to the House of Lords, whereupon Mrs
Crichton appointed Henry Brougham to be her legal counsel in London.

Duncan took some hope from the fact that the government had
appointed a Royal Commission to report on the Scottish universities.
One of its members was Henry Home Drummond of Blair Drummond,
a judge and a personal friend of Thomas Duncan. While in London
in 1827 Henry Duncan had introduced Drummond to Brougham.

There was a time in 1827 when Duncan feared the plan would
not succeed, and he thought of having a theological college in York,
which would be used to educate Presbyterians and Episcopalians,
although he did not entertain this notion for very long as it was abun-
dantly evident that the trustees would not let the Crichton money out
of Dumfries. It is difficult to escape the conclusion that Duncan was
clutching at straws. Undoubtedly, he was trying to keep the project
alive until the House of Lords made up its mind on the John Crichton
case.

The next idea came from Duncan's friend, the local MP, William
Douglas, brother of the Duke of Queensberry, who came up with the
idea of bringing English and Scottish Episcopalians to study in Dumfries
on the basis that any new institution would have to rely upon the
north of England as part of its catchment area. Brougham was keen
on this proposal but both Chalmers and Lee were highly sceptical.
Andrew Thomson in Edinburgh was also consulted and he worried
about what the Church of Scotland's General Assembly would make
of such an idea. Duncan then abandoned the idea and Douglas withdrew the proposal, the former admitting to Chalmers that he had
been rather hasty in promoting it.[11]

It took until 1829 for the views of the Royal Commission to leak out and Duncan wrote to Lee to express the hope that he was now drafting a constitution for the new college. By this time the idea of bringing King's College Aberdeen to Dumfries had been given up in favour of moving Aberdeen's other higher education institution, Marischal College. *The Edinburgh Evening Post* was thoroughly hostile to the idea and Duncan wrote letters rebutting its criticisms.

Chalmers, having taken up his post in Edinburgh University, had again made his support for the scheme perfectly clear, but his personal position was reiterated: he would not become the principal. John Hope-Johnstone, who went on to become a long serving MP for Dumfriesshire, agreed to accept the role. Evidently Lee had not written a constitution and that task fell to Duncan. Hope-Johnstone settled to his task with alacrity, writing to presbyteries asking them how many students they would be able to send to the new institution and then raising a public subscription for the library. He was clearly taking charge of the project.

Meanwhile relations between Mrs Crichton and Duncan were not going well. She had decided to give John Crichton the £10,000 that he had been wanting all along, notwithstanding the decision of the House of Lords that had found against him. She also decided to give £10,000 to Lord Strathallan which, he claimed, he had been promised by James Crichton. Brougham and Duncan were horrified by these decisions. Mrs Crichton wrote to Hope-Johnstone about Duncan in October 1829:

> I could not help being a little vexed with all that nonsense between him and Brougham about York – and I am afraid he is rather hurt with me at present. I was sorry for it, because he means well – and would do anything to serve us – but his kindness has put me into so many scrapes.[12]

Duncan may have been 'hurt' but that did not deter him from getting on with the job in hand. Two weeks later he wrote a very lengthy letter to Hope-Johnstone in which, inter alia, he stated that 'the scheme must be modified by considerations connected with the extent of the funds, as well as by circumstances of a local and more general nature'. His primary concern was with the finances. He had calculated that the £85,000 that Mrs Crichton was then prepared to give would generate income sufficient to endow twelve professorships at a salary of £200 per annum, while the principal could be paid £350. There were to be chairs in Latin, Greek, logic, mathematics, natural philosophy, Hebrew, church history and theology. A principal would be the tenth chair and he together with the professors of Hebrew, church history and theology would constitute the Divinity Faculty. Duncan was clear that these ten chairs were indispensable to the new institution. Buildings would have to be provided by government and by public subscription. There is nothing to suggest that Duncan was contemplating one of the chairs for himself.

The succeeding passage is highly revealing of Duncan's views on education, his critique of the existing university system and of the challenges faced by Christians in an increasingly secular world. He evidently held his views very passionately and saw the opportunity to found a new university as a vital part of his personal philosophy and of the challenge to reconcile the best of the Enlightenment with his religious beliefs:

> It does appear to me, however, that there is one highly injurious omission in all our Universities, as they are at present constituted, or rather as the classes are taught, which I cannot but consider as altogether unaccountable in a country like this, whose system of education is in its original character essentially religious. I allude to even the semblance of any provision for the Christian instruction of the youth while attending Philosophy classes. This is then more to be regretted on account of the age at which they usually enter college, that critical period of their lives when they first begin to think, and to form opinions for themselves, and when they are but too apt to regard all they have been previously taught on the subject of Religion as Nursery Myndries and childish superstitions. It is surely strange that at the very

time when it is considered most expedient to present to their opening minds, on every other subject, enlarged and enlightened views, that subject should be thrown out of sight which is confessedly the most sublime and the most important of all. And it certainly does not remove the inconsistency of such a plan that this happens to be the very time chosen for teaching the higher branches of classical literature, of which all the abominations of Heathen Mythology, and, still more unhappily, of Heathen morality, forms an inseparable part. Nor is it possible to forget that teachers who have devoted their lives to the study of the classics, are but too frequently so enamoured of ancient manners and opinions as in a great measure to lose sight of the purer and more exalted sentiments which ought to characterise a Christian age; or at best, to consider the teaching of these sentiments as no part of their duty.

This defect in the education system could be remedied, according to Duncan, by the principal providing

two courses of lectures – one, to the classical students on the defects of heathenism, both in its mythology and morality, as compared with the enlightened principles of Christianity, and the other, to the students of Natural and Moral Philosophy, on the principles of natural and revealed theology.[13]

Duncan then turned his thoughts to the remaining two chairs. The limited nature of the trust funds together with local considerations made him think it inadvisable to have a school of law or medicine but he was very keen on teaching jurisprudence. His own experience in the University of Glasgow, where he had been taught by John Millar, had affected him profoundly. Millar's lectures on government did more to open his mind to the philosophy of history 'than any other study in my life'. The occupant of this chair, if appointed, would also be required to teach political economy.

The final chair would be devoted to chemistry although the professor would also be required to teach geology, another subject dear to Duncan's heart. There is no escaping the conclusion that Duncan's plan for the university was entirely influenced by his own experience of education as well as by his life experiences. It would have been strange if it had been otherwise.

Having expounded his views on the curriculum and the professors Duncan then returned in this letter to the subject of finances. He anticipated that the university would grow in years to come and funds would be required to pay for expansion. He proposed, therefore, that class fees paid by students would be disbursed in part to the professors, to encourage their industry, and another part would be held back by the university to pay for bursaries and future developments.

Further bursaries would be provided by Mrs Crichton and Duncan suggested measures by which they could be allocated to, and awarded by, local presbyteries. It is evident that Duncan envisaged a major role for the church in running the new establishment. But there was one aspect of how that influence would work that gave him cause for concern. It was a concern that would come to dominate the remainder of his life, not in respect of the Scottish universities but of the church itself.

In the final section of this letter he dealt with the question of patronage. He was clear that all members of the Divinity Faculty should be chosen from among the clergy of the Church of Scotland, but he had growing concerns about how the selection process might work. The whole question of patronage was one that had exercised minds in the Scottish church since the Reformation in the sixteenth century, it being the process by which ministers were chosen by local heritors (landlords) or by the Crown, thus depriving local people of the right to choose their own minister. It was an issue that would eventually split the Church of Scotland, although there had already been a number of schisms, especially in the sixteenth century, concerning this very subject. It was also an issue that would cost Duncan dearly; ultimately it was a question about power and influence.[14] Duncan was worried that if the professors owed their appointments to local heritors, then the latter might be able to exert undue influence on the university. This was a bold position for Duncan to take, as local heritors were among the supporters of the proposed institution. His concern and his solution were outlined in the concluding paragraph of the letter:

> For obvious reasons which it is unnecessary and might be invidious to detail, the patronage should not be placed in the hands of a single private individual, or of a corporate body, or of the Senatus Academicus; and I must be permitted to add that there are also insuperable objections, not less obvious, to the vesting of this power in the Crown. After much thinking on this subject, I cannot suggest any plan, *likely to be adopted*, which would afford a more reasonable prospect of an intelligent impartial and patriotic exercise of the right of patronage than the appointment by the Crown, of Commissioners in whom this power should be vested, chosen from among different orders of society, whose various views and habits might counteract each other so as to prevent any sinister influence, and whose separate walks in life might render combination difficult for effecting any interested object.[15]

When the Royal Commission expressed its support for the idea of a new university, Mrs Crichton wrote to the Prime Minister, Robert Peel, offering £85,000 in support. At this stage Brougham seems to have been playing a double game, although it is not at all clear what his motives were. He hinted that the government was unlikely to accept the idea of a new university despite the fact that Peel had decided to support the Royal Commission's findings. Consequently he believed that this would involve a move of one of the older institutions of higher education. He was, at that time, busily involved in establishing what would become the University of London.

The substance of the constitution that Duncan then drafted is contained in the long letter to Hope-Johnstone and was then submitted to the Royal Commission. Chalmers had been in London and had conversed with Peel on the subject. The Royal Commission's report was finally published on 28 October 1830. Its language was high-minded and it clearly favoured a university in Dumfries, arguing that it was

> essential to keep in view the peculiar and beneficent character of the Scotch Universities, that they are intended to place the means of the highest education in Science and philosophy within the reach of the humble ranks of life, while, at the same time, they are equally adapted to educate and enlighten the youth of the highest class of society [. . .] we should consider it to be one of the greatest misfortunes [. . .] if [. . .] any material bar should be opposed to the full participation of the benefits of University education by all whose means and prospects can render such education of the smallest use to them.[16]

It was at this time that the Whig Party came back to power with Lord Melbourne as Prime Minister and Brougham as Lord Chancellor, but the subject of a new university in Scotland was not uppermost in the agenda of the new government. Time dragged on and the Royal Commission produced a follow-up report in 1832, but by then Mrs Crichton was cooling on the subject.

The Marquess of Queensberry told Duncan that Mrs Crichton was 'worn out and even disgusted with the various harassing delays which have taken place and with want of support which her benevolent plan has met with in influential quarters'.[17] Duncan was not surprised. Mrs Crichton had been a widow for almost ten years and so his own feelings of frustration must have been running very high. He wrote to Brougham in September 1832 to say that unless Mrs Crichton received a favourable answer to her proposal she was likely to withdraw it in favour of using the money to set up a lunatic asylum in Dumfries, something Duncan felt was highly desirable but could be provided by public subscription. Consequently, both institutions could be established.

The two men met at Brougham's Westmoreland home the following month, spending some time refining their ideas about how a university could be structured and administered. But it was not time well spent. Brougham became ill shortly afterwards and could not provide more help. Mrs Crichton, who had not entirely given up the idea of a university, wanted Duncan to go again to London but he did not. So by March 1833 Duncan's hope of realising his dream was diminishing rapidly. Brougham had told Hope-Johnstone that the government had refused permission for the new English universities in Durham and London to award degrees. They could not, therefore, be expected to make an exception for Dumfries.

Duncan envisaged the Church of Scotland's General Assembly permitting Dumfries College to be a School of Divinity in which case the government might be persuaded to grant a charter. But again, he was clutching at straws.

In the summer of 1833 Mrs Crichton refused to have a meeting with Chalmers who was on his way to London, a sure sign she was distancing herself from the project. Duncan and Chalmers then realised that their dream of a university in Dumfries would not come to fruition and began to discuss other uses for the money. Duncan had a further meeting with Brougham in Westmoreland, where they discussed church politics and the bequest.

The Dumfries Times, with heavy sarcasm, reported on what happened next:

> A correspondent informs us that the destination of this fund has at length been resolved on £30,000 to go to the establishment of a lunatic asylum for Dumfries and Galloway; of the remainder one portion goes to further endow the theological chair of Edinburgh; and a second goes to fund bursaries for young men educated in Dumfries. The larger part of the funds will still remain for their most rational object-division among the Trustees.[18]

That was essentially what happened. The asylum opened in 1839, the year in which Duncan became Moderator of the General Assembly of the Church of Scotland. It was a tumultuous time for the church but Duncan doubtless found time to reflect on the failure of his grand scheme. That he had invested so much of his intellectual and physical energies in this project was the measure of the man. When he believed something to be right and desirable, provided that it was consistent with his Christian beliefs and his wider view of the world, then he would pursue it no matter what it cost him.

Whether or not Duncan's status in the community was enhanced or tarnished seems to have been of little, if any, concern, to him. And by the time that he understood that the university would never happen his attention had already turned to other projects. His wife had died earlier that year but there was little prospect of him becoming an old man living his life in quiet solitude. His family and friends were also supportive; both of his sons being ministers. Duncan's energies were undiminished and he was working on what would be his *magnum opus*. His contribution to the campaign to end slavery, however, would be much more productive.

Chapter 11
Campaigning against Slavery

Henry Duncan was conscious that there was a growing number of problems in the fast-changing society in which he lived. Many of these could be laid at the doors of war, industrialisation, agricultural reform and urbanisation. Duncan was a well-read man with a wide circle of correspondents in business, government and in the churches, so he was, therefore, well positioned to take an interest in affairs of state and society. He was also a man whose Christian faith motivated him to try and make a difference wherever he could.

At first sight Duncan's selection of slavery as a subject worthy of his reforming zeal might seem strange; after all he was a minister in a small Scottish parish. But some of his formative years were spent working in Liverpool, a city intimately connected to the slavery business and where a sizeable number of slaves had lived.[1] And it was a period in which the anti-slavery movement gained momentum. Moreover, the bank in which he worked was also connected to the slavery business. The Heywood brothers, who established the bank, had made their fortunes in the slave trade and Liverpool was a major centre for building slave ships. Consequently, Duncan, even though he had never visited the West Indies, would have had a good working knowledge of the trade and the problems it created.

Duncan's formative years were spent in Liverpool and then at the universities of Edinburgh and Glasgow where the senior professors, men of the Enlightenment like Francis Hutcheson in Glasgow and Adam Ferguson in Edinburgh, were known opponents of the slave trade. The Speculative Society in Edinburgh, of which Duncan became a member, also debated the subject and voted against it.

In 1788 the Law Lords in Edinburgh, giving their judgement on the Joseph Knight case, declared that there should be no slavery in Scotland.[2] Nevertheless, numerous Glasgow merchants had extensive interests in West Indian plantations and it was only in 1799, the year in which Duncan's ministry commenced, that bonded servitude in Scottish coal mines came to an end.[3]

The anti-slavery movement, which really got under way in 1788, is often depicted as a movement of the London intelligentsia, but the reality is that there was a strong groundswell of opinion against the trade throughout the whole country, not least in Scotland, where university professors and church leaders (usually the same people) began to raise arguments against slavery. From 1788, universities and presbyteries petitioned parliament to bring an end to the trade. One of the presbyteries involved was Dumfries, of which Duncan's father, George, was a member.

The problem for churchmen was that the Bible was somewhat ambivalent on the subject, and there are many instances, especially in the Old Testament, where slavery is treated as part of the normal way in which societies were organised. In the late eighteenth century this inconvenient fact for the reformers gave rise to arguments that the Bible had been mistranslated and that where it said 'slave' it should have said 'servant'. By 1788 a sufficient number of Church of Scotland ministers had got themselves to the position where they were able to bring the matter to be debated on the floor of the kirk's General Assembly. This concluded that they 'think themselves called upon as men, as Christians and as members of the National Church to declare their abhorrence of a traffic contrary to the rights of mankind and the feelings of humanity'. The Assembly went on to express the wish that 'the wisdom and mercy of the legislature may be speedily exerted for the relief of that unhappy portion of their fellow creatures'. Subsequent General Assemblies expressed themselves even more strongly against the trade.[4]

Petitioning of parliament, from various sources, continued throughout the 1790s and the slave trade was eventually 'abolished' in 1808. This piece of legislation, however, only abolished the trade, not the institution of slavery, which continued in the British Empire for many years to come. This was in spite of the campaigning of William Wilberforce and Zachary Macaulay, who felt that the legislation of 1807 had left the job half done.

Duncan was clearly on the side of the abolitionists and in 1814, as clerk of Annan Presbytery, he sent a petition to the Prince Regent condemning the fact, at the end of war, that France would resume its involvement in the slave trade.[5] But the return of Napoleon from Elba quickly pushed such concerns to the side-lines.

The campaign to abolish slavery as an institution was relaunched in the 1820s. As a result, various government Orders in Council were issued designed to ameliorate the conditions under which slaves were held in British territories. Macaulay's publication, *The Anti-Slavery Reporter*, soon had 20,000 subscribers and was demonstrating that the planters were ignoring these government instructions. In return, the journal *John Bull* attacked Macaulay, claiming that his publication's claims about the conditions of slaves were false and that they had been concocted in 'Bible dinner snuggeries and Godly tea drinkings'.[6] Clearly the fight was on, and people on both sides of the argument prepared themselves for what was to come.

It was at this stage that Henry Duncan's old friend Henry Brougham, MP and leading light in the Whig Party, re-entered the fray. He thought that however problematic the situation of slaves they were nonetheless capable of improvement 'not only of body but of mind sufficient to render their improvement and high refinement a matter of absolute certainty under a proper system of management'. He went on to outline a system of management that did not depend on the lash. He confessed himself surprised that people did not recognise the 'gross impolicy' of cruelty and went on to develop an argument based on economics that the most unprofitable plantations were not those with poor soil but 'uniformly those which are cultivated by negroes subjected to a cruel and stingy system of management'.[7]

He and Duncan corresponded frequently about various issues and met regularly, most often at Brougham's estate, Brougham Hall in Westmoreland, north-west England, i.e. a relatively easy commute from Ruthwell. The two men were of one mind and believed that abolition of slavery would not of itself produce an improvement in the conditions of the slaves. They were in favour of a gradual approach to abolition, which was, indeed, the position of most of the reformers.

In Duncan's view any approach to reform, whatever the subject, had to recognise that the obvious solution to a problem was seldom simple and it was always necessary to consider, and provide for, the process of reform, i.e. in moving from a problem to a solution cognisance had to be taken of what might happen after legislation had been passed.

Duncan's personal contribution to the debate was a series of eleven letters sent to Sir George Murray, who in 1829 was Colonial Secretary.[8] They were originally published anonymously in the *Dumfries Courier* but W. R. K. Douglas persuaded Duncan to have them issued in the form of a series of letters to Murray. A London publisher subsequently published the letters in pamphlet form in 1830.[9]

In the introduction, Duncan expressed the hope his letters would be influential in addressing such a difficult subject. He also wished that 'in stretching a little beyond the immediate line of his professional duties as a minister of the gospel he has, at least, not been deviating from the service to his Divine Master'.

He set out his hostility to slavery in the first letter:

The very name of slavery is happily so abhorrent to the inhabitants of this free and Christian land [. . .] That slavery should ever have been permitted to exist, under the sanction of Britain, is itself a fact deeply humiliating to our national pride.

But Duncan was also concerned at some of the inflammatory language being used by those hostile to slavery and at what he thought were the impractical measures, such as sending the slaves back to Africa, being proposed by some campaigners, although he did go on to support the creation of Liberia.[10] He worried about the 'fatal consequences which might arise from hasty and violent measures, originating in an uninformed zeal and misguided benevolence'. He continued:

Everyone sees the absurdity of sending the negroes back to Africa; and it will, I think, require no great effort of reasoning to shew, that immediate manumission, in any shape, could not fail to be a curse instead of a blessing-that it would add injury to injury, and would crown all, by preparing, for a whole people, inevitable ruin, under the insidious and insulting name of a boon.

This argument was in the mainstream of anti-slavery campaigning at that time. The problem was that 'everyone' did not see the absurdity in some of the arguments in favour of abolition and there was a wide range of opinions as to what should be done.

Duncan turned to the Bible for his second letter and pointed out the mainstream view that there was nowhere in the scriptures where slavery was proscribed. Nevertheless, the argument was developed that slavery was wrong and that the condition of the slaves should be improved until they could be regarded as 'brothers'. That would be the appropriate time for 'manumission' (the act of slave-owners setting their slaves free) for

the negro population of the West Indies are not at this moment in a condition to be benefitted by freedom; that they may and ought to be brought into this condition; that they are in actual process towards it; that this process should be accelerated by every legitimate means; and that, when the period shall arrive in which emancipation shall cease to be an injury to them, it will, from that moment, become an act of injustice and criminality to withhold it.

It was this, and similar passages in the third letter, which were later used to accuse Duncan of being on the side of slave owners. Duncan was aware of the difficulties that had existed in Haiti twenty-five years earlier when there had been a revolt of the slaves and an independent republic was declared. This knowledge was, almost certainly, what brought him to a position where he believed that amelioration of conditions for slaves followed by manumission would be the best policy.

Duncan's fourth and fifth letters were primarily about the gradual improvement in the condition of the slaves and the duties of Christians who had not bought them but nevertheless found themselves in possession of slaves. This may well have been written in deference to his friend and associate W. R. K. Douglas MP, who having married in 1824 came into a fortune of £3,000 per annum that included revenues from slave-owning plantations in Tobago. In the sixth letter he put forward an argument that the time would arrive when emancipation would be in the best interests of the planters, believing that black people, just like whites, would respond positively to economic stimuli, i.e. a reward for their labours. But, he added, 'The difficulty lies in the transition.'

The subject of religion, and in particular Presbyterianism, was the subject of the seventh letter, where Duncan argued that, as many of the white people in the West Indies were Scots or Scots-Irish, the government should establish Presbyterianism, alongside Episcopacy, as the recognised religion. This argument was based on the system of schooling that was an integral part of the Presbyterian ethos and which, Duncan believed, was eminently suited to the improvement of the people, including the slaves.

Duncan's concern for public duty and the responsibilities of the planters dominated the eighth letter, in which he laid the blame for the current situation at the door of the whole of society:

> In common candour and honesty let the blame be shared by the whole community – by the government which for centuries sanctioned the traffic in human beings, which enacted laws for its protection, which shared in its profits, – by the whole body of the people, who, till modern times, complacently looked on, without one remonstrance, nay, with concurrence and approbation.

Letters nine and ten dealt with issues concerning people of mixed race and with slavery elsewhere. Duncan was especially concerned that the trade in slaves continued in other countries – he mentioned Cuba and Brazil – and that this was damaging to British trade. The Royal Navy had the right to stop and search ships on the high seas but the United States and France did not concede this right. French ships were apparently the major transporters of slaves from Africa. Duncan asked: 'Where is benevolence – where slumbers religion –, that such enormities should still be permitted to prevail among civilised nations?'

The final letter concerned itself with a wide-ranging discussion on trade and the problems that planters faced in competing with countries where the trade in slaves continued. Duncan was clearly knowledgeable about prices for sugar, cotton and the costs of packaging and freight. Perhaps he obtained this knowledge from his brothers in Liverpool. He concluded:

> The time is arrived when the question, in all its bearings, must force itself on the public attention, – and that the country looks confidently to their firmness and political sagacity for the suppression of such overwhelming evils; – in the West Indies, by the restoration of amity and confidence between master and slave, and between the white inhabitants and the mother country – in Africa by the final abolition of that traffic which has for so long been the opprobrium of humanity – and in Britain, by the establishment of a wise and paternal system of government, which may impart its blessings equally to all, and which may unite in the bands of mutual sympathy every class of His Majesty's subjects in every quarter of his vast dominions.

The reviews of Duncan's pamphlet were not favourable. His old friend Andrew Thomson, with whom he had had conversations in the company of Brougham about slavery and for whose *Christian Instructor* magazine he had written articles, turned on him. Thomson was minister at St George's Church in the New Town of Edinburgh and was known as a 'powerful and popular preacher',[11] and also a notable anti-slavery campaigner. At a well-attended meeting in the Edinburgh Assembly Rooms in October 1830, motions were called for the eventual abolition of slavery. Thomson rose and welcomed the motions but said that they did not go far enough. He argued, very persuasively, that if the meeting approved the motions they would allow the planters to buy time and to delay the eventual liberation of the slaves.

Chaos ensued and when the meeting was reconvened on 19 October the call was for the immediate freedom of the slaves. Thomson acknowledged there might be violence. 'Give me the hurricane [. . .] rather than the noisome pestilence,' he cried; his speech carried the meeting and, when it was published, turned a large part of the anti-slavery movement towards immediate abolition.[12]

With such a mind-set it was no surprise that he was hostile to Duncan's more gradualist approach. Despite their friendship he went on to accuse Duncan of playing into the hands of the planters. For him, however, the core of his opposition to Duncan was theological and moral, feeling that Duncan, in his letters, had dwelt on the economic arguments and had confined religious matters to one of the eleven letters. In Thomson's view Duncan had devoted too much of his thinking to 'worldly interests and pecuniary consequences'. He went on to conflate Duncan's writings with those of others and concluded that these views had led to 'bad theology, so many misinterpretations of scripture' given by the 'Anti-Abolitionists and by the gradualists-between whom there is very suspicious agreement on this point'.[13]

The review was published in the *Christian Instructor* in January 1831. Its opening lines read:

> Though we had been entirely ignorant of the contents of this pamphlet, we could have had no difficulty in estimating its real merits and value from the reception it has received in certain quarters. It has been welcomed in Jamaica – so we understand – and lauded about as a seasonal auxiliary to the cause of negro oppression. Mr Keith (W. R. K.) Douglas, and other proprietors of human beings, have re-published it in London, and are industriously circulating it from one end of Great Britain to the other.

And what is more decisive still, the 'West India Reporter', which is zealous even to madness for the continuance of slavery, refers to it in these words: 'In Scotland particularly, an eminent clergyman foreseeing the consequences of that rash spirit by which some abolitionists are governed, has explained the subject of colonial slavery on Christian principles'. Such testimonies as these to Presbyter's letters would have convinced us of their unsoundness, even if we had never read a word of them, and determined us to regard them as hostile to the great cause of freedom and humanity. Our previous acquaintance with their author, as one dear to us by reason of his enlightened views and philanthropic labours in other departments, could not have overcome the evidence of his heterodoxy here afforded by the eulogium and the patronage of Jamaican planters, Mr Keith Douglas, and the conductors of the periodical in whose pages his name is recorded with such distinguished honour. These are devoted to the cause of slavery; they are eagle eyed to discover whatever tends to aid or uphold it; and their decided approval and commendation of Dr Duncan's work, leave us no room for doubting that it goes to strengthen the party, and promote the designs of the anti-abolitionists.[14]

Quite what this would have done to the friendship between the two men is unclear as Thomson died of a heart attack at the front door of his manse just as the review was being published. Mrs Duncan wrote to a friend in Jamaica about his death saying, 'What a loss to his family and friends and what a loss to our church. At such a time as this! When the religion of our forefathers seems shaken to the very centre.'[15] A further hostile review of Duncan's work appeared in the *Christian Instructor* a few months later.

The Slavery Abolition Act was passed in 1833 and came into force the following year. It was something of a fudge, and it was not until 1838 that slaves finally became free after a period of forced apprenticeships. Slaves in countries run by the East India Company did not gain their freedom until 1843.

Despite the fact that he had many other battles to fight, not least Catholic emancipation, of which he was in favour, the long-drawn out effort to create a university in Dumfries and the inevitable church politics in which he took a keen and active interest, Duncan never lost sight of the problem of slavery. His very considerable energies were not diminished by the bruising criticism that he received in pursuing the anti-slavery campaign. He might, however, have felt justified in the position that he took, as the abolition of slavery, when it came, was not well handled and produced some of the problems of which he had warned.

This provided Duncan with the opportunity to put the record straight, in case anyone was in any doubt as to his position. In May 1839 he used his role as presbytery clerk to draw up a petition for the forthcoming General Assembly, at which he was to be Moderator. Part of this read:

> It appears from unquestionable evidence that the traffic in human beings between Africa and America, carried on under the flag of nations calling themselves Christian, still subjects at least one hundred and twenty thousand souls annually to the horrors of slavery.[16]

Duncan went on to maintain that murder was rife in this nefarious trade and that when the number of slaves carried off by people from Christian countries was added to the numbers captured by 'Mohammedans', then upwards of half a million people were being trafficked every year. The General Assembly was asked to petition government to bring this trade to an end and thus

> using their influence in wiping off one of the foulest stains that ever disgraced humanity, in freeing the Christian world from a load of incalculable guilt, and in opening to the injured African race the ennobling truths, the substantial blessings, and the elevating hopes of the Gospel of Peace.

The General Assembly, meeting later that month, unanimously approved the petition.

Some years later, after the Disruption of the Church in 1843 and the formation of the Free Church of Scotland, there was another chapter in the involvement of Scottish churchmen with slavery. The Free Church sent a delegation to the United States, including slave-owning states, to try to raise money for the building of new churches, and a college for the training of ministers. In this they were very successful. Many American churches were sympathetic to the Free Church of Scotland as they recognised that what the Free Church stood for – the separation of church and state – they already enjoyed.

At one level it is a little surprising that Duncan was not selected to be a member of this delegation, as savings banks were well established in the United States and Duncan's role and reputation in this movement were widely acknowledged. It may, however, have been his anti-slavery writing that precluded him from this group.

The visit to slave-owning states gave rise to a sustained campaign in Scotland, ably led by an escaped slave, Frederick Douglass, to 'send back the money'. This resulted in much embarrassment and some very subtle arguments and debates from the new church, but the money never was sent back.[17]

It is often forgotten that the British anti-slavery movement was part of a wider effort to abolish slavery, many other countries and some parts of the United States having already abolished slavery by this time. Duncan had, therefore, a relatively small part in the bigger process, but the fact he had involved himself, taken the trouble to inform himself and then had written a series of letters which, when published, amounted to 139 pages, speaks of a man of his time who was not afraid to attract criticism, but who was prepared to speak out in support of a cause in which he passionately believed.

Chapter 12
Ministering in Changing Times

Local and Regional: Personal and Pastoral

While Henry Duncan's campaigns for a university in Dumfries and against slavery were important, the nucleus of his working life remained the parish of Ruthwell. Juggling all his duties and interests appears to have been a challenge, for in a letter to his old friend Robert Lundie (concerning a long-delayed visit to help establish a savings bank in Kelso) Duncan wrote:

> My last was written, as this is, in the hurry and bustle of the printing office, during a short intermission from my editorial labours [. . .] I had the weight of a hundred labours before my eyes. I was harassed with engagements, which rose in long perspective through 'the vista of futurity', and to which I could see no termination [. . .] However, I have now nearly got quit of the most pressing of my *many entanglements*. My new tutor is come home and is likely to give great satisfaction. The printing business is in its usual train, and may be left for a few days to go on by the force of the impulse it has received. My domestic affairs stand in no *particular* need of my presence. My clerical duties may be supplied by the good offices of my neighbours; and a meeting of the parish bank and bible association, which takes place on Saturday, will free my shoulders from the burden of their interests for a short time. I preach at Annan on Sunday before the Bible society of that place. I propose to sleep at General Dirom's, in that neighbourhood, on Sunday night; and

on Monday, wind and weather serving, I will set my sails for Kelso [. . .] Such [. . .] is my present resolution. How far I shall be able to keep up to it, I dare not promise.[1]

In addition to his responsibilities at a local level, Duncan was operating at the upper echelons of church politics, but he never lost sight of his main responsibility, as a parish minister and as clerk to the Presbytery of Annan. Such was his growing reputation he was offered far more lucrative appointments in other parts of Scotland, but he would not leave Ruthwell, where he had formed a strong attachment to the people of his parish.

It was his practice to be involved in whatever was happening in the village. His son recorded, in disapproving tones, that Duncan would assist with 'charity balls' and 'charity theatricals' and that he took upon himself many of the arrangements for these events.[2] He would even attend and regulate the rehearsals. Clearly he was not the kind of man to hide behind the walls of his manse.

Changes were also taking place in Duncan's personal life. His mother, who lived in a cottage he had built on the glebe, died in 1824, and his daughter Barbara went off to school in Edinburgh. His letters to her give full vent to his poetic instincts, his love for his children and his Christian faith:

If I were to now tell you, for the first time, that the years which are now passing over your head, although they warn you, in unequivocal language, that you have here 'no continuing place of abode', are only leading you, step by step, to a new state of existence; that your present life may be compared to that of a caterpillar, which is destined to go down for a time to the grave, and then to burst its cerements that it may assume a new form of being, and instead of grovelling in the dust, sip nectar from the opening breast of the tulip, and repose on the soft and perfumed leaves of the rose, and flutter through the balmy air on painted wings, and bask in the sunny meadow, inhaling sweets from every breath of summer; if, for the first time [. . .]

you were now to be informed that you are born for immortality, and had all the wonders laid before you of that gospel which brings life and immortality to light what a strange and powerful impression it would make on your mind.[3]

Duncan's connection to the *Dumfries Courier* at this stage in his life is unclear, although it is likely he remained one of the proprietors. He was, however, at the newspaper's office one day in March 1831 when Thomas Carlyle entered and found him in deep discussion, on the subject of parliamentary reform, with the local candidates who would stand for election when the 1832 Parliamentary Reform Act was passed. Carlyle expressed some surprise that Duncan was in favour of reform.[4]

Two years later, meanwhile, Duncan endeavoured to establish a new newspaper to be called the *Dumfries Journal*. His efforts were unsuccessful on this occasion but it was not the last time that he would become a newspaperman.

Duncan had a friendly, concerned and gregarious nature. He and Mrs Duncan kept open house at Ruthwell, frequently taking in people in distress, sometimes for months at a time, but there was also a long list of visitors, so many in fact that the Duncans often gave up their bed and went to sleep in the cottage built for Duncan's mother. Among their visitors were Sir David Brewster, Dr Andrew Thomson, Robert Owen from New Lanark, Dr Spurzheim, the phrenologist, with whom he disagreed about the validity of phrenology as a science, Thomas Carlyle, and the geologist Dr Buckland, who later became dean of Westminster. Agnes Duncan was known as a kind, modest woman who enjoyed being the provider of hearty hospitality to her guests.

But by the early 1830s Agnes was not a well woman. Although she was still busy about the house it was evident her strength was failing, and she died of influenza on 28 January 1832 on the eve of a communion service. Both sons, George and William, were elsewhere on ministerial duties and that night Henry wrote to tell them of their mother's death. His letter to William contained the passage:

O my dear Wallace, how many reasons we have for consolation. To be with Christ is far better. I feel at this moment that it is selfish to grieve and I trust I shall be enabled to sustain myself like a Christian. You too, my dear Wallace, stand in need of Christian consolation. Let us comfort one another and pray as I now do most fervently that we may all profit by the dispensation – I will not call it a mournful one, for surely the translation of one we love to a state of endless glory ought not to be esteemed so. But nature is weak and unbelieving – let our prayer be 'Lord I believe, help thou my unbelief'. Let me see you, my dear boy, as soon as you can.[5]

The following morning, a house guest recorded that, at first, Duncan could not speak, but soon gathered his strength and led the household in worship and prayers.

It might be imagined that Duncan's loss would dim his energy and enthusiasm, but this was not the case. His son George recorded that his range of activities, from the bank, the presbytery, the politics of the church and his artistic endeavours, continued as before. Meanwhile George was appointed as assistant minister and successor to the minister in nearby Kirkpatrick Durham.

Duncan's gregarious nature has already been attested but there was also a reflective and emotional side to him. In January 1836 he wrote to his son George:

In reading and reflecting on the useful labour of other Ministers who have been eminently blessed with proofs of spiritual fruits from their ministry, I felt not only my own deficiency, but the low standard of ministerial duty which I had exhibited to my children.

This seems unduly self-critical as, by this time, both sons were ordained ministers. He went on:

My defects lie in a direction somewhat different from yours. I can take up a line of conduct strongly and pursue it perseveringly without being much cooled by obstacles or deterred by disappointments, and this is just the quality that you seem to want; but then the unhappy tendency of my mind is to look beyond my own immediate and proper duty and to fix for my object on something either not at all connected, or only collaterally connected with my functions as a Minister of the Gospel and especially as a pastor of a particular flock. My parish Bank and newspaper speculations and various other matters which must readily occur to you are instances of this propensity. I do not say that these plans and objects were wrong in themselves; on the contrary, I was actuated not by selfish considerations but by a view to the public good perhaps in them all; but then, if the same energy had been concentrated on my parish, I would have acted far more within the strict line of duty and might probably been more favoured by the blessing of heaven on my labours, and by promoting the best interests of immortal souls. Everything ought assuredly to yield to this, and the longer I live the more strongly does conviction of this truth grow upon my mind. I shall not now be able very far to retrace my steps, though I may yet live to do something, and I am not without hope that I am beginning to do something. The energy of youth and the vigour of manhood are both past, and the 'soft green of my soul' as Burke practically expresses it, is fading into the yellow leaf. But I may live again in my children and it will be no small gratification to me to see them increase as I decrease, till they fill a space in the religious world which their father never occupied.[6]

This is a letter from a man who is contemplating his own mortality, but that is not the whole story, for in another part of this letter he rejoices with his son in his choice of a wife, Belle, who is his helpmate, and eulogises about a good marriage. He also mentions that he is assisting Mary Lundie, the widow of his old friend from Kelso, with a book that she is writing on religious revivals. What he leaves out of the letter is the information that he was planning to marry her.

Duncan's son George maintained that Henry's own spiritual life, and his preaching, grew in strength and intensity as he grew older, but Duncan's self-view, a view shared by many ministers, was that that there was always something else to be done. There were always more souls to be saved and, no matter how much energy and commitment a minister put into the task, it would never be enough.

Throughout his ministry Duncan kept an open door at the manse for all who needed his help, but his main priority was education, especially the Christian education of the young people in his parish. He was not afraid to experiment with new ways of reaching out to his people. He held services in the church, in the school house, in the society room where the bank met, in the school which he had built in a remote part of the parish with the surplus funds from the bank, in people's houses. In the modern parlance his was a 'church without walls'. A Sunday school met in six parts of the parish. In 1832 he opened an infant school in the village, the running of which was entrusted to his daughter Barbara. On two evenings each week he conducted classes for youths in which he encouraged the young men and women to ask difficult questions. His approach to this work was that of a counsellor rather than a teacher. From this class he found the teachers for the Sunday schools and they met once a month in the manse for discussion and planning. Yet, for all this work, Duncan still felt that he had much to do.[7] Nor did he ignore the economic needs of his people. He was still running the bank and the friendly society.

Despite the existence of these institutions, which had been established to address some of the problems of poverty, there were still times when, with great reluctance, local people made application to Duncan for assistance from the parish box. His predecessor as minister had recorded that the Kirk Session had about £25 per year for distribution to the poor and that this had proved sufficient for the purpose. But the inflation of the Napoleonic wars and changes to employment patterns in Duncan's time ensured that this was no longer the case. By the early 1820s the sum available for poor relief was about £34, but in 1823 Duncan had to write to the heritors and ask them for more money.

The tradition was that the poor would be supported by their near relations and would only apply for parish assistance in extreme cases, but such were the economic changes taking place that this was no longer a practical possibility in many families. Most of those applying for assistance were the elderly and those who, through physical disability, were unable to work.

Part of Duncan's problem was that none of the heritors lived in the parish, and therefore had no first-hand understanding of his concerns. Duncan was in the habit of providing assistance from his own pocket, but in his letter on this subject he wrote:

> It is impossible [. . .] to live among so much distress without feeling oneself called on to afford relief to an extent which those who reside at a distance could scarcely believe to be necessary. As one instance of the kind of calls irresistibly made on our humanity, I cannot help mentioning, that within these few days I have felt myself constrained to advance several sums from my own pocket to enable individuals on the very edge of pauperism to pay their rents for their wretched cottages, that they might thus be saved with their families, from falling into absolute beggary.[8]

This letter did not produce the response he desired.

In all of this, Duncan was still determined that the English poor rate system should not become the Scottish system, although the law allowed it and it had been introduced in some parishes. He believed that it degraded people.

One of the local heritors went so far as to suggest that the savings bank scheme had been a failure, taking the view that the increase in economic dependency in the village was a sure sign the bank had not fulfilled the ambitions that Duncan held for it. The same heritor then refused to further engage with Duncan on the subject. Undaunted, Duncan responded to that gentleman's factor:

The Ruthwell Parish Bank was only established in 1810, when by far the greater part of the present paupers were upwards of sixty years of age, and all of them [. . .] were at least fifty-six. I need not say how foolish it would be to expect that poor women (for they are all women except four) should, after that time of life, be able to lay up a provision for old age in a parish bank [. . .] In a number of instances sums have been drawn from the bank to support poor relations, or to pay for the expenses of their sick-bed and funeral, which must otherwise have swelled the amount of the Session's disbursements.[9]

Duncan resorted once again to schemes of assistance and make-work projects to provide temporary employment and for

considerable periods [. . .] he became contractor for the repair of the highway which intersected the parish. And when other resources failed, he called the more independent class of the inhabitants together, and induced them to join him in contributing, according to an equitable scale, for the repair of the parish roads.[10]

Duncan's interest in, and concern for, other people was not confined to his parish. He maintained a wide circle of friends of all ages in whom he took great delight and with whom he corresponded frequently. One of those correspondents was Mary Lundie, the younger daughter of his old friend from Kelso, Robert Lundie. Often signing the letters as 'Uncle Henry', he addressed her as 'My dearest Mary'. It is possible that, as a girl, she had been a pupil in the private school that he ran in the manse, so he had probably known her for a long time. She was in the habit of sending him her literary works for his critical comment and she made some contributions to his *Sacred Philosophy of the Seasons* series of books.[11] On one occasion, Duncan replied to one of Mary's letters and, in doing so, revealed himself as an emotional man who shed tears over what she had written. He went on:

this is a much more equivocal compliment from me, than it would be from most men; for I am unfortunately, as you too well know not only not 'unused to the melting mood', but that mood comes upon me, at times and seasons when no one else would be affected, and people of ordinary nerve are totally at a loss to account for it; while at other times, these very persons would overflow with tenderness, while my heart remained as hard as the nether millstone. You cannot think what annoyance the weakness I am complaining of has frequently been to me- how often both in the pulpit and in private, my lips have been sealed, from a fear of losing self command, when a word or two, expressive of my feelings, might have been useful and becoming- and how often an unexpected and overpowering burst of agitation has shown my weakness to the astonishment, and, I fear, sometimes to the scorn of my hearers.[12]

In other letters, Duncan revealed to Mary his concerns about his faith when he wrote:

the higher that I try to aspire after divine things, and the nearer I draw to the throne of the Eternal, the more deeply I perceive my own weakness and insufficiency, and the dead weight of earthliness which hangs on all my affections.[13]

Mary went to live in the manse at Ruthwell in 1835, her younger brother accompanying her. She suffered from headaches and went there to improve her health, describing the routine as bedtime at 11pm, with the family rising at 7 am or earlier. From 8 to 9am she would read Edward's *History of Redemption*, with prayers and further scripture reading following. Time was then spent drawing and reading Italian or English. Exercise was catered for by walking or riding, and in the evening she learned the Hebrew alphabet. She also wrote her essays for Duncan's *Sacred Philosophy of the Seasons*.[14]

In July 1836 Mary Lundie became Duncan's daughter-in-law when she married his son William, who, earlier that year, had been ordained and inducted to the parish of Cleish in Kinross-shire. As the wedding approached, Duncan wrote to her to express his great joy:

> now that we have at last a near prospect of the fulfilment of that engagement which is to make you in love, as well as in cordial affection, my own daughter, I find a pleasure, which there is no reason to restrain, in cherishing towards you those paternal feelings that have so long been growing round my heart, and have been attached to it by so many roots for so many years.[15]

In this same letter he gave her news about the Sunday schools in Ruthwell and offered advice about the duties of a minister's wife. His joy at this union was short-lived as she died in 1840, but not before having given birth to two children.

In October 1836 Duncan married Mary's mother, also called Mary. She was his junior by fourteen years and had been a widow as long as he had been a widower. Thomas Carlyle might have described her as a 'grey lady', but Sir David Brewster described her as 'one of the most charming and intelligent women I ever knew'.[16] She was a woman of considerable accomplishment, author of several books and a contributor, as was her daughter, to *Sacred Philosophy of the Seasons*. She brought two of her children with her to Ruthwell and Duncan's son George paid her a fulsome tribute in the biography of his father.

The National Church

In his earliest days in the ministry Henry Duncan was in the majority Moderate Party of the church but an incident in 1806, at the General Assembly in Edinburgh, moved him to a position where he was prepared to question and challenge established authority. On this occasion he was invited to a breakfast meeting by Dr Hill, a senior church figure, who rather assumed that Duncan would support the moderate line on whatever was to be discussed at the meeting. Duncan bridled at the assumption of authority displayed by Hill and at the idea that another man knew his mind before he had expressed his views or had the opportunity to do so. Thereafter, while he would support the moderates if what was being discussed seemed sensible and in the best interests of the church, he sometimes found himself on the other side. He was, for example, firmly of the view that the Church of Scotland should establish foreign missions. He spoke up on the subject, but many years were to pass before the moderates came round to the idea. Increasingly he found himself voting with the Evangelical Party.

Support for this party grew steadily in the first quarter of the nineteenth century and it was not long before they felt themselves sufficiently strong to raise once more that ancient problem, as they saw it, of patronage, the practice by which local heritors could appoint ministers with little, if any, reference to the parishioners. Although contrary to Presbyterian tradition the system of patronage had been imposed on the Church of Scotland by an Act passed in the British parliament in 1711. There were many who felt this was in contravention of the 1707 Treaty of Union which had guaranteed freedom from government interference in church affairs. They also thought that it was contrary to the spirit of the Reformation. So long as the moderates in the church were in the majority there was little chance of a real challenge, despite the fact there were numerous breakaway groups in the eighteenth century who left the Church of Scotland because they objected to patronage.

By the late 1820s, Henry Duncan was moving into a position of leadership in the church. He was a Doctor of Divinity and his work in the savings bank movement had brought kudos and respect. He had a wide circle of friends of the same, or similar, mind. He had published a great deal and his various speeches on an extensive variety of subjects at presbytery, synod and General Assembly brought increasing recognition that he was a man of stature who was not afraid to challenge authority. His position was that government and church should be mutually supportive, but that they should recognise appropriate boundaries and not interfere with one another.

The question of patronage in the appointment of ministers rose briefly to the surface in 1827. Henry Brougham wrote to Duncan on the subject:

> My great regret at the unlucky accidents which have prevented our meeting is increased by the reflection that there are some subjects of discussion which it is really very essential we should come to an understanding upon, especially Kirk Patronage, because it is necessary to put the Government betimes in a right train; and I had reckoned on Dr T [Thomson] and us having it all talked over at Brougham.[17]

Duncan lost no time in committing his thoughts to paper, and in a lengthy letter to Brougham in October 1827 pointed out that the Church of Scotland 'has no human head, and that the ecclesiastical power ought in no respects, but in matters purely civil, to be in subjection to the secular'. He went on to remind Brougham of what had happened when the government had issued a proclamation regarding prayers for the Royal Family which, due to the scandal in 1820, were to exclude Queen Caroline. Church ministers in Scotland bridled at being told by government who they should and should not pray for, and the proclamation was widely ignored. Brougham forwarded Duncan's letter to the Home Secretary, Lord Lansdowne.

Church leaders took government interference in their affairs very seriously. And the tradition of resisting intrusions had long been exercised. Duncan was to make a habit of it. There had been a tradition in the Church of Scotland of appointing a young minister to succeed an older man, especially when the incumbent was infirm and unable to perform all of his duties. In such cases the new minister was appointed as 'assistant and successor', but the Home Office had decided that, in cases where the Crown held the patronage in a parish, this would no longer take place. In January 1832, Duncan wrote to the Marquess of Queensberry enclosing a letter he had sent to James Brougham, brother of the Lord Chancellor, in which he referred to the 'impolicy of the rule'. He claimed to have the support of many church leaders, including Dr Chalmers and Dr Inglis. It was a minor skirmish, but it does suggest there was a heightened consciousness of government infringements into Scottish church affairs and an increased willingness to resist.

Clearly patronage was to be the battleground, the right of presentation of a new minister, where, in one third of the parishes, this was reserved to the Crown. Duncan felt strongly that the manner in which these rights had been exercised had the tendency to 'degrade the clergy, and to alienate the minds of the people peculiarly alive to everything connected with religion'. His reasoning was that many patrons exercised their rights as a means of social control, while some also used it as a means to gain political influence; especially as Crown patronage was not actually exercised by the monarch but by government ministers.[18]

Duncan, at this time, had little sympathy with those in the church who favoured a complete abolition of the patronage system. He was looking for a middle ground which would restore rights to the congregations to 'call' their minister without removing the rights of heritors. He did not say how this could be achieved, but urged Brougham to proceed cautiously. In keeping with his friend Thomas Chalmers, Duncan believed in a 'godly commonwealth' in which church and state were separate but working together for the common good.

Duncan and Andrew Thomson were also in correspondence about the subject. They, with Brougham, had been fellow students at Edinburgh University, and Duncan had written articles for the *Christian Instructor* that Thomson edited from his manse in Edinburgh's New Town. They were old friends and remained so despite differences over some of the more arcane religious questions. In March 1828, Thomson wrote to Duncan from his family home in Sanquhar, Dumfriesshire, inviting Duncan to go with him to London, where he was to occupy Edward Irving's pulpit for a few weeks. There, he added, 'we shall settle the affairs both of Church and State? Or would you prefer meeting me in Manchester?'[19] Duncan accepted this invitation, but discussions on the matter subsided before being raised again, with some vigour, a few years later. They also visited Liverpool on the way home to raise funds for a new Presbyterian church, motivated by the fear that, without their own church, Presbyterians would join the Unitarians.

Duncan developed his thinking on the subject into a series of letters that were sent to Lord Melbourne, the Home Secretary, later published in the *Christian Instructor*. Further letters were sent to Lord Lansdowne, a leading politician, who, like Brougham and Thomson, had also been a fellow student at Edinburgh University. In 1832, by which time Brougham was Lord Chancellor, he wrote to Duncan asking him to again expound his views on the subject. His object, as George Duncan understood it, was to restore 'the Establishment to the affections of the people of Scotland'.[20] This concern for the affection of the people was an indication of government concern about the various reform movements that were spreading throughout the United Kingdom at this time. There was a palpable fear of revolution.

Duncan's response to Brougham was not to his liking: 'I cannot quite say that I go along with you, and I think the difficulties in the way of so entire an abandonment of Crown patronage are not to be surmounted.'[21] Duncan had proposed what he called a non-intrusion settlement of the problem. His idea was that when a vacancy occurred in a church, where the patronage was vested in the Crown, the heritors should meet with the elders and propose one or two candidates for the charge. The Crown officers would then choose which they preferred and that person would then be presented to the congregation. But the call to be the minister there would only be sustained if a majority of heads of families in the congregation subscribed to the call. Brougham felt that this plan gave 'the choice entirely to the congregation and leaves the patron no real voice except in the case of no choice being made for a long time'.[22] This proposal, therefore, was rejected as Brougham could not bring himself to propose it to the Crown because it involved the giving up of the absolute right of patronage. Duncan was asked to think again.

However, this was not a matter that could be settled simply by correspondence between Brougham and Duncan. It was a matter of national importance and one that would split the Church of Scotland. The whole question was debated at length in the courts of the church, presbyteries, synods, the General Assembly and the pages of news-papers; places where ministers, elders and patrons could air their views and their ideas. There were many opinions: some wanted to do nothing, others wanted to dispense with patronage entirely while many, including Duncan, continued to look for a compromise.

In December 1832, Duncan wrote again to Brougham suggesting that the Crown should advise presbyteries of its intention to present a candidate, whereupon the candidate would be invited to preach to the congregation, who would then be asked to approve or disapprove. If there were any dissenting voices, a vote would be taken of heritors, elders and heads of families, and if the vote was against the candidate then government should be advised by presbytery. It followed that it was up to government to decide what to do next.[23] It was not much of a shift from his earlier position, and suggests not only that he under-stood that a compromise was necessary, but that government was unlikely to shift its position by more than a small degree.

This was a subject to which Duncan returned in May 1833 when the subject was discussed by Annan Presbytery. A petition to the General Assembly was drawn up in which the hand of Duncan is evident. The argument was that patrons *present* a minister, congre-gations *call* a minister:

> the voice, or as it is usually named the call of the people in the appointment of a minister, has always been regarded by the Church as a salutary check on the exercise of Patronage [. . .] it appears highly expedient that it should now be restored to its original force.[24]

By 1834 the Evangelical Party were in the majority at the General Assembly and the whole issue of patronage was coming to a head. It was not a simple matter, and was as much to do with the Church of Scotland's right, as a Presbyterian church, to decide its own fate on spiritual matters as it was with the practicalities of patronage. Never-theless, patronage was the question on which the battle was fought. The Assembly passed the Veto Act, its general provisions stating that

The General Assembly do declare that it is a fundamental law of this Church, that no pastor shall be intruded on any congregation contrary to the will of the people [. . .] that if the major part of the male heads of families, members of the vacant congregation shall disapprove of the person in whose favour the call is proposed to be moderated in, such disapproval shall be deemed sufficient ground for the presbytery rejecting such person, and that he shall be rejected accordingly.[25]

The Moderate Party were not happy and refused to give up the fight. George Cook was leader of the moderates and strongly objected to the Veto Act, writing extensively on the subject. Duncan, who had been active in drafting this legislation and securing its passage through the General Assembly, took great objection to the position adopted by the moderates. In a lengthy document he took issue with what Cook had written. The format was a series of letters, published as a pamphlet, much like his anti-slavery letters, except that the language was immoderate. Gone was the Henry Duncan of well-chosen, polite and gentlemanly address; here was a Henry Duncan with venom. Referring to Cook's comments on Part Six of the Act, he wrote:

you come forward with a long and black catalogue of evils to flow from it, which, if but a tithe of them were anywhere but in your own excited imagination, would render the measure the most iniquitous, the most disastrous, and the most absurd which ever was invented by the ambition, the injustice, or the folly of human beings. The enumeration of these evils in your own words will, of itself, I think be sufficient to show, that there must be in your statements or reasonings, or in both combined, exaggeration and special pleading of the most extravagant kind.[26]

Duncan went on to heap scorn on Cook's statements in a highly polemical but powerfully argued diatribe, much of which was about who had the power to do what. The argument was not confined to patronage;

the qualifications of ministers were also a matter of contention.

One of Duncan's objections to patronage was that many patrons were not even members of the Church of Scotland:

> Some of them being adherents of the English Church, Arminian in their creed and attached to an Episcopal order and a prescribed liturgy, – and others, whatever their own faith may be, having been accustomed to regard the humble but pious labours of a zealous clergy with no favourable eye.

Such people, Duncan considered, were not fit to present a new minister to a parish.

And in one of those strange accidents of history, Duncan's younger son, William Wallace Duncan, got caught up in the controversy. He was a candidate for the vacant charge at Urr in nearby Kirkcudbrightshire. Having been duly nominated by the Crown, there was some local opposition to his candidacy. Henry Goulbourn, the Home Secretary, had written to Henry Duncan to say that he had duly submitted the name of William Wallace Duncan to the king who had been 'graciously pleased to approve thereof, and I have only to express my hope that the result of his labours will be to improve the condition of the Parish and to reconcile the differences which at present prevail'.[27] The fact that Goulbourn wrote to Henry Duncan suggests that the father had written to the Home Secretary in support of his son's candidacy, as he had done on other occasions in support of his elder son, George, and of his brother, Thomas.

The 'difficulties' alluded to in this letter were extensive. The wrangling over the candidacy of William Duncan took two years. Having been presented by the Crown a small majority of the heads of families voted in his favour, but there was a second candidate in the frame and a sufficiently large minority against William that appealed to the presbytery. Arbitration took a long time. Meanwhile some of William's supporters died giving his opponents a slight majority. They appealed to the Synod claiming that Duncan, 'his relatives and friends [had] canvassed and made use of undue, unconstitutional and unclerical means to obtain and make effectual the Crown presentation in his favour'. To save further trouble, young Duncan beat 'an honourable retreat'.[28] The matter was not resolved with his withdrawal, and when Rev. George Burnside was eventually inducted to the charge some of his office bearers resigned at his first meeting of the Kirk Session.

William had seen the irony in the situation and in a letter to his brother George he wrote:

> What will the people do? Let us not forget that they may reject me – and what then? This will be the cause of anxiety now. How queer if that measure [the Veto Act] the carrying of which my Father has so strenuously advocated should prove fatal to his son! Such things however have happened and may be again.[29]

William's uncle Thomas was close to what was happening and wrote to George Duncan, saying:

> William will have difficulties to struggle with. The radicals are calling out that the appointment of any man, however unexceptionable in himself, if [word obliterated] is not the man of the majority, is unconstitutional and worthy of a despotic government, and ought to be resisted.[30]

Clearly, the political temperature in Urr was running at a high level, as it did in many other parts of Scotland in the years to come. Meanwhile, William was settled in the parish of Cleish in rural Kinrossshire, where he had served for a short time as assistant minister and where his call was unanimous.

Yet the initial reaction from government to the passing of the Veto Act was favourable. Lord Brougham, in the House of Lords, spoke about the whole question of church patronage in Scotland being put to rest. Brougham, however, was closer to the situation and to the people than many of his fellow peers and it is highly likely that most members of that House had little understanding of the issue or of the deeply held feelings in churches all over Scotland.

Duncan's contribution to the debate and to the Veto Act was considerable:

> If any man in Scotland was the real parent of that measure, which had such memorable consequences, it was the minister of Ruthwell; and in all the controversies to which it gave rise, up to the time of the Disruption, the same minister took a prominent part.[31]

The Veto Act was an attempt to find a middle ground and, as with all such cases, those who were on the extremes of the argument saw it as an unsatisfactory compromise and were determined to oppose it. As in the case at Urr there were those who were unwilling to allow patrons, especially the Crown patron, to have anything to do with the nomination process. Perhaps the reforming spirit of the age had something to do with this stance, but equally there were those on the patrons' side of the argument who viewed any diminution of traditional powers as something to be resisted.

Duncan was evidently disappointed that the Veto Act did not always work in the ways that he had intended. But he continued to believe that it had merit and that, given time, it would deliver what was hoped for and bring a harmonious solution to a vexatious problem.

The pressures of church politics and the continuing pressure that he imposed upon himself, not least in the production of his *magnum opus Sacred Philosophy of the Seasons*, took a toll on his health and in the winter of 1837–8 he was quite unwell with bouts of anxiety. Duncan put this problem down to advancing years, and resigned himself to the fact that he was no longer a young, vigorous man.

The rumour that he heard towards the end of 1838, therefore, filled him with great concern. He was to be nominated to be Moderator of the General Assembly of the church in 1839. Fortunately, his health recovered sufficiently for him to accept the role. The offer of election to the moderatorial chair was viewed as a great honour, as an acknowledgement of past service and as a cap on a distinguished career. But, given the deep divisions within the church at this time, it was unlikely to be a role from which Duncan would be able to derive much joy.

The Veto Act still did not work in the way that Duncan had hoped. Relations between church and government were strained, and it is difficult to escape the conclusion that this situation had arisen because the Anglican Church of England was an established church which was, in effect and practice, an arm of the government. There was little understanding in Westminster of how different the Presbyterian Church of Scotland was or, at least, of how different some of its leaders wanted it to be.

In March 1838 the Court of Session in Edinburgh considered the case of a minister who had been rejected by the congregation in Auchterarder in Perthshire. The court decided, by a majority of eight to five, that the Veto Act was invalid. This decision was appealed to the House of Lords where that judgement was upheld. The decision of the Lords contracted within the narrowest limits the right of presbyteries to decide on the qualifications of ministers being presented to a charge, so denying them in effect the right to give effect to the wishes of congregations. This must have come as a double blow to Duncan as, not only had he been the architect of the Veto Law, but his old friend Brougham, despite having welcomed the Act in 1834, now led the attack upon it in the House of Lords.

Worse was to follow. In the parish of Marnoch in north-east Scotland the Crown had nominated a new minister, who, when he was presented to the congregation, was rejected by all but one member. The presbytery prevaricated and did not declare the candidate's nomination unsuccessful until prompted to do so by the General Assembly. The government seemed to accept this decision without apparent difficulty and duly presented a new candidate. He was accepted by the people whereupon the original candidate, encouraged by the decision in the Auchterarder case, sought, and was granted, an interdict from the Court of Session, which had the effect of preventing the Presbytery of Strathbogie, where Marnoch was situated, from doing anything to induct the new minister to the charge to which he had been elected by the congregation. This put the church and the courts at loggerheads. The stage was being set for a major confrontation.

Both cases came before the General Assembly that Duncan chaired in May 1839, and there were others in the pipeline. One of those was at Lethendy in Perthshire, where the presbytery had ignored an injunction from the Court of Session and had proceeded to induct a minister to the vacant charge. While the General Assembly convened, the ministers of the presbytery, who had inducted the new minister, were being threatened with charges of contempt of court.

It was the custom at the General Assembly for some of the commissioners to join the moderator for breakfast each morning, and Duncan made the point of introducing a period of worship before the meal. His son recorded that this could take 'half an hour previous to the commencement of the repast'.[32] His intention was to impress upon the commissioners that the Assembly should never lose sight of the fact that it was a church assembly and not a political one. As moderator he set the tone for the proceedings.

The assembly commenced on 16 May 1839 and ran until 27 May. Much of the business was routine, but Duncan was pleased to see the Church of Scotland agree to set up a foreign mission, a subject that was dear to his heart and for which he had long campaigned. This was also the time when the Associate Synod, a group which had broken away from the Church of Scotland in the eighteenth century, rejoined. There was an agreement to establish and endow chairs of biblical criticism in all four Scottish universities. The Assembly was also concerned to convert the Jewish people to Christianity. But the major issue to be dealt with was the relationship between the church and government. A church committee had already investigated this matter; their report was laid aside and the assembly declared that

it is deeply impressed with the unhappy consequences which must rise from any collision between the civil and the ecclesiastical authorities, and holding as their duty to use every means in their power, not involving any dereliction of the principles and fundamental laws of their constitution, to prevent such results, and having appointed a committee for the purpose of considering in what the way the National Establishment, and the harmony between Church and State may remain unimpaired, with instructions to confer with the government of the country if they should see cause; and now feeling that it is inexpedient to take any step which may tend to embarrass the proceeding of the Committee then appointed [. . .] direct the Presbyteries to report all disputed cases to the next General Assembly.[33]

There was still hope that a split in the church could be avoided, but the positions were becoming more deeply entrenched.

A local newspaper recorded that Duncan's chairmanship of the proceedings had been conducted in 'a manly and impartial manner'.[34] Nevertheless, Duncan wholly agreed with the position that had been taken and in his opening and closing addresses to the Assembly he made clear, in the presence of the Lord High Commissioner,[35] Lord Belhaven, that the church could do nothing other than resist all encroachments, from whatever quarter, on its freedom to make all decisions on religious matters.

Meanwhile the relationship between the Church of Scotland and the civil powers continued to deteriorate. This manifested itself in a number of ways, often very petty. Duncan was nominated by the church to head a deputation to go to London to congratulate Queen Victoria on the occasion of her marriage to Prince Albert. It was the tradition for such deputations to be received by the monarch 'on the throne'. On this occasion, however, Duncan learned from a government minister that his deputation would only be received in a private audience with the queen. Duncan viewed this as being disrespectful to the Church of Scotland and refused to hand over the letter. There was impasse, and Duncan threatened to return home with the letter still in his possession. This was enough to change the government's mind as they had no wish to damage their reputation further in Scotland. Queen Victoria duly received Duncan and his deputation in the traditional manner.

Early in 1840 Duncan persuaded a by no means unanimous Annan Presbytery to petition both Houses of Parliament on the subject with the words:

they cannot doubt that this church possesses the right secured by the revolution settlement and ratified by the act of union to exclusive jurisdiction in all spiritual matters including every question relating to the trial and ordination of ministers, from whence it appears to them that the civil courts cannot lawfully review her decisions except as far as relates to civil effects, nor issue orders and injunctions to the church courts, nor coerce them by pains and penalties.[36]

In the spring of that year Duncan went to Strathbogie, where the situation was becoming increasingly difficult. A majority of ministers in the presbytery there had obtained an injunction to allow them to induct a minister against the wishes of the congregation and the General Assembly. The ministers were duly suspended, and the church organised a number of minsters to go there to serve in the parishes of the deposed preachers. Duncan was among those who went despite the advice of his friends and his brother Thomas. He was fully prepared to go to prison if arrested. A messenger-at arms[37] followed him to a country inn where he served him with a copy of the interdict: 'The act was performed with downcast looks and stammered apologies as by one ashamed of his office.'[38] Doubtless the legal powers in Scotland had little appetite for prosecuting the Moderator of the General Assembly. Duncan had gone there, knowing full well that an interdict was in place, and that by preaching there he would be breaking the law. It was, quite simply, an act of civil disobedience. But he believed he was acting for a higher power and was only doing what he had been ordained to do.

Some of Duncan's colleagues in Annan Presbytery used his absence to record their disagreements with his position, which they regarded as 'far from being a fundamental law of the Church is by universal confession a total novelty in our ecclesiastical procedure'. The four members who took this position acknowledged that they were conscious of the support that they had received from the state in carrying out their ministerial duties.[39]

All this happened against the backdrop of a spiritual revival. Begin-

ning in Kilsyth, near Glasgow, in the summer of 1839 it soon spread
to many parts of Scotland. Open-air preaching again became the order
of the day as churches were often too small to accommodate the
numbers of people who wanted to listen. Duncan saw the benefit of
this in Ruthwell, as attendances at church and Sunday school rose
markedly.

He also saw it in his sojourn in Strathbogie. A letter to his wife
dated Monday 11 May 1840 paints the picture:

> Yesterday I preached to a crowded audience [. . .] The people
> were most attentive, and evinced an interest in everything that
> was said, which was extremely gratifying. At half past two I
> attended the Sabbath school founded by Mr Lewis of Leith.
> There are about 120 scholars and seven teachers, whose hearts
> seem to be in their work. What especially struck me is that there
> were so many lads and lassies of the age of those who attend
> our Friday and Saturday classes; many of them very intelligent
> and ready with their answers. I taught a girl's class while a
> number of people gathered round to hear my mode of examining
> and explaining. This lasted about an hour after which I addressed
> the school. At six o'clock we again met for worship, when I
> preached on 'The dead praise not the Lord', to a still more
> crowded audience. I think there must have been nearly one
> thousand present, though I was told that the coldness and threat-
> ening aspect of the weather had kept numbers away.[40]

Duncan spent the remainder of the week preaching and teaching,
visiting the sick and keeping up his correspondence. He caught a cold
that kept him in bed for a day. He was clearly reaching the limits of
his physical powers, and when he travelled to Edinburgh where, as
retiring moderator, he was required to open the 1840 General Assembly,
his voice was not strong enough to make himself heard.

On his return to Ruthwell, Duncan continued to converse with his
colleagues in presbytery, and with friends, about the state of the church
and about what was likely to happen if some accommodation could

not be reached with the civil powers. On numerous occasions he broke down in tears at his fears for the church's future, and he began, once more, to contemplate the state of his own faith faced with his mortality. In a letter to his step-son, George Lundie, who was doing missionary work in Samoa, he wrote:

> I feel the feebleness of age yearly pressing on me more and more, and am like the man in the iron apartment, who had the inexpressible horror of finding the limits of his prison narrowing day by day, with the certainty of being inevitably crushed to death by the diabolical machinery. But I know that the machinery here is not diabolical, but, on the contrary, moved by a fathers hand.[41]

Despite his apparent feebleness, however, Duncan accepted an invitation to go to Glasgow to speak to the students in the mechanics institute about geology. He took pleasure in speaking about one of his oldest interests and felt some relief that, for a time, he could think about something other than the state of the church. At the request of the students the lectures that he gave there were printed and circulated.

Duncan's trip to Glasgow was a pleasant interlude in a troubled time. He viewed Brougham's decision in the House of Lords, acting as a court of appeal, as something of a betrayal, and wrote to him in November 1841, conceding that he had made his decision on a point of law but remonstrating that it had caused a great deal of damage to the church. By this time there was little doubt in Duncan's mind that if things continued as they were then there were many ministers and members who would leave the Church of Scotland. The letter did not contain much of Duncan's traditional, polite and complimentary turns of phrase, rather it was direct to the point of bluntness. If it was a 'cri de coeur', it was also a 'cri de guerre'. A reference to the Covenanters of the seventeenth century was 'de rigueur' for such a letter:

> Your Lordship cannot be so sensible as one who lives on the spot, and who converses daily with the people, of the utter ruin

which this church would sustain, if it were held, in ecclesiastical affairs, to be subjected to the supremacy of the civil courts. Unless the two jurisdictions are kept apart, our Scottish establishment must fall to pieces. There is now, as in the days of the Covenanters, a very deep conviction, that no religious institution can deserve the name of a Church of Christ, which does not strenuously maintain what used to be the rallying cry of our forefathers – 'Christ's kingly government in his Church;' and I assure you, that if the clergy were to abandon this ground, they would soon be deserted by their flocks.

Let me assure your Lordship, that you could not possibly do anything that would endear you more to your native land, or would confer on Scotland a greater national blessing, than by giving your hearty support to some liberal measure, that may free the church from the unhallowed trammels of meddling powers from without-whether they be the patrons or the civil courts. You cannot fail to remark the recklessness with which patrons are at present acting in forcing unacceptable presentees on reclaiming parishes. They are precipitating a crisis, the result of which they are little aware of. Never was there a period when the call for an enlightened and liberal act of the legislature was more imperative.[42]

It seems clear that Duncan was again struggling to find a solution that would satisfy both sides. Given how far the civil authorities had travelled down their road, there was no likelihood of a change of direction or of the church meeting the government at a crossroads; they were travelling in diametrically opposite directions. A breach was, by then, inevitable and interested parties were making preparations.

The Moderate Party in the church, still led by George Cook, was considering its position. They were aware there was a groundswell of public opinion in favour of the independence of the church, but they continued to look for ways in which the movement towards schism could be halted. The traditional method was to appeal to people's pockets, and that is what they did. They began to talk about any ministers leaving the church losing their manses, their stipends and, in many cases, endowments provided for the support of ministers. They made it clear that anyone leaving the church would not be taking any material assets with them.

It is easy to gain the opinion that everyone at Westminster was either hostile or indifferent to the needs of the Scottish church, or that the church itself was divided into two well-defined camps, but this was far from the case. In the House of Lords, Lord Aberdeen introduced a Bill which was not to the taste of Duncan and his friends but they believed that, with some amendments, proposed by Sir George Sinclair, it might meet their requirements. Their hopes were dashed when Sir Robert Peel refused to support the Bill, and in August 1842 another decision in the House of Lords made the law clear: presbyteries would be subject to civil penalties if they enforced the principles espoused by the Evangelical Party. By this stage, they had ceased to be called the 'Evangelical Party' and had become, the better to identify with their cause, the 'Non-Intrusion Party'. Within this group there had been some defections, around forty of whom tried to work out another form of accommodation with government. Duncan was vexed by their defection and maintained that they did more harm than good as, by 1842, the 'non-intrusion' ministers, faced with this opposition, had simply become more entrenched in their position and gained a majority in the General Assembly.

Duncan, as a former Moderator of the General Assembly, was entitled to attend each year and he was there in May 1842 when the assembly voted clearly in favour of non-intrusion principles. He was back in Edinburgh in November of that year for a 'Convocation' of those who were hostile to government intervention in church affairs. About 500 attended this meeting addressing the simple question of whether the civil authorities should be resisted in their encroachments into church affairs. From all accounts the proceedings were conducted in harmony, although a few dissented and left the hall. George Duncan recorded that the ministers pledged to 'maintain their principles, even though at the loss of their ecclesiastical status and emoluments, a feeling of joy and gratitude pervaded the brethren which no temporal success could possibly have afforded'.[43] The die was cast; there was no going back.

The challenge for the minsters, who were now highly likely to break away from the Church of Scotland, was to explain themselves to their parishioners and try to persuade them to follow their leader into a very uncertain future. Duncan's response was to publish a pamphlet that he used as the basis for his teaching among his congregation over the next few weeks. He titled the pamphlet *Letter from the Minister of Ruthwell to his flock, on the Resolutions adopted at the late Convocation.*[44] It was a lengthy document in which he set out the history of what had been happening in the national church, the theological arguments for spiritual independence, the political and constitutional arguments, and some reflections on what had happened in parishes where there had been dissension and difficulties. His conclusion anticipated what would happen next, but there was also a boldly expressed contempt for those ministers who did not come out in support of non-intrusion. He argued that

> should the most faithful of your ministers be forced, by conscience, to renounce a religious Establishment, enslaved and degraded by the usurpation of the Civil Power, a separation would be instantly made between the two great classes of professing Christians. The careless and indifferent would remain behind, while those who valued religion and religious privileges, would go out along with their beloved pastors, and rally round them with an interest not unlike that with which our forefathers followed their persecuted ministers to the retired glen and the wind beaten mountainside.[45]

This further reference to the Covenanters perhaps suggests there was some wish fulfilment going on in Duncan's mind. He was such an admirer of them, their heroic struggle for their principles and their suffering at the hands of a government persecutor, that he wished to be like them. If this is true, then it was not long before his wish was fulfilled. Nothing short of a new Reformation would suffice for Duncan. He finished his pamphlet with the words:

> Glorious prospect! Happy consummation! Oh! If this be the way in which our Heavenly King has decreed that he shall confound the wisdom of the wise, and cause the wrath and the worldly policy of misguided men to praise him, then let the storm burst and the bolt fall! Which of us would not hail our temporal calamities with gratitude and regard it as all joy that we were counted worthy to suffer in such a cause![46]

It was one thing to speak to his own congregation but Duncan recognised the need to speak to a wider audience. Drawing upon his earlier experience with the *Courier*, he started *another* new newspaper in Dumfries, this time called the *Dumfries Standard*, to ensure the views of the evangelical non-intrusion group were well understood by the populace.

The first item carried by the *Standard* was a notice of a breakfast of ministers and elders who supported the principles of the Evangelical Party to be held in the George Temperance Hotel on 4 April. The paper also included the death notice of Duncan's young friend, Rev. Robert Murray McCheyne, in Dundee. It was published on 29 March 1843, just six weeks before the Disruption; the new newspaper would not be short of material.

Chapter 13
Disruption and Death

The Disruption of 1843, a major schism within the established Church of Scotland, not only had a major impact on Scotland's national kirk but upon Scottish civic life in general. It was, however, a widely anticipated event, many ministers, elders and members having come to the conclusion that, in view of the government's continued interference in the spiritual affairs of the church, there was no other solution.

Preparations had been made, money had been raised, and on 18 May 1843 approximately 400 ministers left the Church of Scotland to form the Free Church of Scotland. Henry Duncan, as we shall see, was at the centre of these tumultuous events.

The Disruption happened against a backdrop of growing religious conviction among many sections of the population. The church, and particularly the Evangelical Party, had got round to addressing the needs of a shifting population. During the time Thomas Chalmers was convener of the committee on church accommodation (1834–9), some 222 new churches were built, largely to meet the needs of congregations in the growing towns and cities. Duncan was also a member of this committee. In those same years, offerings for the work of the church had increased fourteen times.[1]

The Church of Scotland had left its eighteenth-century lethargy behind. It was in the 1830s a vibrant, expanding organisation, and some of the eighteenth-century seceders rejoined. Society as a whole was changing. There had been major reforms in parliament and pressure for more radical politics was never far from the surface; trade unions and other working-class organisations were being formed; the savings bank movement was developing quickly; voluntarism was growing as people, with increasing amounts of leisure time, took active roles in churches and civic society.

In the closing years of the 1830s there had been various cases in the courts where the Veto Act had been tested and found against. On one such occasion a presbytery had tried to defy the law of the land and been threatened with imprisonment by the Dean of the Faculty of Advocates. On the same occasion, the Lord President of the Court of Session commented that those who opposed the rule of law had no option but to adhere to the law of the Church of Scotland as interpreted by the courts or leave the church: 'I see no remedy. Either they must submit to the law, or they must retire from the Church.'[2]

At the General Assembly in 1841 the matter was debated yet again and a motion calling for the abolition of patronage was defeated by only six votes. By the following year, faced with the continued opposition from the courts, sentiment had shifted and the vote to abolish patronage was passed by 216 votes to 147. Patronage was said to have been 'attended with much injury to the cause of true religion in this Church and Kingdom'.[3] At this same Assembly a document, some 5,000 words in length, was introduced. It was a 'Claim of Right' composed by an Edinburgh lawyer, Alexander Dunlop, who maintained that the position of the church was guaranteed by statute and by the oath taken by the sovereign at her coronation, but that it was now being undermined by the courts. Hope for any kind of negotiated settlement was fast evaporating.

By that time meetings had been taking place all over Scotland to discuss this particular issue, but minds had been made up and closed. There was no way back. In the Synod of Dumfries there had been a vote which the moderates had won:

Hot words had passed [. . .] and those who ultimately became Free Churchmen arose and left the synod. Dr Duncan sat still, with his face covered, till the bustle of departure was over, then rose and took leave of his old associates with the meekness of wisdom which belonged to him. His poor dear brother (Thomas Tudor) still minister of the New Church (Established), who had never in life before parted from him, laid his head on the table and sobbed aloud, and many were moved.[4]

Thomas did not 'come out' in the Disruption but both of Henry's sons, George and William, followed their father into the Free Church.

Duncan may have been able to leave the synod with some dignity but his feelings took hold later. His wife wrote of his distress a year before the Disruption. Believing, as he did, that state interference in church affairs was 'unscriptural and illegitimate', he could become quite emotional when talking about this subject. 'So keen was this feeling in him that more than once he had to stop,' she recalled. 'It was remarkable that he was never overcome to that extent in the other villages, but in the society room in Ruthwell he could not command himself.' Mrs Duncan continued:

> For forty years he had wedded his affections to his people. The room he had procured for the male and female friendly societies, and there were carried on many of his useful operations. There he had helped them about their ballots for the militia in war time. There, in time of threatened invasion, he had aroused his volunteers. There, in times of scarcity, he had planned with them the bringing of ship-loads of Indian corn and potatoes, and there the stores had been distributed. There he had first unfolded his opening scheme of a savings bank for his own parish. There he had many times examined the village Sabbath school; and there, times uncounted, he had met with them of an evening to worship God. Two evenings in particular, when he was completely overcome, there sat before him those whose spiritual condition he had never been able to influence, and when he looked on them he wept. From the time, however, when the Home Secretary's harsh and ill-considered replies to all the Church's requests proved to him that we had nothing to look for from Government, his natural fortitude was restored to him. He felt that each must take their own place, and stand in their own lot. He warned his people firmly and affectionately, but he never failed again.

Bearing this in mind we can understand the calmness with which the farewell service was quietly gone through at Ruthwell on the last Sabbath before the Disruption.[5]

Thomas Carlyle, who wrote to his wife Jane, confirms Mrs Duncan's description of her husband's emotions:

Henry Duncan of Ruthwell is building a new non-intrusion church [. . .] which he calls 'Kedar's Vale': is not that affecting to one's heart? Duncan they say preaches 'with tears', but the mass of the people do not seem to mind it in this quarter.[6]

When Duncan went to Edinburgh for the 1843 General Assembly, his parishioners sent a petition after him in which they tried to persuade him to stay, arguing that this was in fact a proxy 'call' and that this meant he was in a 'popular settlement'. His reply was brief, expressing surprise and disappointment that they had not really understood the issue. For Duncan, the issue was not so much about whether a minster had the full backing of his parishioners. Patronage and the nature of the 'call' were the issues on which the battle was fought; the real issue was about government interference in the spiritual affairs of the church.

The government, meanwhile, rejected the Claim of Right. There was deadlock. Duncan forecast what would happen in a letter to his son George:

My only fear arises from the danger of defection in our own ranks, and I am afraid that the terror of losing their livings would operate on many to induce them, in the hour of trial to desert their principles. I hope none of my children will show the white feather, indeed I *know* they will not.[7]

Duncan was, by this point, an old man and was feeling his years, but there was still plenty of life in him. He remarked on how little fatigue he felt as he went about his duties, but perhaps adrenalin enhanced his energy. On the morning of the Disruption, in the company of his son George, he wrote to his wife from Edinburgh, knowing well what that day would bring: 'A noble spirit prevails among us all. We are of one heart and one soul; and what will come this day, will strike to the heart of Scotland.'[8] It already had. So certain were the leaders of the evangelicals that a split would occur they had raised substantial amounts of money to erect new churches and a training college for ministers.

The General Assembly duly met in St Andrew's Church in George Street, Edinburgh. The building filled up quickly and there were large crowds in the streets as tension mounted. The queen's representative, the Lord High Commissioner, entered and was duly received by the commissioners. Since 1841 this role had been taken by the Marquess of Bute who was known for his opposition to non-conformity. And although he had no right to speak in debates, or to vote, it is highly likely that he made his views known in the many meetings that took place around the Assembly.

Prayers were offered by the moderator, Dr Welsh, who was an old friend of Henry Duncan. There was silence. Welsh stood and said:

> Fathers and brethren, according to the usual form of procedure, this is the time for making up the roll, but in consequence of certain proceedings affecting our rights and privileges – proceedings which have been sanctioned by Her Majesty's Government, and by the Legislature of the Country – and more especially in respect that there has been an infringement on the liberties of our Constitution, so that we could not now constitute this Court without a violation of the terms of the union between Church and State in this land, as now authoritatively declared, I must protest against our proceeding further. The reasons that have led me to come to this conclusion are fully set forth in this document which I hold in my hand, and which, with the permission of the House, I will now proceed to read.

Permission was duly given and Welsh, having summarised the complaints of the church, concluded:

We are not responsible for any consequences that may follow from this our enforced separation from an Establishment, which we loved and prized, through interference with conscience, the dishonour down to Christ's Crown, and the rejection of his sole and supreme authority as King in his Church.[9]

Welsh laid his protest on the table, bowed to the Lord High Commissioner and walked to the door followed by Thomas Chalmers. A loud cheer was followed by stony silence as more than 400 other commissioners, including Henry and George Duncan, rose and left the General Assembly, before proceeding through the streets of Edinburgh to Tanfield Hall where they constituted the Free Church of Scotland. By this act more than 400 ministers rendered themselves homeless, but they were not jobless. They had the task of building new churches and serving their new church, a task at which they met very considerable success. A further 200 candidates for the ministry soon joined the Free Church.

Lord Cockburn, a leading Edinburgh lawyer, recorded his thoughts on what had transpired:

I know no parallel to it. Whatever may be thought of their cause, there can be no doubt or coldness in the admiration with which all candid men may applaud their heroism. They have abandoned that public station which was the ambition of their lives, and have descended from certainty to precariousness, and most of them from comfort to destitution, solely for their principles. And the loss of the stipend is the least of it. The dismantling of the manse, the breaking up of all the objects to which their hearts and the habits of the family were attached, the shutting the gate for the last time of the little garden, the termination of all their interest in the humble but respectable kirk – even all these desolations, though they may excite the most immediate pangs, are not the calamities which the head of the house finds it hardest to sustain. It is the loss of station that is the deep and lasting sacrifice, the ceasing to be the most important man in the parish, the closing of the doors of the gentry against him and his family, the altered prospects of his children, the extinction of everything that the state had provided for the decent dignity of the manse and its inmates.[10]

In Ruthwell a site had been selected for a new church, not actually in Ruthwell village but close by. The land had been donated by Dr James Buchanan, Professor of Theology at New College (the new Free Church college in Edinburgh). Duncan had already arranged for someone to preach there and he asked his wife to circulate handbills advertising the coming services. He also asked her to have the whin (gorse) bushes removed from the site and a tent was to be erected which was primarily designed to protect the preacher, rather than the congregation, from the elements. Having been a parish minister for forty-three years Duncan now felt himself to be a 'Gospel missionary' who could preach anywhere.[11]

It was not long before Mount Kedar Church, in Mouswald, was under construction. The foundation stone was laid on 1 August 1843, a very inclement day, by William Garvin of Hilhat, one of the elders and master of Duncan's masonic lodge, St Ruth. There was a large attendance but James Buchanan, who had gifted the land, was not able to be there.

Duncan busied himself in raising money for the new church and manse, but he also had other responsibilities, and until the new church was built services were conducted by Duncan and guest preachers in the open air. By the end of 1843 the sum of £300 had been collected in the 'tent' and at other meetings of which £100 had been disbursed on the new building. Within a year the roof was being erected and the building made watertight. A school house was also under construction. Duncan, despite many concerns, nevertheless found time to write to his son William in Peebles and advised him to make some changes to the architect's drawings for his new church there.[12]

Kirk Session meetings were held with Duncan and three elders present, and one of their first tasks was to deal with a case of an unmarried mother. The irony in this case must have struck Duncan quite forcefully as the 'guilt was committed in the manse of Lochrutton where she was a servant' and where he had been born.[13] A more pressing task, however, was to build up the congregation. A list of the adherents of the new church dated August 1843 listed nineteen names from Mouswald, fourteen from Dalton and forty-five from Ruthwell. This last group included his sister and her husband Walter Phillips, factor to the Earl of Mansfield and Agnes Muir, who had been his servant in the manse at Ruthwell. Other names were later added in pencil.[14] Duncan's son claimed that half the parishioners who had worshipped with him in Ruthwell joined the Free Church at Mount Kedar,[15] and he himself recorded that 115 people had attended communion.[16] At any rate it was a very promising start.[17] Duncan continued to preach on a regular basis and also got into the habit of doing so in the open air at Caerlaverock, where he sometimes drew a crowd of 200 people. He also preached in a barn.[18] Sabbath schools were established in Mouswald and Dalton, and weekday evening classes for religious instruction were set up in various villages. Duncan had support in all this. His assistant Mr Brown, his wife Mary and Mr Bryant, the schoolmaster, all took their share of the teaching.

The first General Assembly of the Free Church was held in November 1843 in Glasgow. Duncan was there to support his friends and seek ministers to serve other churches being erected in Dumfriesshire.

By this time Duncan was already seventy years old and it is doubtful if he ever intended to be minister of the new church in the long term, although he clearly served it well judging by the amount of fundraising he undertook. He also loaned some of his own money to the building fund. By November 1845 a new man, Rev A. Brown, who had acted as his assistant in forming the new church, had been installed as minister.

Meanwhile Duncan had another pressing problem to deal with – where were he and Mrs Duncan to live? The manse, to which he had devoted so much of his energy and so many of his creative talents, had to be given up. Mrs Duncan recorded the event:

On the previous evening his eldest son and two little grandsons had arrived to look again at the birthplace of one and a scene which he wished the other two to remember if they should live to be old. On the next day we had agreed to meet and eat our last mid-day meal in the dear old parlour, which for forty-three years had witnessed much hospitality and kindness. But Dr Duncan and his son had gone to look after the workmen at the rising church. Noon, one, two, three o'clock passed. We were in despair it would be night. The people who were working suggested the idea that he could not bear to take leave of the house, and did not mean to return. We dined without them, and the last chair was placed on the cart, when, cheerful and hungry, they returned to the door of the dismantled dwelling. A message from a sick man had drawn them to a distance of eight miles, and, little occupied about where or how he should be lodged, he had pursued his ministerial work as if no removal had been in the way. Yet he was bent on making the best of our discomfort. Next morning when he found rain pouring into our new pantry, he returned quietly to the home of his early happiness to bring a bit of lead, which he had observed in the rubbish of the garret, that with it he might stop the hole that was adding to our discomfort, We smiled at the incident, as proving how far they were mistaken who thought he had indulged in anything like sentimental sorrow for what he had resigned.[19]

A visitor on that day was none other than Duncan's old friend Thomas Carlyle, by then a famous man himself. He wrote to his wife, Jane, that night, 23 August 1843, from Dumfries:

Among my sad thoughts was one that I ought to call for poor old Duncan of Ruthwell. Five and twenty years ago I used to know his Manse well, and he was one of the earliest friends I had; he is now old, a Non-Intrusion 'martyr,' about to quit said Manse: in spite of John I decided that we ought to call. Admire my firmness of purpose, I pray thee! We found the old Manse, much *bushier* than twenty years before; the old Dr somewhat barer; – just in the act of flitting towards 'Kedar's vale'; a new Wife was there, a stern grey woman (a professed admirer of mine): we sat down among the wreck, and talked half an hour not unpleasantly: I was right glad that I had gone. I shall be in that room probably no more: how many that I knew there are already gone out of it; Mitchell, the kind first Mrs. D. &c &c! It was in that room that the dying Burns looked out upon the setting Sun, and said, 'Let me see him yet a little while.'[20]

There was no place for Duncan and his household to go to in the village of Ruthwell but an old friend, Miss Dickson, agreed to share her cottage with them in nearby Clarencefield.[21] It was a temporary arrangement, and within four days of their moving out they had nowhere to go. Duncan and his wife used to console one another by saying 'that our Father knew we could not in our climate live under a hedge'.[22] The possibility of moving to Edinburgh to help with the central organisation of the new church was being considered but, one night, he went to hear a will being read and it became clear that an old labourer's cottage, in Clarencefield, on the turnpike road between Dumfries and Carlisle, was available. The local people turned up to get it in order, including whitewashing its walls. Nor would they accept any payment for their work. It was ready by the due date and they moved in. Mrs. Duncan reckoned that the motivation of at least some of those who helped was a desire to keep Duncan in the district; they did not want their old friend to go to Edinburgh.

The cottage contained a room, a kitchen and a bed closet. Behind the cottage lay a quarry with 'unsightly rubbish mounds and great pools of water'. Duncan entertained some friends to dinner and afterwards asked them to accompany him to the drawing room. Much puzzlement ensued until he took them outside declaring: 'My drawing room is the great drawing room of nature.' Just as he had done at the manse he had landscaped the area by planting larch and spruce, building a small bridge and laying some paths. There was also a field beside the quarry. Its owner, without saying anything, cut a hole in the hedge so that Henry and Mary Duncan could walk there. Mrs Duncan described it with these words:

> we could walk in a very pleasant place, and often escaped from the smoke of the house to the green field, with its little plots of wild roses and honeysuckle; and there, with our books we were as happy as we could have been in the garden, whose every graceful nook was so endeared to us.[23]

Duncan had retained the services of his old gardener James Veitch, and together they set about planting the garden to make the whole place more attractive.

When his daughter and son-in-law James Dodds, who had also come out in the Disruption, came to visit, Duncan is recorded as saying: 'They talk of sacrifices; I never can feel that I have made any. I never was more happy. I have all that my necessities require. The only thing that would have made me unhappy would have been to act contrary to conscience.'[24]

In addition to giving up his church, manse and glebe, Duncan also had to give up his customary mode of transport, a phaeton, (a two-horse, four-wheeled carriage) and prepared to do his work on foot which, given the more dispersed nature of his congregation in the new church, would have made life extremely difficult. The situation was resolved when his brothers in Liverpool provided him with a 'low gig' – a much more modest form of transport than that to which he had been accustomed.

All these changes seem to have energised Duncan. His wife later wrote that

> his energy was never greater; his youth seemed to be renewed – his labours were more abundant – and when he returned late and cold from distant prayer meetings during that severe winter [1844–5] in the little open gig he would not allow us to express any concern as if he were exerting himself beyond his strength.[25]

Yet there were also genuine concerns about his health. He believed he had a heart problem and had gone to Leamington Spa before the Disruption to recover, while on his return he had complained of vertigo.

Duncan's relationship with many of his former parishioners was problematic, as it was for all the ministers who had come out in the Disruption. The split in the church had been hugely divisive when it came to friendships and families, not least the traditional bond that existed between a minister and his parishioners, especially when that bond had endured for such a long time, as it had in Duncan's case. In an earlier age such breakages might have led to bloodshed but, despite highly charged emotions, there were no recorded incidents in any part of the country. Very often feelings were expressed in petty ways in incidents where, for example, there was some minor vandalism around the manse and glebe, or builders' merchants would refuse to supply materials for the erection of Free Churches. Duncan had held meetings in the Clarencefield school but the 'establishment' soon denied access. He was even prevented from holding meetings in the school house that he had erected with surplus funds from the bank, so he resorted to having them in the freemasons' lodge that could seat sixty people. There was also an unsuccessful move to unseat Duncan's old friend, Sir David Brewster, then Scotland's leading scientist, as principal of St Andrews University, on the grounds that he had come out in the Disruption and his role had to be filled by a Church of Scotland minister. The Lord High Commissioner to the General Assembly, the Marquess of Bute, sacked one of his gardeners who went over to the Free Church, and there were many more examples of unhelpfulness, discrimination, personal rivalries and vindictiveness. Scotland was indeed shaken to its foundations.

In Ruthwell some of the people were initially outraged at what Duncan had done, and at what he was doing in building a new church. But

As time rolled on the necessities of some of those who had been most angry against him led them to seek help from their old friend. It was curious to observe that if there was any change in his demeanour at all it was visible in an increased desire to do them service.

On one such occasion a small child had died and there was, as yet, no replacement for Duncan in the parish church to take the service. The father asked Duncan to officiate. In all probability he had been the minister who had baptised the child:

His prayer was so full of love for those who had divided from his ministry, that some of the women, unable to contain themselves, rushed out of the house, and wept it out together with their Free [Church] friends.

The churchyard was some distance away and Duncan took the child's body and placed it in his small gig. He walked, leading the horse, to the internment and

Even the [. . .][Church of Scotland] wives who thought he should not have been invited and the Free Church wives who thought he should not have accepted the invitation, were at least agreed on this, that their old friend was their old friend still, and bore the same Christian heart to them all.[26]

It seems that both Duncan and his wife had a rosier view of Duncan's health than was warranted. In March 1844 he wrote to his son William and conceded he was not well. Much of the local preaching was being undertaken by Mr Bonar and Duncan began to feel that he had been 'cast aside'; winter in the cottage had taken its toll and the prospect of going to live in Edinburgh became a reality in November 1845. Rev. Brown had been inducted as his successor in Mount Kedar, but Duncan was most reluctant to go. He wrote: 'If they take me from my people, they may just lay me on the shelf. My energies, such as they are, are gone, and I really think that if I be transplanted I shall wither and die.'[27]

His intention was to go to Edinburgh for the winter and return to Ruthwell in the summer.

In the event, Duncan went to Edinburgh and worked with Thomas Chalmers and others in building up the new church, but he missed the daily routine of parochial duties which had been his mainstay since 1799. When his health was sufficiently restored, he made a trip to England, visiting his daughter and sons en route. Barbara was married to Rev. James Dodds in Belhaven, near Dunbar, while William was busy building the Free Church in Peebles, and Duncan lent a hand in getting the savings bank there re-established while adding a children's bank. George had accepted a call to the Presbyterian Church, North Shields, in the north of England. Duncan greatly enjoyed the visit to his children and his growing number of grandchildren.

The main purpose of the trip was to raise funds for his new church and manse at Mount Kedar, and in this Duncan was highly successful. He preached in crowded churches, and at one meeting he was asked if the Disruption and the rise of the Free Church was not the result more of passion than of principle. His interrogator went on to ask, in the light of this, if he had any regrets. Duncan replied with a question, 'Can a man regret having the grace to act up to his principles?' before adding, 'No, God forbid. Were I placed in similar circumstances to-morrow, it would be my only happiness to do as I have done.'[28] In the process of making this trip he over-taxed his health and strength but ignored the advice of family and friends to slow down. Duncan went on to raise funds in Liverpool, Manchester and Salford and even opened a new church in Chester.

One of the friends Duncan visited in Manchester later recorded that he

> looked wonderfully well, and had his usual cheerful and benev-
> olent smile. When I spoke however of the length of time that
> had elapsed since we had met, and of the many changes which
> had taken place, and inquired respecting his health, he told me
> he felt few of the infirmities of age, but that in walking through
> crowded streets he had a peculiar sensation at his heart; he was
> convinced that there was disease there, and that his call would
> be sudden.[29]

Duncan understood that the money that he was raising for the manse at Ruthwell would be for the benefit of his successor.

While in England Duncan became reacquainted with young men who had been boys in Ruthwell but who had gone south to make a living. He also involved himself in the affairs of the recently formed Evangelical Alliance. His final visit was to his brothers in Liverpool and his nephews escorted him to the train to begin his journey home to Ruthwell. He journeyed with John Cropper of Liverpool and they spoke of old times in that city and old friends before turning their conversation to matters of religion.

Returning to Scotland, Duncan stopped in Ruthwell to visit with friends and to oversee the work at Mount Kedar. When news of his arrival spread through the village people came out to greet him and he visited many, preaching whenever the opportunity arose. He also took the opportunity to visit the grave of his first wife.

One evening Duncan was conducting a service in the house of one of his old parishioners who had not joined the Free Church, a sure sign that people were beginning to overcome the hard feelings of 1843. His text for the sermon was from Zechariah 3, 'For behold the stone', but as he preached his voice became faint and he slumped in a chair. He was carried to the house of his sister and brother-in-law at Comlongan Castle, and while he seemed aware of all that was happening around him he was unable to speak. Duncan lingered for two days and died on the evening of 12 February 1846. Neither his wife nor his sons arrived in time to be at his deathbed.

Earlier that day one of the women of the village wrote to a friend:

We were in expectation of seeing once more our venerable and dear minister and he has come – but I think it is to end his days in Ruthwell.

Comlongan avenue has been crowded these two days. One stream of people going very mournful-like down, the other coming up. The parish is in deep affliction, and so they may. But I hope he is going to that happy land above, where there is no sorrow, and where the Lamb will wipe away all tears from his eyes. He has spent a long life-time in the service of his Heavenly Master.[30]

The funeral service was conducted on the green at Comlongan Castle and attended by a large number of mourners, including ministers from various branches of the church. Duncan was buried in the yard of the church where he had served the people of the parish for more than forty years, in a place close to the manse where he had lived for so long and from which his principles had led him away. There was a memorial service in Mount Kedar Church the following Sunday where one of his old friends Rev. Robert Brydon of Dunscore preached a sermon on the text 'The path of the just is as the shining light.'

It was not long before people began to think about how Duncan's life and his contribution to society could be commemorated. His parishioners erected a stone memorial to him near the church at Mount Kedar,[31] while his brother Thomas, notwithstanding that he had not come out in the Disruption, built a sizeable office for the Dumfries Savings Bank.

He also commissioned a local stonemason to carve an eight-foot-high statue; this still stands and is locally known as 'the Stane Man'. It depicts Henry Duncan with furrowed brow, clutching a Bible to his chest and wearing pastoral garb. Underneath an inscription simply reads:

HENRY DUNCAN, D. D.

1774 – 1846

FOUNDER OF SAVINGS BANKS 1810.

Chapter 14
Conclusion

Henry Duncan is best remembered today as the founder – some would say 'the father' – of the savings bank movement, and indeed his extensive correspondence and two editions of his pamphlet did much to set the movement on its way. But, importantly, he was not alone in promoting the idea. His adversary in Edinburgh, John Forbes, published several editions of his own pamphlet entitled *A short account of the Edinburgh Savings Bank, containing directions for establishing similar banks, with the mode of keeping the accounts etc.* His intention was that others would follow the Edinburgh model which was, in some respects, a little simpler than the Ruthwell model.

Yet it was Henry Duncan who was widely acknowledged as the father of the savings bank movement.

Before long there was quite an extensive library of books and pamphlets about savings banks. In 1830, John Tidd Pratt published a book with the title *The History of Savings Banks in England, Wales and Ireland*. Nothing was said about Scotland except that in the preface he wrote:

> It appears, therefore, on the whole, that though some institutions similar both in their principles and details, had been formed before the parish bank of Ruthwell, yet it was the first of the kind which was regularly and minutely organized and brought before the public: and further, that as that society gave the impulse which is fast spreading through the kingdom, it is in all fairness entitled to the appellation of the Parent Society.[1]

There were similar publications in North America and in 1876, Emerson W. Keyes, who had been deputy superintendent of the banking department of the State of New York, wrote and published a two-volume history of savings banks in the United States.[2] Having reviewed many of the experiments prior to the formation of the Ruthwell Bank, Keyes wrote:

> The name of Rev Henry Duncan, in association with the establishment of Savings Banks, deserves more than merely incidental mention [. . .] That he first conceived the idea is not claimed, but he probably did more than any other man, perhaps more than all others, to reduce the idea to practical form, and to impart to it success.
>
> And yet in a sense, he is claimed as their *founder* in that he 'originated and organized the first self-sustaining bank, and succeeded in so arranging his scheme as to make it applicable not to one locality only, but to the country generally'. The amount of travel, correspondence and public speaking performed by Dr Duncan in connection with, and for the establishment of these institutions was, for that period, immense. It is but just to say that but for such efforts as he put forth, and upon some basis or plan as well considered and practicable as his, Savings Banks would not have been organised to any considerable extent at so early a period, or, if organized, would not, for want of practical plans of operation, have been successful.[3]

Modern American writers on the subject also acknowledged Duncan's role in the formation of the movement. A recent Templeton Foundation publication noted that

> many of the first incorporated savings banks in the United States cite the Ruthwell Bank as their model. Whatever the particular institution that served as the model, it was European voluntary organisations and 'friendly societies' that provided the inspiration for their state-incorporated American counterparts.[4]

Duncan's right to be thought of as the founder of the savings bank movement was further cemented in 1910. His great grand-daughter, Lady Sophy Hall, produced a biography, and the Edinburgh Savings Bank, once Duncan's nemesis, organised a conference to celebrate what the organisers considered the centenary of savings banks: 'Many came from a distance, from the Savings Banks of Paris, Lyons, Bordeaux, Brussels, Amsterdam, Rotterdam, Neuchatel, Sydney, Melbourne, Auckland, Philadelphia, Brooklyn and New York. Others sent messages.'[5]

Former Prime Minister Lord Rosebery also sent a message:

Let the spirit of Duncan of Ruthwell speak once more among us. For thrift is at the root of independence and self-respect, two vital principles in our national life, more especially in the life of an ambitious and aspiring people like ours.[6]

The conference heard from G. Stuart Patterson, president of the Western Savings Bank of Philadelphia, that there were then 642 mutual savings banks in the United States.

When the bi-centenary of the formation of the Ruthwell Bank came round in 2010 there were two conferences in Edinburgh. The first took place in the hall where the General Assembly of the Church of Scotland now meets, a building which also houses the divinity school of the University of Edinburgh. This was also one of the buildings for which Duncan raised money, as it was formerly the theological college, the Assembly Hall and a church for the Free Church of Scotland. A second conference for savings bankers from many parts of the world was held in the Sheraton Hotel in Edinburgh the following day. On both occasions the role of Henry Duncan as founder of the savings bank movement was generously acknowledged. It has also recently emerged that the Egyptian founder of the first Islamic bank based his model on savings banks that he had visited and studied.

Duncan's contribution to the movement is all the more remarkable in that it was achieved without any form of central organisation; no head office and no staff. His success in setting the savings bank movement under way was due to two factors. First was the self-belief and energy that he devoted to the enterprise. This was contagious, with his brother, then his friends and correspondents following his example. Second was the power of ideas: many people were looking for ways to reduce poverty, ameliorate the worst effects of the agricultural and industrial revolutions, reduce the burden of helping the poor and help poor people to lead more independent lives, and the savings bank idea appealed as a way of doing all of these things. Moreover, Duncan also believed that through the medium of savings banks and related activities working people would come to feel less alienated from society and would become more actively involved citizens. Having a savings bank account would, therefore, help to moderate some of the radical ideas and activities that were percolating through society. Thus the popularity of the savings bank idea spread throughout the United Kingdom and then to many other parts of the world where it still thrives today. The savings bank in Ruthwell reached its peak of deposits in 1835 and continued in existence until the 1870s, when it was absorbed by the Annan Savings Bank. The friendly society was still active in 1871, by which time the population of the parish of Ruthwell, which had reached a peak in 1821, had declined by a quarter.[7]

Duncan, however, was well aware that the savings banks had not solved all the problems of poverty, although he never expected they would. What he, Thomson and a large number of others had set out to end was pauperism, i.e. 'the support of the poor by charitable dona-tions'.[8] His efforts were 'directed to succouring the victims of a harsh society while leaving unquestioned those principles on which that society was constructed'.[9] Nevertheless, Duncan was conscious that savings banks had helped a very large number of people, in many parts of the world, to meet the financial challenges in their lives. Perhaps, more than any other person, he deserves credit for inculcating the virtue of thrift in the psyche, not just of the Scots, where it became well embedded, but in the mind-sets of many people internationally.

Henry Duncan deserves his reputation as founder of the savings bank movement. He is also acknowledged as the man who preserved the Ruthwell Cross, which now stands within Ruthwell Church where he served as minister. It attracts visitors from all around the world.

The Free Church of Scotland, that he helped to found in 1843, eventually found common cause with the Church of Scotland in 1929 and, with notable exceptions, the two were reunited. The congregation at Mount Kedar eventually merged with the congregation in Ruthwell, where services are still conducted. Patronage and government interference in church affairs are things of the past – congregations call their own ministers.

The Crichton Campus, once the home of the hospital for the mentally ill, established in the 1830s with a bequest, is now a university campus where the University of Glasgow, the University of the West of Scotland and the Open University offer degree programmes. It is also the home of Dumfries and Galloway College, which is the natural successor of the mechanics institute that Duncan helped found.

The British government brought an end to slavery in the Empire just a few years after Duncan's letters on the subject were published.

Duncan's literary works are not read today, although some are available as e-books and as print copies from electronic sources. Nevertheless, they are a remarkable tribute to a man of his times whose energy, talents and money were put to use in the public interest without hope of any personal financial advantage. The inventory of his estate showed that he was worth £1,400 at the time of his death, including £37 held in the Ruthwell Bank.

Henry Duncan lived in interesting times. Changes in politics and agriculture, the industrial revolution, the growth of cities, the Napoleonic wars, problems in church politics and the revolution in transport all occurred in his lifetime. Notwithstanding that he lived in a remote part of Scotland, his part of the country was nevertheless connected economically and socially to what was occurring in other parts. He understood what was happening through his very wide circle of friends and correspondents. He was also a well read man although, given the workload that he carried, it is difficult to know how he managed to keep up to date with all that was taking place. That he did so is a tribute to his determination that the things he cared about – his family, his congregation, his church and his friends –

should be the focus of his energies and his care.

He was, in the words of Thomas Carlyle, 'the amiablest and kindliest of men; to me pretty much a unique-the one cultivated man whom I could feel myself permitted to call a friend'.[10] It was an appropriate epitaph that resonates with Duncan's concluding words in his novel.

And now, my patient friend, whoever thou art, that has borne with me to the end of this long story, I bid thee heartily and gratefully farewell.

Postscript

Long before Henry Duncan's death in 1846 the savings bank movement had become a vital part of domestic culture in the UK and many other parts of the world. In many families it became established practice to open an account in a savings bank for every newborn baby.

But, by the late twentieth century, society was changing. Savings banks came under increasing pressure to adapt. The coming of computing technology to banking made it possible for salaries to be paid into bank accounts forcing savings banks to invest in computers and to offer current accounts to their customers. There was also the problem of inflation in the 1970s and 1980s which seriously impacted on thrifty habits. By that time many of the smaller savings banks had merged with larger organisations.

And when the Page Committee on National Savings reported to Parliament in 1973 it revealed that some of Britain's savings banks were struggling to survive. What followed was the creation of regional trustee savings banks (TSBs) as the 73 remaining banks entered merger agreements with their neighbours. In Scotland a few banks that had been formed under Henry Duncan's Act of 1819 remained independent. But, within a few years, only Airdrie Savings Bank remained, as the others sought membership of their local TSBs or the embrace of commercial banks.

The mutual status of the regional TSBs came under increasing pressure as they tried to compete with the commercial banks and their need for capital led, in the mid 1980s, to their amalgamation into one bank, TSB Group plc, and then to their privatisation. Within a decade, however, discussions were under way with Lloyds Bank about a possible merger which was effective from 1995 making the new Lloyds TSB PLC Britain's largest bank by market share.

All went well until the financial crisis of 2008. HBOS, on the verge of failure, was taken over by Lloyds TSB at the Government's behest. The European Commission acknowledged the need for this rescue operation but maintained that it breached their rules about government assistance for business and insisted that Lloyds TSB sell some if its assets. The decision was then made to demerge TSB, which in 2013 became an independent bank.

The new TSB bank included all of Lloyds TSB branches in Scotland, many more in England and all Cheltenham and Gloucester branches. These were challenging times in which to launch a new bank. The low interest rate regime and heightened compliance costs put considerable pressure on the bottom line. However, TSB set about to bring Local Banking back to Britain with the mindset of a 'challenger' to bring more competition to UK banking and ultimately make banking better for all UK consumers.

The new TSB was successful, and it became an attractive partner for Spanish Bank Sabadell, itself in the European savings bank tradition. A union of the two banks was achieved in 2015.

There are many echoes of Henry Duncan in the new TSB – most notably how it is focused on the communities in which it serves. And when the bank launched in 2013, it even created a cartoon of Duncan for its advertising campaign which extols his ideas and ideals.

At the time of writing, Airdrie Savings Bank, the last of the old guard of savings banks, is bowing out of the banking business. Its small size and high costs made it impossible to remain viable in the long term. In looking for another bank to take over its lending, it chose TSB, which now stands as the natural successor to Henry Duncan and his ideals about community banking.

Henry Duncan might struggle to recognise TSB as the natural outcome of his hopes for the parish bank that he founded in 1810. It is highly likely, however, that he would be proud of it.

Appendix 1
A Contemporary Account
of Henry Duncan

The source of this contemporary account of Henry Duncan, almost certainly, is James Dodds, a native of nearby Cummertrees, who was schooled in the Ruthwell Manse, assisted with the newspaper and went on to become a minister. He married the Duncans' daughter Barbara in early 1843 and came out with his new father and brothers-in-law in the Disruption later that year.

A Contemporary Account of Henry Duncan
(G. Duncan, *Memoir of Henry Duncan*, 201–9)

A native of a parish adjacent to Ruthwell, I heard much about Dr Duncan from my boyhood, and early formed an exalted idea of his character. As far back as my early recollections extend, he filled a large space in the public eye of the South of Scotland, and stood prominent among all his brethren, not only as a talented clergyman, but as an enlightened and public spirited man. Before I knew the meaning of benevolence, I heard of his active and original methods of promoting the interests of his parishioners, and seeking the good of his country.

I can remember hearing people say of young men who wanted a friend or patron to help them to a situation, or push them on in the world, that if they could get Dr Duncan of Ruthwell to take them by the hand success would be sure to attend them. I may also mention that a similar good name attached to his amiable and gentle partner, whose kindness of feeling and strong good sense, and charity to the poor, endeared her to all the country round.

The first time I saw Dr Duncan was on the occasion of a masonic festival in the town of Annan where he preached to a large assembly of free-masons and other in the parish church. As a boyish spectator, rather than an intelligent hearer, I mingled with the audience; but I was soon arrested by the fine personal appearance, the elegant language, and the affectionate delivery of the preacher. His text was 'Let us not be weary in well-doing, for in due season we shall reap, if we faint not'. I can recall nothing of the sermon but its general impression, which remained with me after other sermons I heard at that period were forgotten. Indeed the text, the sermon and the preacher, were in a manner fixed upon my heart and memory, and formed together an era of my youth.

I can well remember when I was first introduced to Dr Duncan, and had the privilege of conversing with him. The natural gentleness and unassuming dignity of his manners, at once won my respect, and put me at my ease. I could feel little diffidence in his company, though I had cause to be diffident enough. The subject of conversation was the improved, or what has been called *the intellectual* system of teaching. He spoke as upon a favourite topic, and like one who knew the philosophy of education. I had been in Edinburgh, and had visited the Sessional School, then in the zenith of its fame. He spoke of that seminary as realising views he had long cherished, and done his best to recommend. I had already known, though I knew better afterwards, that the author of 'The Cottage Fireside', was one of the first to advocate more sensible and philosophical ways of managing and teaching the young. Its lessons on education are the most valuable portion of that pleasing and useful little book.

In the summer of 1829 I went to reside under Dr Duncan's roof, and from that period a friendship, I may say an intimacy, began, which death, I trust, has only suspended. Thenceforth I had every opportunity of judging of the character and inner life of one, whom from my boyhood, I had learned to venerate.

Both for internal and external attractions, few Scottish manses could compete with that of Ruthwell. The genius of its benevolent and accomplished master was felt and seen within and without its walls.

When I first saw the manse and its premises, its lawns adorned and sheltered with trees, its numerous gravel walks gracefully winding and skilfully prolonged, its pond or artificial lake, reflecting a white rustic bridge, and many living flowering ornaments on its borders; its garden, or rather series of gardens, divided from each other by tall, thick beech hedges, with the garden house, composed of slabs of red sandstone that had served to rectify some scientific errors of the day, and made no small sensation in the geologic world; and a runic monument, almost unequalled in Britain, and the delight of northern antiquaries; I could hardly credit the accounts I received of the former uninteresting condition of the place and its neighbourhood.

The society at the manse was of a very varied description, embracing almost a constant succession of guests throughout the year. A more hospitable roof could not be found. It was at Ruthwell Manse, I think in the summer of 1831, that I first met with Dr Chalmers. He was on his return from London, and was in high health and spirits, having not only enjoyed the opportunity of giving expression to his favourite philanthropic views before the senators of the day, but also having visited many of his English friends, and made numerous pleasant journeys over a great part of England. I was profoundly struck with the affability, the beaming benignity, the geniality of mind and manner, of that great man. The friendship between Dr Chalmers and Dr Duncan was most cordial on both sides. A community of views and feelings on most topics, civil and ecclesiastical, and a common benevolence that longed for the elevation of the lower classes of society, bound them together as friends and fellow-churchmen by the strongest ties. Dr Duncan's love and admiration of his illustrious friend were unbounded; and I have heard Dr Chalmers say that it was an honour to the Church of Scotland that she numbered among her ministers the originator of Savings Banks.

I have often thought that the description of a month, a week, or even a single day at Ruthwell Manse, about the time that I speak of would present a most interesting specimen of Dr Duncan's spirit and character, and an excellent *section* of Scottish clerical life. The society, the conversation, the employments of the day, the books read or discussed in the evening, were of a superior stamp, and indicated the philosopher, or philanthropist, the

Christian minister, and the man of letters. At prayers in the morning, after reading the chapter, he usually addressed a few affectionate words, or appropriate questions, to the young gentlemen who resided with him, who were always, I may say literally, treated as children of the family. He sometimes also read a paper from 'Sturm's Reflections', that he might introduce in a becoming manner the *works* along with the word of God. It was, I believe, in connection with this practice, that the idea first arose in his mind, which he afterwards admirably carried out in his 'Sacred Philosophy of the Seasons'. His forenoons were usually devoted to study, if indeed some poor parishioners soliciting advice or assistance, or some Savings Bank depositors, coming to increase or diminish their store, left him the necessary leisure. At mid-day he received visitors, walked with his guests, or performed parochial duties at a distance. A public meeting in Dumfries, a meeting of the Presbytery in Annan, or some communion engagement in a neighbouring parish, would frequently take the Pastor from his home for the day: and I can well remember the joy with which the rattle of his returning phaeton was hailed by the different members of his household, and, among the rest, the boys would start to their feet to welcome 'Uncle Henry'.

I cannot help speaking of his skilful hand; indeed a hand more skilful and versatile I never saw. His feats of manual and artistic dexterity were numberless and amazing. What is called a *mechanical turn* is not uncommon; but he had something much higher than an accomplishment of that kind. His was not merely the ingenuity which delights to construct or mend a child's toy, repair a domestic disaster, or make as good as new some out-of-door implement – all such feats he easily could and did perform, with rare delight to himself and to the great satisfaction of others. But he possessed in a remarkable degree that fineness of eye, and power of hand, which characterise the artist. He made exquisite models and figures in clay, was an excellent draughtsman, and had a fine appreciation of the beauties of painting. Numerous plaster of Paris casts, and elaborate models of the Runic monument, all executed with the nicest skill and precision attested the vigour of that *constructiveness* which was one of his leading characteristics. After being deprived by advancing years of several of his teeth, by the loss of which his utterance was somewhat affected, and having been disappointed by professional unskillfulness he even became his own dentist, and succeeded to his perfect satisfaction again and again in this self-taught profession.

I have alluded to the tasteful grounds and gardens with which he surrounded the manse. The improvement of these was his favourite amusement. The alteration of a road, the giving of a new bend to a walk, the thinning of a belt or clump of trees, the lopping off a few branches from the favourite ornaments of the lawn, or the transplantation of a few shrubs, or flowers, was to him a prized relaxation, and was always directed with characteristic taste and skill. In executing all such operations he had a ready agent in his worthy and faithful old gardener, James Veitch, a man who had a great deal of poetry and feeling in his composition, and loved his master with no common love, entered into all his tastes, and zealously executed his orders. He also clung to him in days of trail when many proved faithless. He died in his service and never did master more honour a faithful old servant.

Dr Duncan's ministerial character, when I first knew him was daily deepening in earnestness and power. His labours for the highest welfare of his people had begun to become more spiritual and more abundant than they once were; and it was only what might have been expected, immediately before and after Disruption times, while the love of some of his brethren was waxing cold, his only grew warmer; and that, while others halted in their work, his labours became more numerous and blessed than ever. In visiting the sick, attending to the wants of the poor, and ministering generally to the temporal and spiritual necessities of his people, he was the faithful, tender-hearted, and anxious pastor. He himself felt and confessed many deficiencies, but I continually saw the strongest proofs of his fidelity. His pulpit ministrations, if not eminently popular, were replete with earnestness and fervour; his doctrine was strictly evangelical; his delivery was always affectionate, often animated and impressive; his whole style and manner were eminently unaffected. The literary merit of his discourses was always high. Nothing could exceed the lucid order of the arrangement and the flowing beauty of the language. So excellent his taste, so great his talent for composition, that anything awkward or inelegant never dropped from lips or pen.

His scientific attainments were of no common order as his writings show. I never knew any unprofessional man of science who had a better acquaintance with the different kingdoms and general system of nature. He had a decided turn for natural history; was versed in the general principles, and, to a certain extent, in the minute details of geology; and always cherished an enthusiastic love for astronomy. He could read the constellations of the starry heavens with the eye of a practical astronomer, and delighted to expatiate on the glories of the material universe. Of the sublime and beautiful in nature he had a deep and lively perception, his natural sensibility being quickened by pious feeling and intellectual refinement. The splendour of a starry night, a grand or lovely landscape, or the sublime phenomenon of a thunder-storm, would often affect him to tears. I never saw such deep and lively emotion in any lover of nature. It was a general belief in the parish and neighbourhood that the minister of Ruthwell delighted in a thunder-storm; and while others were filled with terror, he was wont to exclaim, as the thunder rolled overhead 'How glorious'.

Dr Duncan's correspondents were of all classes, and would range from the Lord Chancellor of England to the humble native of Ruthwell who had gone to push his fortune in another part of the country. The same pen that one night wrote learned letters to high personages on Scottish ecclesiastical law and church politics, would probably next be engaged in advocating the cause, or directing the conduct of some former parishioner. No young man setting out in life, or wife or widow inquiring after husband or son in a distant land – no person, in short, who could appeal to his benevolent nature, ever appealed in vain. At the expense of many a tedious correspondence, and many a sum of money lent, or given, he conducted the business, or pleaded the cause of the widow, the orphan, the deserving, and the friendless. I often thought that his benevolence peculiarly delighted in literary efforts of this kind. He was certainly most ardent and untiring with the pen; and I need scarcely say, with the purse too. The matchless facility and elegance with which he wrote letters of every description, was one of his most remarkable accomplishments, and often struck those near him with amazement. After being wearied perhaps with the business of the day, he would often throw off, at a sitting, letters, no matter on how delicate or difficult subjects, that were perfect models of expression.

Appendix 2
The Church of Scotland – a Guide

I am hopeful this book will be read in many parts of the world by those who may not be familiar with Presbyterian church governance or with some of the terminology that is used to describe Church of Scotland activities and processes. This short guide is offered as an aid.

Popularly known as 'the Kirk', the Church of Scotland is Scotland's national church. It was formed as a Presbyterian church in the Reformation in 1560 and struggled throughout the seventeenth century to retain its Presbyterian form of church governance against kings in London who would have preferred an episcopal form of government, with the monarch as head of the church and with bishops as regional heads. The view of the Kirk was that there could be no human head of the church and matters were organised so that no individual could exercise any undue influence or control. Consequently, there were no bishops or archbishops and this remains the case.

The coronation of King William of Orange and Queen Mary in 1689, together with the Act of Union of the Scottish and English parliaments in 1707, ensured that Presbyterianism would remain the organisational form of the Church of Scotland.

Ministers

Ministers are ordained preachers who are 'called' to their church by the congregation, although in Henry Duncan's time this was a controversial matter as local heritors, i.e. landowners (or the Crown), often saw it as their responsibility – and right – to decide who should be the minister even if they were not themselves members of the Church of Scotland. Heritors based this claim on the fact that they were responsible, at parish level and working with presbyteries, for the maintenance of church property.

Ministers were responsible for preaching on Sundays, administration of the sacraments (baptism and communion), conducting marriages and funerals, and for maintaining high moral standards among their parishioners. They had a great deal of freedom to decide how matters should be organised in their parish but were not allowed, unless invited, to exercise their ministerial functions outside their own parish.

In return for their services ministers were paid a stipend, which in Duncan's time could be paid in cash and kind. They were also provided with a manse in which to live and a 'glebe', which was an area of land which they could farm.

Church Government

There were four levels at which the church was organised: kirk sessions, presbyteries, synods and the General Assembly.

Kirk sessions existed in every parish church and were the governing bodies at local level responsible for all church activities except worship, which was the sole responsibility of the minister. Kirk sessions comprised the minister and a number of elders who were ordained lay people. Meetings were usually chaired by the minister who, in this capacity, acted as moderator. In the early nineteenth century kirk sessions were responsible for administering poor relief in each parish.

Presbyteries were groups of churches, organised geographically, that met monthly. Attendees were ministers and a representative elder from each member church. A typical presbytery in the nineteenth century might comprise eight to ten churches, and they were responsible for ensuring that church property was well maintained, that parish schools were provided with teachers and that any breach of good moral behaviour was investigated. They were presided over by a moderator, i.e. one of the ministers, who was elected for six months or a year.

Synods were groups of presbyteries, often organised on a county basis with much the same responsibilities as presbyteries. They were discontinued in the twentieth century.

The General Assembly traditionally meets in the third week of May each year, presided over by a moderator who is elected for a one-year term. It is the law-making body of the church and comprises an equal number of ministers and elders. It hears reports from its various committees and decides to accept or reject the proposals from these bodies and may also accept or reject amendments from the floor of the Assembly.

Appendix 3
Henry Duncan's Poetry

The source of the verses on Burns is a photocopied document in the Savings Bank Museum in Ruthwell. The verses are clearly taken from a published volume as they are in printed form and are described as 'Appendix II'. However, the compiler notes that a final verse in the manuscript from which he/she was working was so faded as to be undecipherable.

The Music of the Year is Hushed
Air – 'Maggie Lauder'

The music of the year is hushed
In bonny glen and shaw, man,
The winter spreads, o'er nature dead,
In winding-sheet o' snaw, man;
O'er burn and loch the warlock, frost,
A crystal brig has laid, man,
The wild-geese, screaming wi' surprise,
The ice bound wave ha'e fled, man.

Up curler! Leave your bed sae warm,
And leave your coaxing wife, man,
Gae, get your besom, trickers, stanes,
And join the friendly strife, man;
For on the water's face are met,
Wi' mony a merry joke, man,
The tenant and his jolly laird,
The pastor and his flock, man.

The rink is swept, the tees are marked,
The bonspiel is begun, man;
The ice is true, the stanes are keen;
Huzza! For glorious fun, man.
The skips are standing on the tee
To guide the eager game, man;
Hush! No a word – but mark the broom,
And take the steady aim, man.

How stands the game? It's eight and eight;
Now for the winning shot, man,
Draw slow and sure, the ice is keen,
I'll sweep you to the spot, man.
The stane is thrown, it glides alang,
The besoms ply it in, man,
Wi' twisting back the players stand,
And eager, breathless grin, man.

A moments silence, still as death,
Pervades the anxious thrang, man,
Then sudden bursts the victor's shout,
Wi' hollas loud and lang, man;
Triumphant besoms wave in air,
And friendly banters fly, man,
Whilst, cauld and hungry, to the inn,
Wi' eager steps, they hie, man.

Now fill ae bumper – fill but ane,
And drink wi' social glee, man,
May curlers on life's slippery rink
Frae cruel rubs be free, man;
Or should a treacherous bias lead
Their erring steps a jee, man,
Some friendly inring may they meet,
To guide them to the tee, man.

Verses on the Memory of Robert Burns

PORTENTOUS sigh'd the hollow blast
That sorrow freighted southward past;
I heard the sound, and stood aghast
In solemn dread;
The mournful truth is told at last,
And Burns is dead.

Ah, sweetest minstrel, Nature's child,
Could not thy native woodnotes wild,
Thy manly sense, thy manners mild,
And sprightly glee,
The dreaded tyrant have beguiled
To set thee free?

Unfriended, desolate and young,
Misfortune o'er thy cradle hung;
And penury had check'd thy song,
But check'd in vain;
Till death with unrelenting wrong,
Has closed the strain.

Thus midst the cold of winter's snows,
The bright and naked snowdrop blows;
Its pure and native beauty glows,
And charms the eyes,
Till past some ruthless spoiler goes,
And crops the prize.

But not for them, O Bard, the lot
In cold oblivions shade to rot,
Like those unhonoured and forgot,
The unfeeling great;
Who knew thy worth, but hastened not
To soothe thy fate.

Whilst love to beauty pours the sigh,
Whilst genius shall with nature vie,
Whilst pity from the melting eye
Shall claim regard
Thy honour'd name shall never die,
Immortal Bard!

But oft as winter o'er the plain
Shall pour at eve the beating rain,
The hind shall call his little train
Around the fire,
To listen to some thrilling strain
Of thy loved lyre.

Whether to heaven's eternal King
Thou strike the deep-resounding string,
Whilst rising on devotion's wing,
Hope soars above
To happier realms of endless spring
And boundless love.

Or whether lighter strains beguile
The moments of relaxing toil,
Biding on labour's front the smile
Of pleasure sit;
The roof re-echoing all the while
To native wit.

Or if wild Fancy seize the rein,
Whilst horror thrills through every vein
And sprites and elves, an awful train,
Their orgies keep;
And warlocks o'er the frighted plain
At midnight sweep.

As works the spell the fairy band
Aghast in mute attention stand;
Again thou wav'st thy magic wand
Of power so rare,
And all the scene of Fancy plann'd
Dissolves in air.

Thins, too, the charm of social hearts,
Where wit its vivid lightning darts,
And, answering keen, to age imparts
The fire of youth,
Whilst from the fierce encounter starts
The spark of truth.

Old Coila first, whose braes among
Thy infant hands the wild heart strung,
Shall flourish in thy deathless song
With lasting fame;
And Ayr shall henceforth roll along
A classic stream.

But thou, O Bard, in silence laid,
Oh, what shall soothe thy pensive shade
For youth and genius ill repaid
With bounty scant,
And hours of sorrow unallay'd
And toil and want?

See on thy song, as loud it swells,
The lordly thane delighted dwells,
Or to his fair his rapture tells,
By thee inspired;
His bosom, as the strain impels,
Or thaw'd or fired.

Appendix 4
Thomas Tudor Duncan

Duncan's younger brother Thomas was a source of friendship throughout his life. He was also of immense assistance in a number of the projects in which Henry became involved. Ultimately they thought differently about the events that led to the Disruption, although that does not seem to have disturbed their mutual respect.

Thomas Tudor Duncan

Thomas Tudor Duncan was born at Lochrutton on 24 June 1776. He received the same early education as the rest of the family, tutored at home before going to school in Dumfries with Henry. From there he went to Edinburgh and St Andrews universities in his teenage years, before deciding to study medicine.

Having received his medical degree from the University of Edinburgh in 1803, Thomas decided not to become a doctor and, having also studied sufficient theology, was licensed to preach by the Presbytery of Annan in June 1803 (to assist him in his studies, he had received a bursary from the presbytery). He became minister at Applegarth the following year but did not remain there. He was the king's presentation to be minister at the New Church (Greyfriars) Dumfries, on 20 June 1806.[1] No sooner had he been inducted when his father became ill and Thomas was appointed to assist him as presbytery clerk in February 1807. He went on to serve in that capacity and then as moderator on several occasions. The presbytery was quite a small one with an average attendance of around ten people, so it is not surprising that he became moderator more than once. Shortly after his becoming assistant clerk, Thomas received a letter from Lochrutton to say that his father was dying and that Mrs Duncan was worried about what to give him to eat and drink. Henry was on his way to Lochrutton and Thomas was urged to join him.

Like his brother, Thomas was an enthusiastic freemason and was chaplain of the Old Lodge of Dumfries for many years.

His initial reception by the parishioners in Dumfries was less than friendly. When he preached after his induction even his friends were not impressed, and his parishioners held a meeting from which the minute reads:

[H]e is not a minister whose experience, manner of communicating religious instruction or influence and authority in discharging the various important duties of the pastoral office – or the pastor of a congregation – of more than three thousand souls. This is the unanimous opinion of the meeting.[2]

It was a very shaky start but Thomas persevered, and in 1814 a public dinner was held in his honour at which he was presented with an elegant silver water and coffee pot. On that occasion the speeches expressed the appreciation of the congregation of Thomas 'as a minister and as a man'. He had clearly put the initial reservations of his congregation behind him and settled into the role of a parish minister.

To some extent Thomas lived his life in his brother's shadow, but there can be no doubt that Henry would have been hard pressed to achieve what he did without help from his brother. This was especially the case with the newspaper and the bank. The exact extent of his input is uncertain, but we know that he worked closely with Henry on the production of the newspaper and was a useful source of copy, especially for local news. He went on to follow his brother's example and establish a savings bank in Dumfries, and it was this bank that Henry chose to hold up as an exemplar in the 1816 edition of his pamphlet.

Thomas married Frances Brooks of Everton Hall, Liverpool, in June 1807. She was the daughter of a West Indian slave-owning family and they had four sons, one of whom died in infancy. Frances died suddenly in September 1837 and her death seems to have had a profound effect on Thomas's health, as the presbytery were so concerned about him that they decided he should have an assistant.[3] This would normally only happen when advanced old age or imminent death prevented the incumbent minister from carrying out his duties.

The assistant, however, was never appointed and Thomas appears to have made a full recovery. In church matters he seems to have been a man of high principles who took his responsibilities very seriously. On one occasion, when he was clerk to the synod, he complained about the poor attendance and on another occasion, when a minister's baby was delivered seven months after the wedding, the presbytery debated the matter and decided to do nothing about it. Thomas registered his objections.[4]

His principles, however, did not lead him to leave the church at the time of the Disruption in 1843. This involved a major split with Henry to whom he had been very close his whole life. Despite Henry's departure and that of his sons, both of whom were ministers, neither Thomas nor his son Joseph came out. Joseph took the opportunity of the many vacancies occasioned by the Disruption to move from Applegarth to the parish of Torthorwald, which was within the Presbytery of Dumfries.

Shortly after Henry's death in 1846, Thomas commissioned a new building for the Dumfries Savings Bank and a statue of Henry that was erected, and still stands, above it. The statue, 8.5 feet high, was carved by a local man called J. Currie at a cost of £80, raised by local subscription.

Thomas lived well beyond his brother Henry, and died in 1858 while still the minister in New Church.

Notes

CHAPTER 1 INTRODUCTION

1 T. M. Devine, *To the Ends of the Earth*, London, 2012, 48.
2 P. Aitchison and A. Cassell, *The Lowland Clearances: Scotland's Silent Revolution, 1760–1830*, Edinburgh, 2012, 25.
3 J. Burns, *Fire and Light*, New York, 2013, 3.
4 Aitchison and Cassell, *The Lowland Clearances*, 92.

CHAPTER 2 BIRTH AND BOYHOOD

1 George J. C. Duncan, *Memoir of Henry Duncan, Minister of Ruthwell*, Edinburgh, 1848, 5.
2 Ibid., 4.
3 Ibid., 8.

CHAPTER 3 BANKING IN LIVERPOOL

1 Dr and Mrs Currie. Duncan's hosts in Liverpool.
2 R. D. Thornton, *James Currie: The Entire Stranger and Robert Burns*, Edinburgh, 1963, 161–3.
3 Ibid., 162.
4 Duncan, *Memoirs of Dr Henry Duncan*, 15.
5 C. C. Booth, *Dumfries and Galloway and the Borough of Liverpool: The Curries and the Duncans. Proceedings of the Dumfries and Galloway Antiquarian and Field Naturalists Society*, LXXVII, 2003 (Booth was a great-great-great grandson of Henry Duncan).
6 Anon., *Arthur Heywood Sons and Company, 1773–1883*, Liverpool, 1949, 11–12.
7 Ibid., 11.
8 S. Hall, *Dr Duncan of Ruthwell: Founder of Savings Banks*, Edinburgh, 1910, 21–2.
9 There is nothing really to suggest that literary and artistic talents are incompatible with a banking career, as the lives of Robert Service, the Yukon poet, and James McBey, the official World War I artist, attest.

10 Quoted in A. L. Drummond and J. Bulloch, *The Scottish Church, 1688–1843*, Edinburgh, 1972, 156.

CHAPTER 4 UNIVERSITY EDUCATION

1 S. J. Brown, 'Historical Context within Scotland and its Kirk: Henry Duncan, Savings Banks and Evangelical Social Reform', Proceedings of the Henry Duncan Bi-Centennial Conference, Edinburgh, 2010, The Centre for Theology and Public Issues, 8.
2 A. Broadie, *The Scottish Enlightenment*, Edinburgh, 2011, 14.
3 Duncan, *Memoir of Henry Duncan*, 27.
4 P. H. Scott, 'Introduction', in J. Galt, *The Member and the Radical*, Edinburgh, 1996, xii.
5 G. A. Johnston, *Selections from the Scottish Philosophy of Common Sense*, Ithaca, NY, 2012, 12.
6 Duncan, *Memoir of Henry Duncan*, 148.
7 After Duncan's death, and in correspondence with George Duncan, Brougham cast doubt on Duncan's membership of the Speculative Society. However, the official history of the Society clearly states that Duncan became a member in 1798. Anon., *A History of the Speculative Society of Edinburgh, 1764–1904*, Edinburgh, 1905.
8 Duncan, *Memoir of Henry Duncan*, 27.
9 Brown, 'Historical Context', 9.

CHAPTER 5 EARLY YEARS IN MINISTRY

1 Duncan, *Memoir of Henry Duncan*, 29–30.
2 Scottish Records Office, CH2/13/3. Presbytery of Annan minutes, 3 July 1799 and 7 August 1799.
3 1801 Census. Dumfriesshire returns.
4 Aitchison and Cassell, *The Lowland Clearances*, 2.
5 J. Butt and K. Ponting (eds), *Scottish Textile Industry*, Aberdeen, 1987.
6 Anon., *Georgian Dumfries and Galloway, 1750–1830*, Dumfries and Galloway Libraries, n.d.
7 Aitchison and Cassell, *The Lowland Clearances*, 11, quoting C. A. Whatley in T. M. Devine (ed.), *Conflict and Stability in Scottish Society, 1700–1850*, Edinburgh, 1990.
8 A. Bold (ed.), *Rhymer Rab: An Anthology of Poems and Prose by Robert Burns*, London, 1993, 23, quoting J. Mackay (ed.), *The Complete Letters of Robert Burns*, Ayr, 1987, 125.
9 Henry Duncan to Mrs Craig, 23 January 1799, quoted in Duncan, *Memoir of Henry Duncan*, 33.
10 www.electricscotland.com/history/dumfries/history51.htm (accessed 10 July 2014).
11 A. Smellie, *Biography of R. M. McCheyne*, Fearn, 1995, 19–20.

12 Dumfries and Galloway Archives, CH2/1284/16. Presbytery of Dumfries minutes, 8 August 1803.

13 S. Hall, *Dr Duncan of Ruthwell*, 34–5.

14 Duncan, *Memoir of Henry Duncan*, 42–7.

15 S. Brown, 'Historical Context within Scotland and its Kirk'.

16 Lloyds Bank Archives. Letter Henry Duncan to George (perhaps Joseph) Sturge, 18 June 1839.

17 I. Devlin and J. Carter (eds), *Albaniche: A History of the Galloway Rifle Volunteers*, Dumfries, n.d.

18 Duncan, *Memoir of Henry Duncan*, 46.

19 Ibid.

20 Lloyds Bank Archives, TSB 73/1/4. Rules and minutes of the Ruthwell Friendly Society, 20 October 1800.

21 Aitchison and Cassell, *The Lowland Clearances*, 99–100.

22 *Glasgow Mercury*, 13 March 1783, quoted in David J. McLaren, 'David Dale, Scott Moncrieff and the Royal Bank of Scotland in Glasgow, 1783–1806', *Scottish Business and Industrial History*, 27.2, July 2012, 66.

23 C. A. Whatley, 'Custom, Commerce and Lord Meadowbank: The Management of the Meal Market in Urban Scotland c.1740–c.1820', *Journal of Scottish Historical Studies*, 32.1, 2012, 1–27.

24 Ibid., 16.

25 Savings Bank Museum. Rules and minutes of the Ruthwell Friendly Society, 30 January 1801.

26 Duncan, *Memoir of Henry Duncan*, 40, and Hall, *Dr Duncan of Ruthwell*, 31.

27 Hall, *Dr Duncan of Ruthwell*, 41.

28 Duncan, *Memoir of Henry Duncan*, 52.

29 Henry Duncan was not the only person upon whom Deborah Darby had a profound influence. She was also influential in the life of the prison reformer, Elizabeth Fry.

30 Duncan, *Memoir of Henry Duncan*, 55–7.

31 Ibid., 60.

32 Ibid., 84–7.

33 Dumfries and Galloway Archives, CH2/1284/16. Minutes of Dumfries Presbytery, 3 February 1807, NS 7/4/1807.

34 Duncan, *Memoir of Henry Duncan*, 87.

35 Ibid., 91.

36 Ibid., 88–9.

37 Hall, *Dr Duncan of Ruthwell*, 78.

38 The Carlyle Letters Online (CLO), B. E. Kinser (ed.), Duke University Press, 2007. Letter Thomas Carlyle to James Johnston, 8 January 1819, http://carlyleletters.dukeupress.edu//online_project (accessed 8 October 2013).

39 CLO, letter Thomas Carlyle to Robert Mitchell, 27 November 1818.

40 Ibid., letter Thomas Carlyle to Thomas Murray, 1 February 1814.

41 Ibid., correspondence between Henry Duncan and Thomas Carlyle, 13, 16 and 19 September 1827.

42 Duncan, *Memoir of Henry Duncan*, 83.

43 Ibid., 246.
44 The *Dumfries and Galloway Courier* survives as the *Dumfries Courier*.

CHAPTER 6 THE BANK

1 J. MacKay, *The Complete Letters of Robert Burns*, Ayr, 1987, No. 215, quoted in Alan Bold (ed.), *Rhymer Rab*, Black Swan, London, 1993, 213.
2 Savings Bank Museum, letter signed 'Philopenes' to *Dumfries Courier*, May 1810.
3 Duncan, *Memoir of Henry Duncan*, 34.
4 Ibid., 34.
5 Savings Bank Museum. Petition by Mary Duncan to Lord John Russell requesting a pension, March 1847.
6 Duncan, *Memoir of Henry Duncan*, 36.
7 E. W. Keyes, *A History of Savings Banks in the United States from their Inception in 1816 down to 1874, with Discussions of their Theory, Practical Workings and Incidents, Present Condition and Prospective Development*, Boston, 1878, 38–45.
8 Early American Imprints Series 2, No. 45617.
9 Duncan, *Memoir of Henry Duncan*, 42.
10 TSB Archives, Lloyds Bank. H. Duncan, *An Essay on the Nature and Advantages of Parish Banks: For the Savings of the Industrious*, Dumfries, 1815, 19.
11 Hall, *Dr Duncan of Ruthwell*, 54.
12 TSB Archives, Lloyds Bank. Letter from H. Home Drummond to Thomas Duncan, 16 January 1815.
13 H. Duncan, *An Essay on the Nature and Advantages of Parish Banks: For the Savings of the Industrious*, Edinburgh, 1816 (Nabu Public Domain Reprint, 2012), 5.
14 Duncan, *An* Essay, 1816, 4.
15 C. W. Munn, *Airdrie Savings Bank: A History*, 10.
16 Dumfries and Galloway was one of the last areas of the country where country people were still paid quarterly.
17 Duncan, *An Essay*, 1816, 6.
18 Ibid., 8.
19 Ibid., 27.
20 Ibid., 23.
21 Ibid., 32.
22 J. H. Forbes, *Observations on Banks for Savings*, Edinburgh, 1817.
23 G. Duncan, *Memoir of Henry Duncan*, 109
24 Cited in Duncan, 109.
25 CLO. Letter from Thomas Carlyle to Robert Mitchell, 31 March 1817 (accessed 8 October 2013).
26 H. O. Horne, *A History of Savings Banks*, London, 1947, 47.
27 Cited in Duncan, *Memoir of Henry* Duncan, 115.
28 TSB Archives, Lloyds Bank, Acc. 2011/1/8/2. Statement of Account for Janet Dinwiddie, Murraythwaite.

29 Savings Bank Museum. Annual report, 1822.

30 The meeting room for the church elders.

31 Hall, *Dr Duncan of Ruthwell*, 8.

32 M. Andersson, 'Savings Banks and Economic Development: Sweden in the 19th Century', *Perspectives*, 63, September 2011, World Savings Banks Institute and European Savings Banks Group, Brussels, 30.

33 Quoted from the Political Register in Hall, *Dr Duncan of Ruthwell*, 69–70.

34 Duncan, *Memoir of Henry Duncan*, 116–25.

35 TSB Archives, Lloyds Bank. Letter from W. R. K. Douglas to H. Duncan, 4 June 1817.

36 TSB Archives, Lloyds Bank. Letter from H. Duncan to W. R. K. Douglas, 3 July 1817.

37 Savings Bank Museum. Letter from A. Munnochie to W. R. K. Douglas, 9 March 1818.

38 TSB Archives, Lloyds Bank. Letter from Rev J. Thomson to H. Duncan, 27 January 1818.

39 TSB Archives, Lloyds Bank. Letter from H. Donaldson to H. Duncan, 30 March 1818.

40 Savings Bank Museum. Letter from H. Donaldson to H. Duncan, 30 March 1818.

41 TSB Archives, Lloyds Bank. Letter from H. W. Smith to H. Duncan, 17 April 1818.

42 Douglas's involvement in the Bill is not mentioned in the official online history of parliament.

43 TSB Archives, Lloyds Bank. Letter from H. Duncan to W. R. K. Douglas, 1 June 1818.

44 TSB Archives, Lloyds Bank. Letter from H. W. Smith to H. Duncan, 31 July 1818.

45 *Land Transport on Dumfries and Galloway, 1790–1930*, Dumfries and Galloway Libraries.

46 Responsible for Indian affairs.

47 TSB Archives, Lloyds Bank. Letter from H. Duncan to A. Duncan, 28 February 1819.

48 TSB Archives, Lloyds Bank. Letter from H. Duncan to R. Lundie, 22 February 1819.

49 TSB Archives, Lloyds Bank. Letter from H. Duncan to A. Duncan, 28 February 1819. Mitchell was the tutor in the manse school and Phillips was his brother-in-law and factor to the Earl of Mansfield.

50 Quoted in *The Economist*, 10 August 2013.

51 TSB Archives, Lloyds Bank. Letter from H. Duncan to A. Duncan, 9 March 1819.

52 H. Dundas to R. Lundie, 10 March 1819, quoted in Duncan, *Memoir of Henry Duncan*, 131–2.

53 H. Duncan to R. Lundie, 1 April 1819, quoted in ibid., 133.

54 Duncan, *Memoir of Henry Duncan*, 134.

55 TSB Archives, Lloyds Bank. Letter from H. Duncan to W. R. K. Douglas, 13 April 1819.

56 TSB Archives, Lloyds Bank. Letter from I. A. Leslie to H. Duncan, 30 April 1819.

57 TSB Archives, Lloyds Bank. Letter from H. Duncan to W. R. K. Douglas, 7 June 1819. And Gale Document U3603615235, circular letter to the managers of Banks

for Savings in Scotland, comprehending some observations on the Parish Bank Act, 1820.

58 Circular letter to the managers of Banks for Savings in Scotland, comprehending some observations on the Parish Bank Act, 1820.

59 TSB Archives, Lloyds Bank, Acc. 2010/43/10. Draft of parliamentary Bill.

CHAPTER 7 PRESBYTERY AND POLITICS

1 National Records of Scotland CH2/13/3. Presbytery of Annan Minutes, 3 July 1799.

2 National Records of Scotland CH2/13/4. Presbytery of Annan Minutes, 8 August 1803.

3 National Records of Scotland CH2/13/4. Presbytery of Annan Minutes, 3 July 1805.

4 National Records of Scotland CH2/13/4. Presbytery of Annan Minutes, 15 April 1813.

5 G. Duncan, *Memoir of Henry Duncan*, 83.

6 National Records of Scotland CH2/13/4. Presbytery of Annan Minutes, 3 August 1814.

7 National Records of Scotland CH2/13/4. Presbytery of Annan Minutes, 6 January 1815.

8 National Records of Scotland CH2/13/4. Presbytery of Annan Minutes, 1 August 1816.

9 National Records of Scotland CH2/13/5. Presbytery of Annan Minutes, 5 February 1823.

10 Horne, *A History of Savings Banks*, 14.

11 M. Fry, *A New Race of Men: Scotland 1815–1914*, Edinburgh, 2013, Location 285, Kindle edn.

12 National Records of Scotland CH2/13/4. Presbytery of Annan Minutes, 15 December 1819.

13 National Records of Scotland CH2/13/5. Presbytery of Annan Minutes, 4 October 1820.

14 Savings Bank Museum, H. Duncan, *A Sermon on the Constitution of the Church of Scotland*, n.p., n.d., 7.

15 Ibid., 14.

16 Dumfries and Galloway Archives Ch2/1284/20. Presbytery of Dumfries Minutes, 17 February 1829.

17 Quoted in S. Hall, *Dr Duncan of Ruthwell*, 106–7.

18 H. Duncan, *Letters on the Principles of Protestantism on a Practical Role of Life*, Dumfries, 1828, 4.

19 Cited in Hall, *Dr Duncan of Ruthwell*, 102–3.

20 G. Hughes, *James Hogg: A Life*, Edinburgh, 2007. Letter from James Hogg to Margaret Hogg, 1 January 1832.

21 National Records of Scotland CH2/13/7/1. Presbytery of Annan Minutes, 4 May 1842.

CHAPTER 8 DUNCAN'S OTHER INTERESTS

1 J. L. Dinwiddie, *The Ruthwell Cross*, Dumfries, 2008, 10.
2 B. Cassidy (ed.), *The Ruthwell Cross*, Princeton, NJ, 1992, 3.
3 H. Duncan, 'An Account of a Remarkable Monument in the Shape of a Cross, Inscribed with Roman and Runic Letters, Preserved in the Garden of Ruthwell Manse, Dumfriesshire', *Transactions of the Society of Antiquaries of Scotland*, 4.2, 313–26 (reprinted 1857).
4 Quoted in Cassidy, *The Ruthwell Cross*, 23.
5 Dinwiddie, *The Ruthwell Cross*, 32.
6 R. T. Farrell and C. Karkov, 'The Construction, Destruction and Reconstruction of the Ruthwell Cross: Some Caveats' in Cassidy, *The Ruthwell Cross*, 35–47.
7 Quoted in Hall, *Dr Duncan of Ruthwell*, 111–14.
8 H. Duncan, 'An Account of the Tracks and Footmarks of Animals found Impressed in Sandstone in the Quarry of Corncockle Muir in Dumfriesshire', *Transactions of the Royal Society of Edinburgh*, 1828 (read 7 January 1828).
9 Quoted in Hall, *Dr Duncan of Ruthwell*, 114.
10 Ibid., 39.
11 Ibid., 89.
12 Dumfries and Galloway Museum. Burns Mausoleum, minutes of Organising Committee, 16 December 1813.
13 Dumfries and Galloway Museum. Burns Mausoleum, minutes of Organising Committee, 20 January 1819.
14 Dumfries and Galloway Museum. Dumfries Burns Club minutes, list of original members.
15 Lloyds Bank Archives. Letter from Henry Duncan to the masonic lodge in Lochmaben, 31 March 1808.

CHAPTER 9 POET AND NOVELIST

1 H. Duncan, *Tales of the Scottish Peasantry*, Dumfries, 1815, v–vii.
2 H. Duncan, *The Cottage Fireside; Or the Parish Schoolmaster, A Moral Tale*, 2nd edn, Edinburgh, 1815.
3 Ibid., 7.
4 Ibid., 21–2.
5 Ibid., 92–3.
6 Ibid., 96.
7 Ibid., 96fn.
8 D. G. Barrie, 'Patrick Colquhoun, the Scottish Enlightenment and Police Reform in Glasgow in the late Eighteenth Century', *Crime, History and Society*, 12. 2, 2008, 59–79.
9 Lloyds Bank Archives. Letter from H. W. Smith to Henry Duncan, 31 July 1818.
10 H. Duncan, *The Young South Country Weaver, or a Journey to Glasgow, a Tale for the Radicals*, Edinburgh, 1821, iii.

11 *New Edinburgh Review*, 1, 1821, 568–89.
12 Savings Bank Museum, Ruthwell. Letter from Henry Duncan to George Sturge, 8 June 1839.
13 http://tinyurl.galegroup.com/tinyurl/TTUB1 (doc. number GALE AHMANL144912680). Nineteenth Century Collections Online, the Corvey Collection, consulted WEB DuBois Library, University of Massachusetts, February 2015. Henry Duncan, *William Douglas or, The Scottish Exiles, a Historical Novel*, Edinburgh and London, 1826, vol. 1, 26, 40 and 46.
14 Ibid., 92.
15 Ibid., 321–2.
16 *Edinburgh Weekly Journal*, n.p.
17 *La Belle Assemblée*, 3.4, 1826, 33–4.
18 *Monthly Review*, 2, 1826, 331–2.
19 *Scots Magazine*, 97, 1826, 706.
20 Hall, *Dr Duncan of Ruthwell*, 97–102.
21 H. Duncan, *Sacred Philosophy of the Seasons Illustrating the Perfections of God in the Phenomena of the Year*, Edinburgh, 1836–7, 4 vols.
22 Ibid., vol. 3, 43–4.
23 TSB Archives, Lloyds Bank. Letter from Joanna Baillie to Henry Duncan, 4 June 1831.
24 Lloyds Bank Archives. Letter from Alexander Duff to Henry Duncan, 12 May 1838.
25 W. F. P. Greenwood, 'Introduction', in *Sacred Philosophy of the Seasons*, viii.
26 Duncan, *Memoir of Henry Duncan*, 261.
27 E. A. Poe, *Essays and Reviews*, Library of America, New York, 1984, 245–7.

CHAPTER 10 A UNIVERSITY FOR DUMFRIES

1 A. Anderson, *Crichton University: A Widow's Might*, privately printed, 2001, 6.
2 Brown, 'Historical Context', 15.
3 These bodies of landowners, originally established to assess and collect a land tax, gradually assumed many of the roles and responsibilities that would, in modern times, by exercised by a local authority.
4 Anderson, *Crichton University*, 12–13.
5 Duncan, *Memoir of Henry Duncan*, 152–3.
6 Dumfries and Galloway Archives, 13/12a, Dumfries and Maxwelltown Mechanics' Institute minute book, 15 March 1825, 25 March 1825 and 26 July 1828.
7 Anderson, *Crichton University*, Chap. 4.
8 Lloyds Bank Archives. Letter from Henry Duncan to Thomas Chalmers, 4 February 1823.
9 Duncan, *Crichton University*, 147.
10 Anderson, *Crichton University*, 20. Letter from Henry Duncan to Thomas Chalmers, 9 December 1823.
11 Ibid., Chap. 8.
12 Ibid., 43. Annandale Estate Papers, letter from Elizabeth Crichton to John Hope-Johnstone, 16 October 1829.

13 Lloyds Bank Archives, Savings Bank Museum 01/08/03–5. Scroll letter from Henry Duncan to Hope Johnstone, 28 October 1829.

14 C. Brown, *Religion and Society in Scotland since 1707*, Edinburgh, 1997, 689.

15 Lloyds Bank Archives, Savings Bank Museum 01/08/03–5. Scroll letter from Henry Duncan to Hope Johnstone, 28 October 1829.

16 Cited in Anderson, *Crichton University*, 54.

17 Ibid., 60.

18 Ibid., 69.

CHAPTER 11 CAMPAIGNING AGAINST SLAVERY

1 In 1772 a legal decision in the Court of King's Bench was taken by the Earl of Mansfield, which found that slavery was not supported by common law. It had never been supported by statute in England, therefore it was no longer legal to have slaves in England.

2 J. Buchan, *Capital of the Mind*, Edinburgh, 2007, 336.

3 B. Duckham, *A History of the Scottish Coal Industry*, vol.1, Newton Abbot, 1970, Chap. 6.

4 I. Whyte, *Scotland and the Abolition of Black Slavery, 1756–1838*, Edinburgh, 2006, 80–1.

5 Scottish Records Office, CH2/13/5. Presbytery of Annan minutes, 3 August 1814.

6 Whyte, *Scotland and the Abolition of Black Slavery*, 129.

7 Ibid., 131.

8 The Rt Hon. Sir George Murray was a Scot, from Perth, who had spent his very successful career in military service, some of it in the West Indies. He was a much respected Quarter Master General for the army during the Napoleonic wars and was subsequently in charge of the Royal Military Academy at Sandhurst before entering politics.

9 H. Duncan, *Presbyter's Letters on the West India Question*, London, 1830 (Cornell University Library Digital Collections).

10 Liberia, on the west coast of Africa, was originally created by the American Colonization Society as a home for freed and escaped slaves from the United States and the Caribbean. It became an independent state in 1847, although this fact was not recognised by the US until 1862.

11 W. Clinkenbeard, *The One Tree*, Edinburgh, 2013, 46.

12 Whyte, *Scotland and the Abolition of Black Slavery*, 197.

13 Quoted in ibid., 200.

14 *Christian Instructor*, January 1831.

15 Lloyds Bank Archives, Acc. 2010/45/18. Letter from Agnes Duncan to Dr James Campbell, 12 February 1831.

16 Scottish Records Office, CH2/13/6. Presbytery of Annan minutes, 1 May 1839.

17 I. Whyte, *Send Back the Money*, Cambridge, 2012.

CHAPTER 12 MINISTERING IN CHANGING TIMES

1 Duncan, *Memoir of Henry Duncan*, 100–1. Letter from H. Duncan to R. Lundie, 11 October 1814.
2 Ibid., 248.
3 Ibid., 193.
4 CLO. Letter from T. Carlyle to J. A. C., 2 March 1831 (accessed 8 October 2013).
5 Lloyds Bank Archives. Letter from H. Duncan to W. W. Duncan, January 1832.
6 Lloyds Bank Archives, Acc. 1010/45/09. Letter from H. Duncan to G. Duncan, 11 January 1836.
7 Duncan, *Memoir of Henry Duncan*, 248–52.
8 Ibid., 164.
9 Ibid., 172.
10 Ibid., 165.
11 She is best known as the author of the hymn, 'Jesus tender shepherd hear me'.
12 Duncan, *Memoir of Henry Duncan*, 254. Letter from H. Duncan to M. Lundie, 5 February 1835.
13 Ibid., 255. Letter from H. Duncan to M. Lundie, 8 November 1835.
14 M. Duncan, *Memoir of Mrs Mary Lundie Duncan by her Mother*, New York, 1842, 211.
15 Duncan, *Memoir of Henry Duncan*, 257. Letter from H. Duncan to M. Lundie, no date.
16 Hall, *Dr Duncan of Ruthwell*, 131.
17 Lloyds Bank Archives. Letter from H. Brougham to H. Duncan, 1827.
18 Duncan, *Memoir of Henry Duncan*, 215–17.
19 Lloyds Bank Archives. Letter from A. Thomson to H. Duncan, 12 March 1828.
20 Duncan, *Memoir of Henry Duncan*, 233.
21 Quoted in Hall, *Dr Duncan of Ruthwell*. Letter from H. Brougham to H. Duncan, 27 November 1832.
22 Lloyds Bank Archives. Letter from H. Brougham to H. Duncan, 27 November 1832.
23 Duncan, *Memoir of Henry Duncan*, 236.
24 Scottish Records Office, CH2/13/6. Presbytery of Annan minutes, 1 May 1836.
25 Hall, *Dr Duncan of Ruthwell*, 140.
26 Lloyds Bank Archives, SBM 1/8/2/2. Letters to G. Cook on the late enactment of the General Assembly relative to patronage and calls.
27 Lloyds Bank Archives. Scroll letter from H. Goulbourn to H. Duncan, no date.
28 D. Frew, *The Parish of Urr*, Dalbeattie, 1909, 270.
29 Lloyds Bank Archives. Letter from W. Duncan to G. Duncan, 26 March 1835.
30 Lloyds Bank Archives. Letter from T. T. Duncan to G. Duncan, 25 March 1835.
31 N. Dinwiddie, *The Life and Times of the Reverend Dr Duncan of Ruthwell, 1774–1846*, Dumfries, 1974, 11.
32 Duncan, *Memoir of Henry Duncan*, 266.
33 British History Online. Acts of the General Assembly of the Church of Scotland, 1839 (accessed 28 November 2014).
34 Duncan, *Memoir of Henry Duncan*, 267.

35 The Lord High Commissioner is the monarch's representative at the General Assembly but is not a commissioner and cannot take part in the debates.

36 Scottish Records Office, CH2/13/6. Presbytery of Annan minutes, 5 February 1840.

37 A legal officer of the Court of Session.

38 T. Brown, *Annals of the Disruption*, Edinburgh, 1892, 35.

39 Scottish Records Office, CH2/13/6. Presbytery of Annan minutes, 1 April 1840.

40 Duncan, *Memoir of Henry Duncan*, 276. Letter from H. Duncan to M. Duncan, 11 May 1840.

41 Ibid., 282. Letter from H. Duncan to G. Lundie, 7 May 1841.

42 Ibid., 288. Letter from H. Duncan to H. Brougham, 16 November 1841.

43 Ibid., 291.

44 Savings Bank Museum, H. Duncan, 'Letter from the Minister of Ruthwell to his flock on the Resolutions adopted at the late Convocation', 12 December 1842.

45 Ibid.

46 Ibid.

CHAPTER 13 DISRUPTION AND DEATH

 1 Drummond and Bulloch, *The Scottish Church*, 233.

 2 Ibid., 236–7.

 3 Quoted in Drummond and Bulloch, *The Scottish Church*, 241.

 4 T. Brown, *Annals of the Disruption*, Edinburgh, 1892, 80. The source for this, and other passages about Duncan was Henry Duncan's wife, Mary.

 5 Brown, Annals, 102, quotes memoir by M. L. Duncan.

 6 CLO. Letter from T. Carlyle to J. Carlyle, 16 August 1843 (accessed 8 October 2013).

 7 Hall, *Dr Duncan of Ruthwell*, 144.

 8 Duncan, *Memoir of Henry Duncan*, 301.

 9 Hall, *Dr Duncan of Ruthwell*, 146.

10 Drummond and Bulloch, *The Scottish Church*, 248.

11 Duncan, *Memoir of Henry Duncan*, 310.

12 Ibid., 315.

13 Scottish Records Office, CH3/1174/1. Minutes of Mount Kedar Free Church Kirk Session, 7 June 1844.

14 Scottish Records Office, CH3/1174/9. List of adherents to Free Church Mouswald, 1 August 1843.

15 Duncan, *Memoir of Henry Duncan*, 307.

16 Ibid., 314. Letter from H. Duncan to W. W. Duncan, 26 March 1844.

17 The church continued there well into the twentieth century.

18 Hall, *Dr Duncan of Ruthwell*, 150.

19 T. Brown, *Annals of the Disruption*, Edinburgh, 1892, 132.

20 CLO. Letter from T. Carlyle to J. Carlyle, 23 August 1843 (accessed 8 October 2013). Robert Mitchell had been the schoolmaster when he and Carlyle were young men.

21 Miss Dickson was the aunt of Rev. R. M. McCheyne, an old friend of Henry Duncan. McCheyne died at the age of twenty-nine just before the Disruption, but he left a lasting legacy in his writings, which are still in print.
22 Brown, *Annals*, 186.
23 Ibid., 188.
24 Ibid., 187–8. This passage was written by Mrs Duncan and includes a quotation from J. Mackenzie, *Life of Dr Cunningham*, London, 1871.
25 Ibid., 376.
26 Ibid., 406, quoting Mrs Duncan.
27 Duncan, *Memoir of Henry Duncan*, 326.
28 Brown, *Annals*, 406.
29 Duncan, *Memoir of Henry Duncan*, 332.
30 Ibid., 344.
31 The monument was created with space for a sarcophagus, but there seems to be no record of his body having been moved there.

CHAPTER 14 CONCLUSION

1 J. T. Pratt, *The History of Savings Banks in England, Wales and Ireland*, London, 1830, xiii.
2 E. W. Keyes, *A History of Savings Banks in the United States from their Inception in 1816 down to 1874* [. . .], New York, 1876.
3 Keyes, *A History*, 18–19.
4 S. Brophy-Warren, 'US Mutual Savings Banks and the Savings Bank Idea: The Virtue of Thrift as an Institutional Value', in D. Blankenhorn et al. (eds), *Franklyn's Thrift: The Lost History of an American Virtue*, West Conshohocken, PA, 2009.
5 Horne, *A History of Savings Banks*, 294.
6 Quoted in ibid., 295.
7 *Georgian Dumfries and Galloway, 1750–1830*, Dumfries and Galloway Libraries, Dumfries, n.d.
8 Drummond and Bulloch, *The Scottish Church*, 174.
9 Ibid., 1.
10 *Fasti Ecclesiae Scoticanae*, vol. 2, Edinburgh, 1917.

APPENDIX 4 THOMAS TUDOR DUNCAN

1 Dumfries and Galloway Archives, CH2/1284/17. Dumfries Presbytery minutes, 20 June 1806.
2 Lloyds Bank, TSB Archives, Acc. 2010/43/10. Duncan letters.
3 Dumfries and Galloway Archives, CH2/1284/21. Dumfries Presbytery minutes, 3 April 1838.
4 Dumfries and Galloway Archives, CH2/1284/18. Dumfries Presbytery minutes, 12 November 1819.

Bibliography

P. Aitchison and A. Cassell, *The Lowland Clearances: Scotland's Silent Revolution, 1760–1830*, Edinburgh, 2012.

A. Anderson, *Crichton University: A Widow's Might*, privately printed, 2001.

M. Andersson, 'Savings Banks and Economic Development: Sweden in the 19th Century', *Perspectives*, 63, September 2011, World Savings Banks Institute and European Savings Banks Group, Brussels.

Anon., *Georgian Dumfries and Galloway, 1750–1830*, Dumfries and Galloway Libraries, n.d.

Anon., *A History of the Speculative Society of Edinburgh, 1764–1904*, Edinburgh, 1905.

Anon., *Arthur Heywood Sons and Company, 1773–1883*, Liverpool, 1949.

Anon., *200 Years of Savings Banks*, Brussels, 2011.

D. G. Barrie, 'Patrick Colquhoun, the Scottish Enlightenment and Police Reform in Glasgow in the late Eighteenth Century', *Crime, History and Society*, 12. 2, 2008, 59–79.

D. Blankenhorn et al. (eds), *Franklyn's Thrift: The Lost History of an American Virtue*, West Conshohocken, PA, 2009.

A. Bold (ed.), *Rhymer Rab: An Anthology of Poems and Prose by Robert Burns*, London, 1993.

C. C. Booth, *Dumfries and Galloway and the Borough of Liverpool: The Curries and the Duncans. Proceedings of the Dumfries and Galloway Antiquarian and Field Naturalists Society*, LXXVII, 2003.

A. Broadie, *The Scottish Enlightenment*, Edinburgh, 2011.

C. Brown, *Religion and Society in Scotland since 1707*, Edinburgh, 1997.

S. J. Brown, 'Historical Context within Scotland and its Kirk: Henry Duncan, Savings Banks and Evangelical Social Reform', Proceedings of the Henry Duncan Bi-Centennial Conference, Edinburgh, 2010, The Centre for Theology and Public Issues.

T. Brown, *Annals of the Disruption*, Edinburgh, 1892.

J. Buchan, *Capital of the Mind*, Edinburgh, 2007.

F. Burdett, *Annals of Banks for Savings*, London, 1818.

J. M. Burns, *Fire and Light*, New York, 2013.

J. Butt and K. Ponting (eds), *Scottish Textile Industry*, Aberdeen, 1987.

R. Cage, *The Scottish Poor Law*, Edinburgh, 1981.

The Carlyle Letters Online (CLO), ed. B. E. Kinser, Durham, NC, 2007.

B. Cassidy (ed.), *The Ruthwell Cross*, Princeton, NJ, 1992.

W. Clinkenbeard, *The One Tree*, Edinburgh, 2013.

C. Compton, *The Savings Bank Assistant: Exhibiting the Whole Machinery of Savings Banks*, London, 1829.

T. M. Devine, *To the Ends of the Earth*, London, 2012.

I. Devlin and J. Carter (eds), *Albaniche: A History of the Galloway Rifle Volunteers*, Dumfries, n.d.

J. L. Dinwiddie, *The Ruthwell Cross* (9th edn), Dumfries, 2008.

N. Dinwiddie, *The Life and Times of the Reverend Dr Duncan of Ruthwell, 1774-1846*, Dumfries, 1974.

A. L. Drummond and J. Bulloch, *The Scottish Church, 1688-1843*, Edinburgh, 1972.

B. Duckham, *A History of the Scottish Coal Industry*, vol.1, Newton Abbot, 1970.

G. J. C. Duncan, *Memoir of Henry Duncan: Minister of Ruthwell*, Edinburgh, 1848.

H. Duncan, *A Sermon on the Constitution of the Church of Scotland*, n.p., n.d.

H. Duncan, *Tales of the Scottish Peasantry*, Dumfries, 1815.

H. Duncan, *The Cottage Fireside; Or the Parish Schoolmaster, A Moral Tale*, 2nd edn, Edinburgh, 1815.

H. Duncan, *An Essay on the Nature and Advantages of Parish Banks: For the Savings of the Industrious*, Dumfries, 1815.

H. Duncan, *An Essay on the Nature and Advantages of Parish Banks: For the Savings of the Industrious*, Edinburgh, 1816 (Nabu Public Domain Reprint, 2012).

H. Duncan, *The Young South Country Weaver, or a Journey to Glasgow, a Tale for the Radicals*, Edinburgh, 1821.

Henry Duncan, *William Douglas or, The Scottish Exiles, a Historical Novel*, Edinburgh and London, 1826. http://tinyurl.galegroup.com/tinyurl/TTUB1 (doc. number GALE AHMANL144912680). Nineteenth Century Collections Online, the Corvey Collection, consulted WEB DuBois Library, University of Massachusetts, February 2015.

H. Duncan, 'An Account of the Tracks and Footmarks of Animals found Impressed in Sandstone in the Quarry of Corncockle Muir in Dumfriesshire', *Transactions of the Royal Society of Edinburgh*, 1828 (read 7 January 1828).

H. Duncan, *Letters on the Principles of Protestantism on a Practical Role of Life*, Dumfries, 1828.

H. Duncan, *Presbyter's Letters on the West India Question*, London, 1830 (Cornell University Library Digital Collections).

H. Duncan, *Sacred Philosophy of the Seasons Illustrating the Perfections of God in the Phenomena of the Year*, Edinburgh, 1836-7, 4 vols.

H. Duncan, 'Letter from the Minister of Ruthwell to his flock on the Resolutions adopted at the late Convocation', 12 December 1842. Held in the Savings Bank Museum.

H. Duncan, 'An Account of a Remarkable Monument in the Shape of a Cross, Inscribed with Roman and Runic Letters, Preserved in the Garden of Ruthwell

Manse, Dumfriesshire', *Transactions of the Society of Antiquaries of Scotland*, 4.2, 1992, 313–26 (reprinted 1857).

M. Duncan, *Memoir of Mrs Mary Lundie Duncan by her Mother*, New York, 1842.

Fasti Ecclesiae Scoticanae, vol. 2, Edinburgh, 1917.

J. H. Forbes, *A Short Account of the Edinburgh Savings Bank*, Edinburgh, 1815.

J. H. Forbes, *Observations on Banks for Savings*, Edinburgh, 1817.

D. Frew, *The Parish of Urr*, Dalbeattie, 1909.

J. A. Froude, *Thomas Carlyle: A History of the First Forty Years of his Life*, London, 1901.

M. Fry, *A New Race of Men: Scotland 1815–1914*, Edinburgh, 2013.

Georgian Dumfries and Galloway, 1750–1830, Dumfries and Galloway Libraries, Dumfries, n.d.

S. Hall, *Dr Duncan of Ruthwell: Founder of Savings Banks*, Edinburgh, 1910.

H. O. Horne, *A History of Savings Banks*, London, 1947.

G. Hughes, *James Hogg: A Life*, Edinburgh, 2007.

G. A. Johnston, *Selections from the Scottish Philosophy of Common Sense*, Ithaca, NY, 2012.

E. W. Keyes, *A History of Savings Banks in the United States from their Inception in 1816 down to 1874, with Discussions of their Theory, Practical Workings and Incidents, Present Condition and Prospective Development*, New York, 1876.

W. H. Kniffin, *The Savings Bank and its Practical Work*, New York, 1918.

Land Transport in Dumfries and Galloway 1790–1930, Dumfries and Galloway Libraries.

J. Mackay (ed.), *The Complete Letters of Robert Burns*, Ayr, 1987.

J. Mackay, *A Biography of Robert Burns*, Edinburgh, 1992.

A. McCreary, *By All Accounts*, Antrim, 1991.

W. McDowall, *History of the Burgh of Dumfries*, 4th edn, Dumfries, 1986.

David J. McLaren, 'David Dale, Scott Moncrieff and the Royal Bank of Scotland in Glasgow, 1783–1806', *Scottish Business and Industrial History*, 27.2, July 2012.

A. Moffat, *The Borders*, Edinburgh, 2007.

M. Moss, 'Henry Duncan and the Savings Bank Movement in the UK', *Perspectives*, 63, September 2011, World Savings Banks Institute and European Savings Banks Group, Brussels.

M. Moss and I. Russell, *An Invaluable Treasure: A History of the TSB*, London, 1994.

J. Z. Muller, *The Mind and the Market*, New York, 2002.

C. W. Munn, *Airdrie Savings Bank: A History*, Airdrie, 2010.

S. G. Osborne, *The Savings Bank: Some Particulars of the Life and Death of 'Old Rainy Day'*, London, 1838.

N. Phillipson, *Adam Smith, An Enlightened Life*, London, 2010.

E. A. Poe, *Essays and Reviews*, Library of America, New York, 1984.

J. T. Pratt, *The History of Savings Banks in England, Wales and Ireland*, London, 1830.

D. M. Ross, 'Poverty and Savings Banks in Mid-Nineteenth Century Scotland', *Papeles de Economia Espanola*, 105/106, 2005, n.p.

L. J. Saunders, *Scottish Democracy, 1815–40*, Edinburgh, 1950.

P. H. Scott, 'Introduction', in J. Galt, *The Member and the Radical*, Edinburgh, 1996, vii–xiii.

A. Smellie, *Biography of R. M. McCheyne*, Fearn, 1995.

J. Smith, *History of the Old Lodge of Dumfries*, Dumfries, 1892.

C. Taylor, *A Summary Account of the London Savings Bank*, London, 1816.

R. D. Thornton, *James Currie: The Entire Stranger and Robert Burns*, Edinburgh, 1963.

C. A. Whatley, *Scottish Society 1707–1830*, Manchester, 2000.

C. A. Whatley, 'Custom, Commerce and Lord Meadowbank: The Management of the Meal Market in Urban Scotland c.1740–c.1820', *Journal of Scottish Historical Studies*, 32.1, 2012.

I. Whyte, *Scotland and the Abolition of Black Slavery 1756–1838*, Edinburgh, 2006.

I. Whyte, *Send Back the Money*, Cambridge, 2012.

Index